Root Cause Analysis in Process-Based Industries

Menachem Horev

Order this book online at www.trafford.com/07-1615
or email orders@trafford.com

Most Trafford titles are also available at major online book retailers.

Printed in Victoria, BC, Canada.

ISBN: 978-1-4251-3977-3

Library of Congress Control Number: 2010902466

We at Trafford believe that it is the responsibility of us all, as both individuals and corporations, to make choices that are environmentally and socially sound. You, in turn, are supporting this responsible conduct each time you purchase a Trafford book, or make use of our publishing services. To find out how you are helping, please visit www.trafford.com/responsiblepublishing.html

Trafford PUBLISHING **www.trafford.com**

North America & international
toll-free: 1 888 232 4444 (USA & Canada)
phone: 250 383 6864 • fax: 812 355 4082

Acknowledgments:

The rights to this book are not mine alone. Indeed, I had the idea to write this book for a long time, but it was my wife Sylvie that told me "If you really wish your book to become a reality, take your time and do it now." I followed her advice and the book eventually became a reality. The process of writing had its ups and downs. I appreciate the constant encouragement and good words of advice that I got from my dear brother Tuvia. The encouragement and support I received from my parents, my father-in-law, and my four children, helped me finish this project.

Over the years, I have had the pleasure of meeting many remarkable people in the semiconductor industry. Some of them had a significant impact on my career, and even without knowing it they took part in the creation of this book. I would like to thank a few of them by name:
Eli Shavit, who has been a great teacher and walked me through my first steps in the world of process engineering,
Yoel Raab, who introduced me to the mind-widening world of process integration and for years we worked together on process problems,
Hamutal Friedlander–Klar, for her special insight and generosity on yield and data analysis over the years of sharing ideas about it,
Yoram Kirschner and Maxine Fassberg, who realized how important this book was to me, and for the freedom and support I received to accomplish it.

I was once told by Ran Kafri, who is a well known professional and a dear friend that "There is something to learn from everyone you meet." Indeed, I have learnt so much from so many colleagues that it is impossible to list them all. So, I thank you all for these seeds of knowledge.

Contents

INTRODUCTION

Root cause analysis: when it all started and who needs it

The human species is unique in its ability to observe a sequence of events, understand the interaction between these events and make use of it. In the dawn of civilization, Homo sapiens observed that there is a repetitive sequence of events that causes plants to grow. We do not know who first watered a seed, hoping for a yield, but this was probably the first human attempt to produce something from a controlled process. This person believed that following a certain sequence of actions would produce a positive result. Sometimes there was no yield at all and this person needed to find the reason for it. Was it over-watering, under-watering, the cold, birds, worms, or other factors which could affect the end results? Today this is called process parameters.

Today's process-based manufacturing sites, such as those in the semiconductor industry, rely on a repetitive pre-planned sequence of operations. The end result should be a product that meets the required specifications.

Problem solving is a routine activity in process-based industries. Although it is sometimes performed by one person, in most cases, teams are required to work together to solve complex problems.

In a typical problem-solving sequence, a few basic steps are required for successful completion of this task. These principal steps are: stating the problem, understanding the current status, identifying the root cause, developing a solution, implementing the solution, and standardizing the solution. Proper completion of one step is required before progressing to the next one. While looking at this short list of steps, two fundamental parts in the problem-solving sequence are apparent. The first part starts with detecting the problem and ends with understanding the cause. This is the root cause analysis (RCA) stage. The second part is the solution stage, which starts with developing a solution and ends after the implemented solution is standardized. The solution development stage cannot start without a proper understanding of the cause of the problem.

This book focuses on the RCA stage in the processing related industry. The aspects related to the solution stage are beyond the scope of this book.

Most of us perform analysis intuitively based on our accumulated experience. Although it appears to be a simple task, finding the cause of the problem is not always so easy and straightforward. I often find that very intelligent and technical teams with inventive and innovative minds get stuck in the root cause analysis stage. As the teams struggle to find the root cause, the problem may continue to take its toll.

When attempting to understand the source of a team's difficulty in confronting RCA, I was surprised to see that in many cases this was not due to a real dead-end situation. It appears that there are two prominent reasons for this.

The first problem is in the rationale behind the tasks intended to collect data. These tasks were derived by short-term understanding, instead of a conscious act directed at establishing a valid model.

The second problem lies in drawing the correct conclusions based on available data. Although a great amount of relevant data was gathered (or maybe because of this), there was no structured way of associating the data with potential causes (hypotheses or models) and drawing the necessary conclusions.

These problems lead to inefficient allocation of resources, unnecessary repetition of data collection, and slow progression in the cause analysis investigation. It is quite clear that there is a lack of basic methodology that addresses these two problems.

RCA can and should be taught. This book intends to save costly learning from experience and to provide a structured guide for RCA to team-leaders, engineers and anyone dealing with it on the way to Problem Solving. It is directed at RCA in the processing industry however, I am sure that anyone dealing with RCA in any discipline would also find significant parts of this book useful.

Navigating the book

I made an effort to structure the book in a way that the reader will not have to take it or leave it. You, the reader, may find some parts more useful than others, and I tried to make it easier for you to fish out these parts from the full text, and to make these parts independently readable. The separation described below may help you to do so.

The Problem Classification chapter aims to familiarize the reader with potential sources and type of problems that may appear in the processing industry.

The basic methodology with its basic supporting tools appears in three chapters: Problem Characterization; Model Building; and Model Validation.

The Data Collection chapter discusses the approach for extracting the most relevant information and knowledge from various data sources.

The Team Tools and Methods chapter deals with group thinking techniques, and covers several common techniques for raising ideas and decision making.

The Recommended Reading chapter consists of a list of suggested reading material. The list is divided into a range of topics that are discussed in the book. This bibliography provides more comprehensive learning for readers interested in broadening their knowledge about RCA and other related topics that are beyond the scope of this book.

It is recommended to read the book from beginning to end the first time. Later on, you may refresh your memory on any topic by going directly to the relevant chapter and section.

Finally, as complete as any book maybe, it will not do the work for you. It is important to remember that there are methodologies and tools but there is no recipe for finding a root cause. Teams should have knowledge, skills, and creativity to gather data, suggest models, and get to the real cause. I hope that this book will make your way to root cause shorter and easier.

Two channels of event investigation

There is often an attempt to gather a team in the very early stage, provide a brief or even vague problem description, and then send the team to collect data. This team will work hard to gather a great amount of data that will evolve as irrelevant, inconclusive, with the need to be re-evaluated, and so on.

Another common method is to run a brain-storming session to suggest models or hypotheses for the problem, while the team has nothing but a general problem statement. The result will be a wide range of suggestions, some of which are very wild and farfetched, leading to a very long list of actions with unclear priorities and directions.

How can this waste of resources be avoided?

There are two investigation fronts that may run in parallel.

The first one is Problem Characterization and the second is Model Building.

Problem characterization is aimed at having information that will define the problem as accurately as possible, and should be based on <u>expected vs. unexpected</u> philosophy that is discussed later. This characterization should provide an indication on problem type, extent and severity. It may even point to the problem source (process step or tool). Fast progress on this front may direct towards a satisfactory way to contain the problem, but in most cases it will not lead to Root Cause understanding.

The other channel is aimed towards root cause identification and is based on <u>model building and validation</u>. This should be performed while having some information about the problem. The suggested models are based on problem characteristics. The data is collected to support or refute suggested models or to assist in building more detailed models. A well-supported model will lead to a solution and will provide enough information to judge the quality of the affected material.

The above separation appears to be somewhat artificial, as the work is usually performed in these two channels in parallel. However, bearing this distinction in mind, it will be easier to understand the rationale behind any data collection task. Problem Characterization usually starts earlier and the collected data supports the Model Building stage, which continues later and is crucial for proper solution development.

While progressing throughout this book, separation of the channels will not be emphasized, however it will be easy to observe that the Problem Classification and Problem Characterization chapters address characterization aspects, while the Model Building and Model Validation chapters cover the modeling aspects. This kind of distinction cannot be made in other chapters, since data items collected in any one of the channels may be used to support and enhance progress in the other channel.

CHAPTER 1

Problem Sources and Classification

This chapter provides an overview of the typical problems appearing in process-based manufacturing sites, without getting into the analytical aspects of these problems. The author assumes that the reader has a very basic knowledge in descriptive statistics, and that will be sufficient to understand the basic terms of the presented issues.

The topics covered in this chapter are:

Process monitoring concept and sources of variation
- o Introduction to processing and controlling issues in semiconductor industry
- o Process noise

Change in process
- o Bounded event
- o Continuous event
- o Sporadic event

Process capability problems
- o The limits placement (working window)
- o Distribution width and shape
- o Interdependency of process parameters

Poor process control coverage
- o Poor sampling method
- o Monitor and product mismatching
- o Unrealized factor

Shift from source identification to cause understanding
- o Component malfunction
- o Human behavioral aspects

Process monitoring and sources of variation

Introduction to processing and controlling in the semiconductor industry

Since this book is based on my experience in the semiconductor industry, I find it necessary to start with a brief explanation of this industry. The introduction emphasizes the importance of proper monitoring and data collection. This extensive monitoring is usually considered as a way for early alert of a line problem to prevent production material loss. However in our case this data collection also plays a significant role in root cause analysis.

Manufacturing modern semiconductors products is a process that involves hundreds of process steps (or operations). Running material through the processing loop may take a few days or weeks, depending on the complexity of the process. Detecting any problem as early as possible and addressing it as fast as possible is a major concern in these semiconductor fabrication sites (Fabs). Naturally, a flaw in the production line could cause significant loss of material, time, and money. Adequate monitoring of production parameters is a matter of survival for these lines. Therefore parameters related to supplies, conditions, treatments and timing are closely checked during processing.

The raw material in the Fab is a round silicon wafer (substrate). A typical process involves many steps, such as layer growing, photo masking, layer etching or polishing; silicon doping, thermal processing and cleaning. The end result is a high number of electronic devices (dice or chips) that are defined over the wafer surface. These wafers are sawed to individual dice and each die will be assembled for use in electronic instruments.

Each silicon wafer carries its own identity number for proper tracking. Usually, 25 wafers are placed in a storage box and moved together from one process step to the next (this is called process lot). In any specific process step, depending on required treatment and the type of machine, the operation may be performed wafer by wafer, on several wafers at once (typically full lot), or in some cases on a larger load that consists of wafers from several lots at once.

To ensure product health, careful monitoring is required for each machine and process parameter in every process step. However this kind of monitoring is time-consuming and sometimes contributes to damage to the product. Therefore it is required to define proper sampling that will track line performance and detect unexpected events as early as possible.

Monitors are classified as Input Parameter Monitors or Output Parameter Monitors. Input Parameters are everything that goes into the machine performing the processing step, while Output Parameters are everything that can be measured on the product emerging from the tool (either on the actual product or on the test vehicle) or at the end of line. All monitoring data is collected, stored and extracted later for review and analysis.

The purpose of all this data collection is to detect any unusual event, either inline or at the end of the line. Once an event is flagged, there is a need to understand its cause and this is where Root Cause Analysis (RCA) starts.

Process noise

We would like to believe that each die, wafer and lot receives exactly the same treatment during any specific process step; however this is not exactly the case. There is always process noise. Each processing tool has it own performance regarding uniformity, stability and repeatability. This variation in performance of a specific process step is an accumulation of all sources of variations: variation over a die (within die variation), over the wafers (within wafer variation), wafer-to-wafer (variation within a lot or load), lot-to-lot variation, and machine-to-machine variation.

Variations of all process steps are reflected on the end products as a variation in product performance. Healthy processes should have a working window in every process step that is wide enough to provide proper yield of functional and reliable products with this noise.

When dealing with certain parameters in a specific process step, we know that not every point will repeatedly provide the exact same value. Ideally we would like all of our measurements to fall evenly on both sides of our target value, with narrow normal distribution.

To better understand the potential sources for process noise of a specific process parameter, let's examine an actual example taken from the semiconductor industry. In one of the steps, a certain thickness of a previously deposited layer is removed from the wafer surface by polishing. The rate of removal (of the material by the polishing) and the duration of polishing define the amount of material that is removed. The polishing rate should be closely monitored so as not to remove too much of the polished layer. What are the potential sources of variation in the polishing rate?

Machine-to-machine variation

For line efficiency, several polishing tools of the same kind are available to run this process and therefore they all run the same process in parallel (Figure 1-1). Even if the machines are of the same model and have the exact same components, there may be slight differences in performance. This could be related to small differences in building the individual components of the tool, small differences incorporated during tool construction, small variations in alignments or in calibrations during maintenance, and so on. The end result could be that the tools are "telling" us that they are doing the same thing, while in fact they are not.

The down force applied during polishing affects the polishing rate. Can we take for granted that the down force indicated by the tool is indeed the absolute correct value? Should we believe that the reason for tool-to-tool polish rate variation is not related to down force just because the tools indicators show a similar number?

Figure 1-1. Machine-to-machine variation

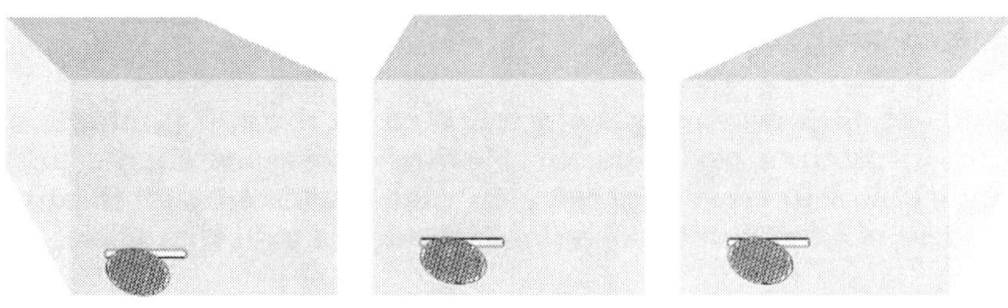

Time-related variation

To prevent the manufacturing line from stopping, routine maintenance is performed to one machine at a time. We may see a change in tool performance as a function of elapsed time or amount of material running on it since its last maintenance.

The polishing pad is worn during polishing and therefore replaced periodically. Is it possible that slow wear-out of the polishing pad is the reason for deterioration in polishing performance over time?

Lot-to-lot variation

Even when running in the same time frame and on the same process tool, there could still be a difference between one lot (batch or load) and another (Figure 1-2). This could be due to inherent instability of the processing tool itself, lot-to-lot variation imported to this process step from previous operations, or even the difference in sitting time (delay) from the previous process step.

The process step that deposits the layer (to be polished) employs two deposition tools in parallel. There is a slight difference between the tools in the refractive index (RI) of the deposited layer. This indicates a difference in layer characteristics (even if all set points of the two deposition machines are exactly the same). Is it possible that the variation observed in polish rate is related to the difference in the density of the deposited material?

Figure 1-2. Lot-to-lot variation.

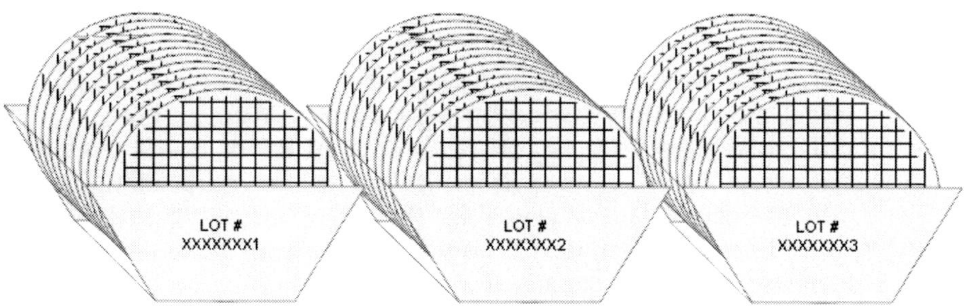

Wafer-to-wafer variation

Wafer processing sequence (wafer order) is another potential source of variation (Figure 1-3). One can assume that within the same lot there will be small wafer-to-wafer variations, as these wafers saw the same tool set and were processed throughout the line together. However, this is not always correct.

In polishing, the typical pad lifetime is hundreds of wafers and pad deterioration is considered to be negligible over one lot. However, could the pad condition of the first wafer be different to any subsequent wafer if the machine stood idle for some time?

Figure 1-3. Wafer-to-wafer variation

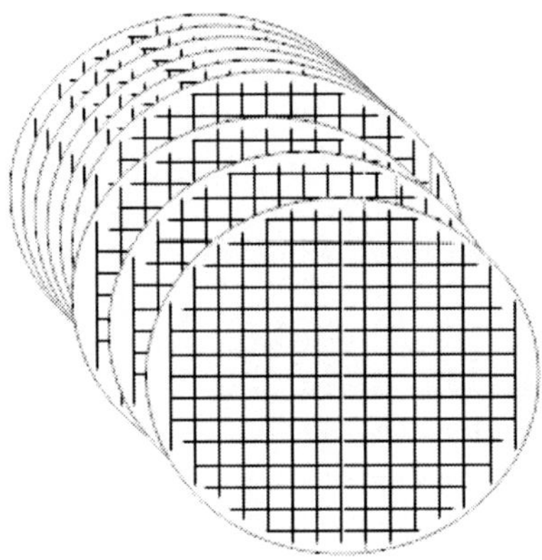

Within wafer variation

The assumption that the entire area of the wafer receives exactly the same treatment is usually not correct. It is quite common for tools to show non-uniformity over the treated area (Figure 1-4). This can be related to geometrical effects, flow dynamics, temperature distribution, and many other factors that could cause region-to-region differences over the same wafer (region-to-region could be center to edge, side to side, top to bottom, or any other effect).
The removal (polishing) rate is not the same at every point over the entire wafer area. Radial non-uniformity (center to edge effect) over the wafer is observed. Is it possible that the abrasive substance (slurry) is carried more efficiently by the polishing pad near wafer edges and less efficiently towards the wafer center?

Figure 1-4. Within wafer variation

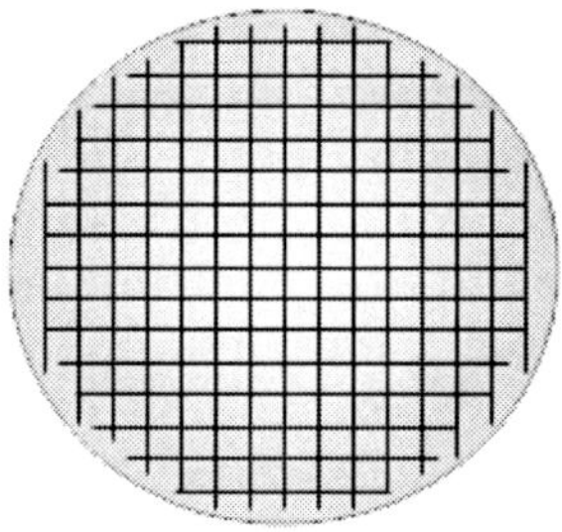

Within die / field variation

The area of one die is indeed small (a few mm per side) however due to a change in the characteristics of underlying topography; local variation in polishing rate may occur (Figure 1-5). The density of underlying layers is defined by circuit functionality. Some circuit blocks are very dense while others have lower structure density. The deposited layer over low density areas will be polished faster than over high density areas. If we will take measurements of 100 points evenly distributed over the entire die area, the results will most probably not show a normal bell shape distribution.

Naturally, picking one measurement site and defining the required polishing time based on this location relies on the assumption that other points with different underlying densities will keep their behavior relative to this measurement point. Could this assumption be incorrect if a softer polishing pad is introduced into the process line?

Figure 1-5. Within die/field variation

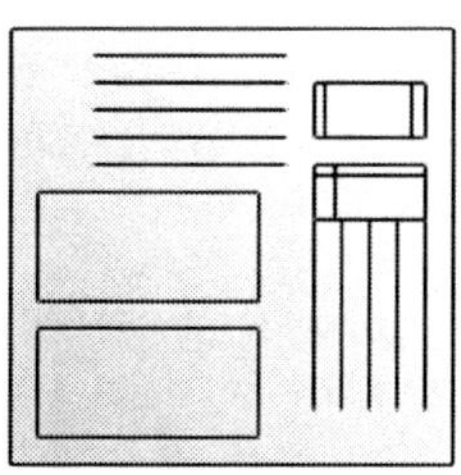

Sampling

As very responsible engineers that care about our customers, we would like our measurements to be taken in a way that will truly cover the entire material being processed. As such, every source of variation should be included in our check.

Based on the above example, if we want to achieve a real representation of each and every point that is being processed just for this specific parameter in this process step, our production line will manufacture measurements, but not sellable products. (100 measurements sites per die) x (100 dice per wafer) x (25 wafers per lot) x (20 lots per day per machine) x (3 machines per operation) = 15,000,000. 15 million measurement sites for one process parameter in one day is a joke, isn't it?

Naturally we use sampling to control our material. By making a few assumptions, early learning and process characterization, the number of measurement sites can be reduced to a reasonable amount. Of course, some information is missing, however with proper sampling, the process will still maintain adequate monitoring coverage.

For example: (1 site per die) x (9 dice per wafer) x (5 wafers per lot) x (20 lots per day per machine) x (3 machines) = 2,700

Indeed, this is significantly less than before, but is still too high to digest easily. Therefore, for the engineer's convenience, this data is aggregated into a lower number of statistical indicators, such as lot average and lot St-dev, which are easy to follow and control. These indicators are usually plotted graphically on charts for better illustration of the process step performance.

When exploring this entire collection of variation sources, it can be seen that a high level statement like "lot average is trending up in the last few days" is only a starting point. You should drill down through all the levels of process noise sources to find the exact reason for this change. Was the entire population changed? Is it due to a few points in the far edge that have wild results?

Problem in process can manifest itself as a change in the performance of a certain monitor within the line, or as a change, or even failure, of products at the end of line. Classification and a brief discussion on process problems and the potential reasons for their appearance are provided in the next few sections.

Change in process

Normal distribution (also known as bell-shape or Gaussian distribution) is the most typical distribution in process parameters. Although there may be other distribution shapes in the processing line, for convenience sake I will limit the discussion on process problems to the normal distribution.

The most common way to follow the performance of certain process parameters is by graphic representation of the measured value according to the processing sequence. When following the sequence of running the material through this process step and recording the monitoring results in order, the trend chart will looks like the one in figure 1-6.

Figure 1-6. Trend chart of normally distributed results.

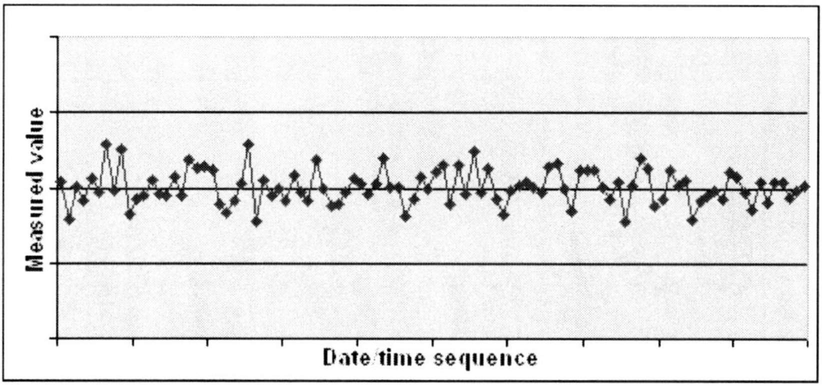

All measured points are scattered around the target value (the center line) with no points above or below the predefined upper and lower limits. This is considered to be a healthy situation and this parameter is well in control.

Since material in process-based industries is run sequentially, a problem is usually detected as a **change** in parameter behavior over time. We consider this unwanted change as an **event** that requires initiation of RCA. This event could be caused by a single or one significant source, but it could also be caused by several conditions that coincided to create the change (the latter is usually more complicated to identify).

Bounded events

A bounded event is a one-time occasion of a specific problem. This type of event is characterized by the fact that it started and finished in the past. The severity of this occasion may vary from negligible impact to large volume loss, however it is clear that the event is over and done. RCA is usually initiated in this case to prevent future reoccurrence of this event, and to assess the reliability related to the affected material.

Bounded event, isolated case:
The simplest case of a bounded event is one lot that is clearly out of the normal distribution for the tested parameter (Figure 1-7). This kind of event is usually not considered to be a reason to initiate intensive RCA, and it is quite common for one person to deal with it.

Figure 1-7. Bounded event, isolated case

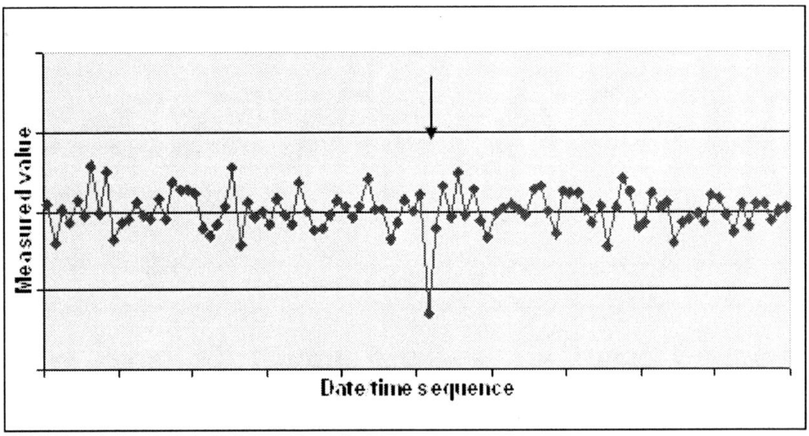

Bounded event, process excursion:
The more frequent bounded event to initiate RCA involves a larger amount of material (Figure 1-8). In this case, it is quite clear that all lots between the start and end of the event (indicated by black arrows) are affected and can be used for analysis.

Figure 1-8. Bounded event, process excursion

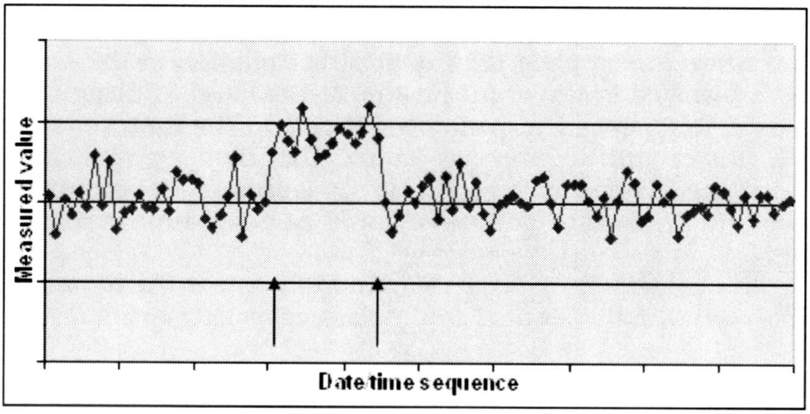

In another typical bounded event, we may find a mix of bad and good material (Figure 1.9). It is more difficult to distinguish the start and end of this event because of the large point-to-point variation within the affected period. It is also more difficult to have a clear distinction between bad and good materials within the event.

Figure 1-9. Bounded event, variation change

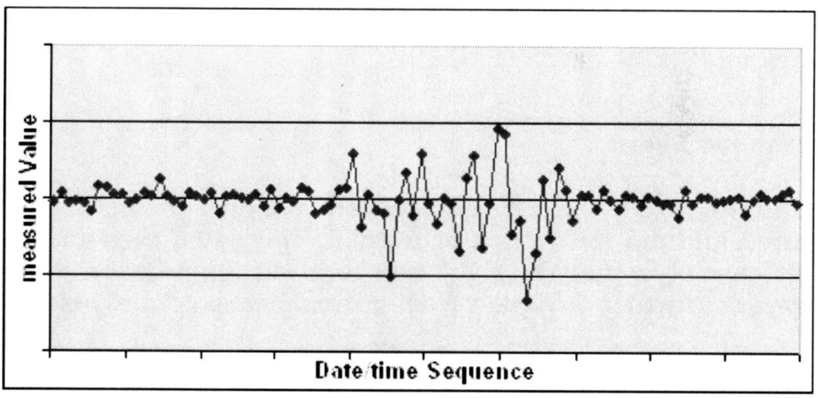

The level of urgency for practicing root cause identification in the case of a bounded event is lower than in other cases, as material currently running through the line is not at risk. However, as long as we do not know the cause of this event, there is a good reason for RCA. First, since we do not know the cause we cannot prevent its reoccurrence, and second, product health is questionable and hard to evaluate without knowing the cause of this event.

The pressure to complete RCA is in direct relation to the amount of material involved in the event (lost or at-risk) and in inverse relation to elapsed time since the end of the event. In the first, management is still upset and concerned about the damage and afraid of reoccurrence, while in the second, management is becoming more confident in line health and considers it as a one-time event.

The main obstacle in RCA for this kind of event is the data available for analysis, which is limited to the data collected during the event.

New data cannot be generated unless you already have a solid model and can deliberately regenerate the same event. In many cases, you have all the evidence pointing towards the root cause, and the only way to prove it is to regenerate the problem. However, you will not always have the chance to do so. You will frequently find yourself in a situation where a conscious decision will be taken not to explore this event further, due to the investment involved or other priorities. Do not be discouraged by this. Record all your findings and conclusions so far and suggest ways for further progress. If this event is repeated, you will have a chance to confirm your findings, either by the new data or by justifying the required investment in the required experiments.

Continuous Event

Continuous event is an unexpected change in behavior that appeared and did not return to normal. The usual reason for RCA in this case is to find the right way to bring things back to normal and prevent further deviation from normal and potential loss.

Continuous event, step function:
Step function is a sudden (abrupt) shift in parameter to a new level (Figure 1-10). From the time of change onwards, the material is stabilized around a new value.

Figure 1-10. Continuous event, step function

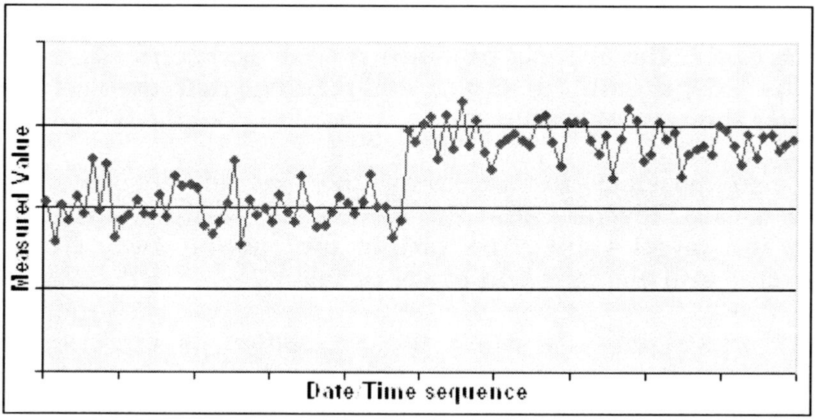

Continuous event, gradual change:
Trend up (or down) is a gradual shift in parameter value to a new level (Figure 1-11). This gradual change may stop and stabilize around certain level or continue and deteriorate to a level that requires stopping the line because the entire material could be worthless.

Figure 1-11. Continuous event, gradual change

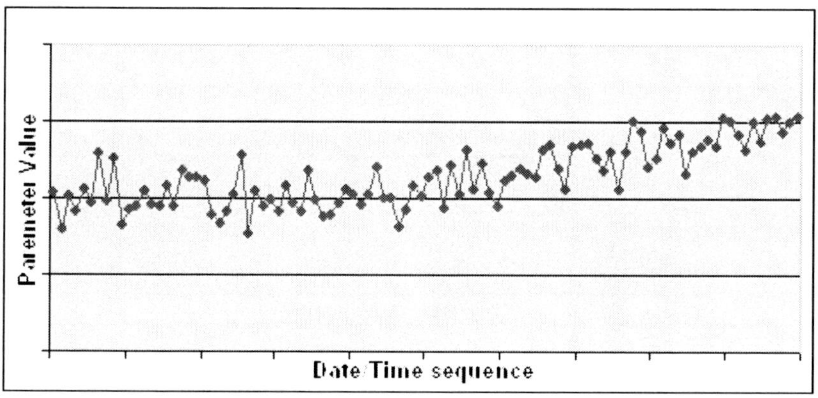

Continuous event, change in dispersion:
When a distribution starts to show a larger spread of process parameter, this is counted as an event. As described earlier, this change may be abrupt while the process is moving from narrow to widespread distribution at a distinct point, or it may occur as a

continuous event, with gradual widening of the distribution with increasingly larger fluctuation of material around the target value.

In some cases, the process becomes noisier symmetrically and the spread is wider around the target, and readings that are both higher and lower than usual appear.

It is also possible to see that the spread becomes wider asymmetrically, meaning that the material is not fluctuating evenly around the target value. The results are moving away from the target value into one direction (up or down).

Another typical case is when the population is dispersed into skewed distribution (asymmetric), while some of the baseline values are still preserved, and more and more material with higher (or lower) values start to appear. An example of a certain kind of asymmetric change in distribution appears in figure 1-12. Abrupt change in spread of results is shown. It appears to have two distinct populations (bimodal distribution) from a certain point on. Part of the material remained as baseline while another part moved to a different level.

Figure 1-12. Continuous event, spread change, bimodal distribution

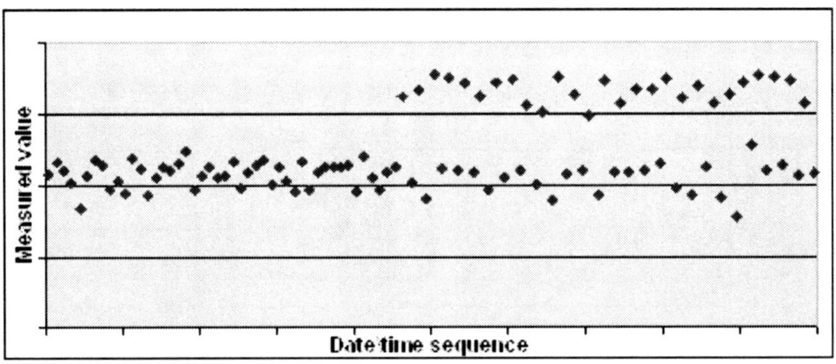

Teams that work on a continuous event are under constant pressure to solve the problem. Usually all are concerned that the line is producing material with a potential risk or with different quality. Sometimes the need to satisfy the demand for frequent updates to management regarding the investigation progress disrupts the team's work. The team members and the leader are too busy trying to explain why they are doing this and that, and less in doing it. Management should keep an eye on what's going on but must be careful not to distract the team from its main task.

From the start of the investigation, the team should be aware that there is a problem in the line, and there should be constant effort to search for a way to contain the problem and minimize damage. Frequently, a problem is contained by applying constraints to the manufacturing line. The leader and team should weigh the relief gained by this containment against the constraint it applies to the line. Keep in mind that containment is usually a temporary act. Once the root cause is found and problem is fixed, all constraints related to the containment should be removed. If new barriers are required to control the line to preventing reoccurrence, it should be part of the decisions related to root cause identification and not as containment "left-over".

Sporadic event

Sporadic (or erratic) events are occurrences that appear repeatedly but without noticeable order or a visible pattern at first glance. This can be shown on the trend chart as intermittent appearance of single readings or as random appearance of clusters with a few successive readings that are not part of the normal population (Figures 1-13 and 1-14).

Figure 1-13. Sporadic event, intermittent single failures

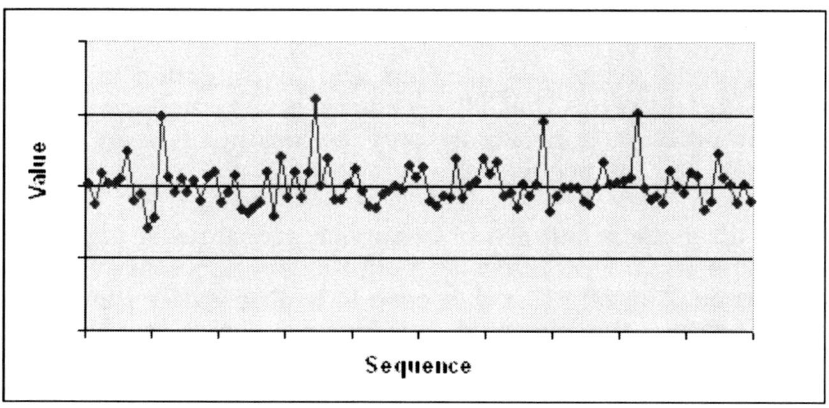

Figure 1-14. Sporadic event, clusters of successive failures

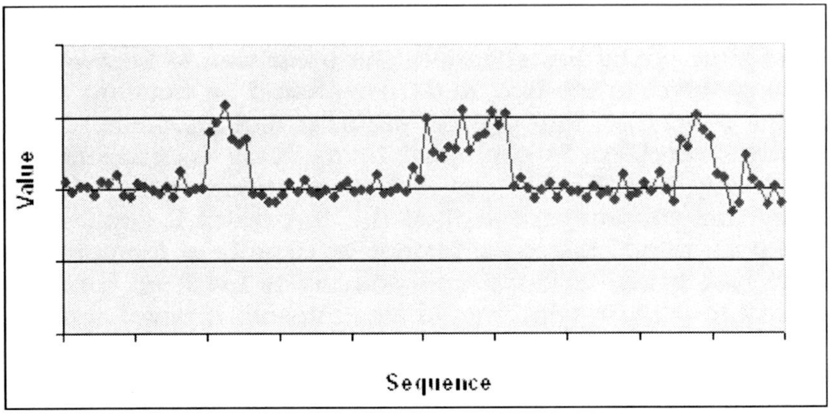

The level of urgency and the pressure applied to the team leader to solve this problem depends on the frequency that the problem tends to appear and the amount of material that is affected in these events. If a negligible amount of material is affected and the problem is known for a long time, it is quite usual not to pay too much attention to it and the management will be reluctant to allocate resources to solve it. The problem is sometimes considered to be tolerable background loss. On the other hand, if this problem appeared recently and/or the impact on line performance is significant, there will be a lot of pressure to solve it. Why? Because there is too much accumulated damage to ignore, and there will always be a dark cloud above, threatening to flood the entire line with bad material.

When a sporadic event is suspected and investigation is planned, the owner should verify that all occasions share similar symptoms. A common problem source can only be assumed if an identical footprint between the occurrences is found.

If there is a repetitive pattern or sequence over time, it implies that some routine treatment or cycled condition is necessary to initiate an occurrence. The effort in this case is to find either the common trigger to initiate the observed occurrences, or to verify whether several coincidental factors are required to cause the problem. Even without observing a repetitive pattern (routine cycle) in problem appearance, a thorough check should be performed to verify whether any common treatment or condition coincides with the initiation of every occurrence.

A saw-tooth pattern is a typical pattern that could be interpreted as an erratic event, but in fact it is a rather typical in process line. There are two basic cases of saw-tooth patterns:

Diminishing saw tooth (Figure 1-15) is a repetitive signature that shows an unusual step to high (or low, or noisier) values at a certain point with gradual change back to normal. The situation is usually an indication of a treatment that requires the tool or system to run differently after it. The tool is in a gradual return to normal with the elapsed time after the treatment, or after processing some material through it.

Figure 1-15. Diminishing saw tooth

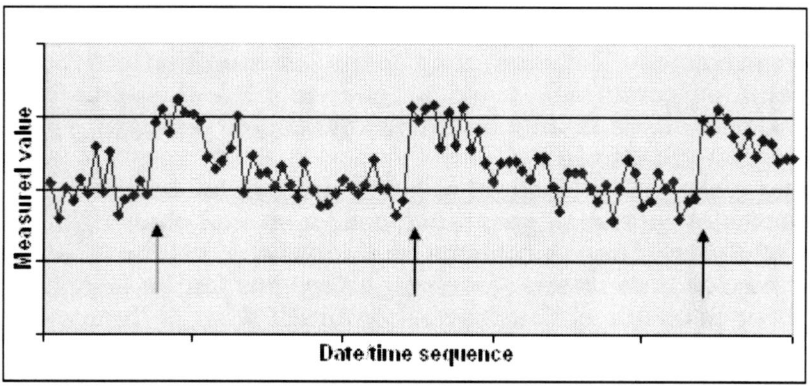

Intensifying saw-tooth (Figure 1-16) is a repetitive signature that shows gradual change over time until a certain point and than abrupt change back to normal. The situation here is opposite in nature to the previous one. The tool or system shows stable performance for a while and then tends to deteriorate (or change) over time. Once the tool or system passes certain treatment it returns to normal.

Figure 1-16. Intensifying saw tooth

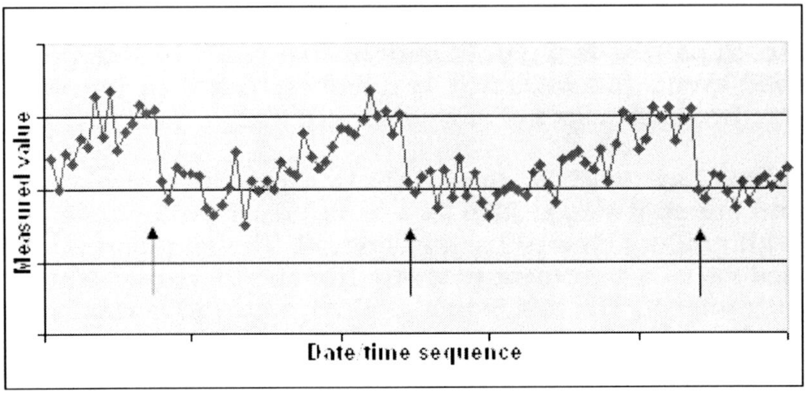

Once a noticeable pattern is observed, and/or a certain treatment that coincides with every occasion is identified, the investigation is in a much better situation. From this point on, the next occurrence may be predicted. The team may focus its attention on the exact treatment (or condition), learn it, change it, and addressing the problem, may check results on the next expected occasion.

Sporadic event with a low level of failure (low signal to noise ratio)
Some cases of sporadic appearance pose a special challenge for root cause analysts. These problems are characterized by a sporadic appearance in time or sequence and a very low failure level (in total number or percentage).You may ask yourself what is the motivation to solve a problem that involves an almost negligible amount of material and requires extra effort to do so. Well, there are good reasons. Imagine that these components are about to be installed in larger or more critical systems and defective components put this larger system at risk. Or, it is suspected that this kind of failure may develop dramatically into a significant threat to the line or product reliability.

To demonstrate this type of problem, the Bathtub Model for reliability will be introduced. Let's look into the typical lifecycle of a product, as shown in fig. 1-17. The X axis represents the service time (or its correspondent reliability test time), and the Y axis represents the number of failing units. The relatively high failure rate on the left (after short service time) is related to "infant mortality", meaning that defective products failed after very short service. Then there is a long period with very few or no failing products, which represent the typical lifecycle with good service of healthy products. On the right side of the X axis there is again a sharp increase in the product failure rate. This region is the product wear out after prolonged service.

Figure 1-17. Bathtub model of product life cycle

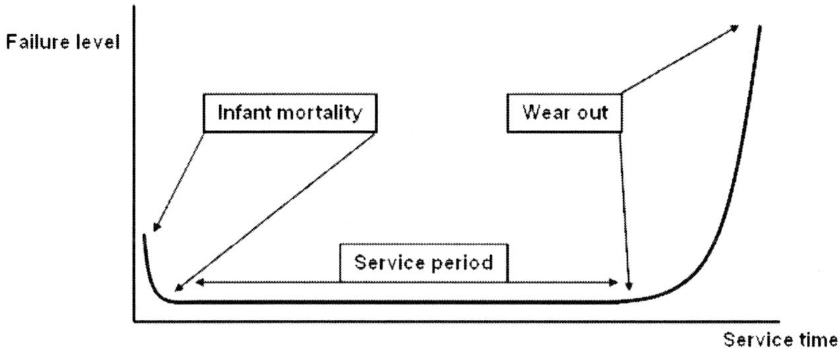

In most cases, it is very hard to acquire data from the customer, and the time to failure under regular service conditions could be long. Reliability tests under harsh conditions are used to accelerate the process, and in a short time, relate the expected product performance under regular service conditions. If necessary, it is possible to use the required test conditions on all manufactured products, filtering out all defective products and preventing infant mortality in the customer's hands. But what if a certain inline problem causes premature failure in products, as demonstrated in figure 1-18?

Figure 1-18. Low level of random failures during service

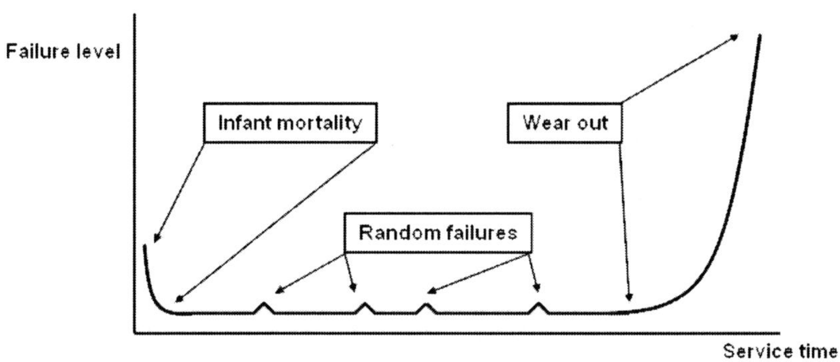

What are the special difficulties in running root cause analysis in low failing level events?

Difficulties in using statistical tools:
The tendency of the problem to fluctuate between no failures to a few failures makes it hard to characterize with the usual statistical methods (we can define it as noisy background level). Due to the low number of failures and the inconsistency of the appearance, there is a poor chance of gaining effective learning by searching for trend patterns or by trying to correlate the problem to certain process parameters.

Difficulties in running and interpreting experiments:
Additional difficulty lies in the poor ability to learn much from short term experiments. The rarity of the phenomenon under investigation will make the experiment ineffective. If randomly selected material is tested, the chance is that there will be no response on this material. Even if you are lucky enough to achieve some signal on the experiment, you will wonder if this is real or just the usual problem fluctuation.

Slow to detect meaningful response:
It is also hard and slow to detect a change in relation to background. Learning this kind of a problem requires a long time or large production volume. Knowledge about the background level is only acquired after enough results have been accumulated. A change or solution will not be observed right away. Again, only after observing the behavior for some time can one conclude whether the applied change was effective (this can be defined as trying to observe low signal from high noise).

As the change in behavior is more dramatic (better signal to noise ratio) the time to detect it will be shorter. For example, if the number of failures per week was very low, but was never 0, and after implementing change there are two consecutive weeks with 0 failures, you can be quite confident that the solution has a positive effect. However this is not always the case and it takes some time and patience to gain a real impression of the impact of a change.

Mixed sources:
It was stated above that a very low number of failures is the problem, and it was assumed that all failures are related to the same source. Once this specific defect or problem is addressed, the

problem will be eliminated. However, what if the failures share the same characteristics, but the problem comes from various sources (mixed sources)?

Sometimes low background level failures with a similar failure mode are caused by different types of defects. If a low level of loss was counted as tolerable background level in the past, not much effort was invested to break this low number of failures at their sources. Once there is an increase in the level of failures, it is impossible to know which of these sources remained at its usual level and which is responsible for the increase in the number of failures (maybe a new one just appeared).

To deal with mixed sources, you need to either understand which of the sources is responsible for the increased failure level (when comparison to past performance is possible) or to learn the current situation by quantifying the sources of failures (when past performance per source is unknown).

The Pareto Chart (Figure 1-19) is a graphic tool that is most useful in defining dominancy and priority. It shows the relative frequency (or count) of each classified item (defect type) and highlights the ones that are most dominant in appearance.

Figure 1-19. Pareto chart of visible defect classification

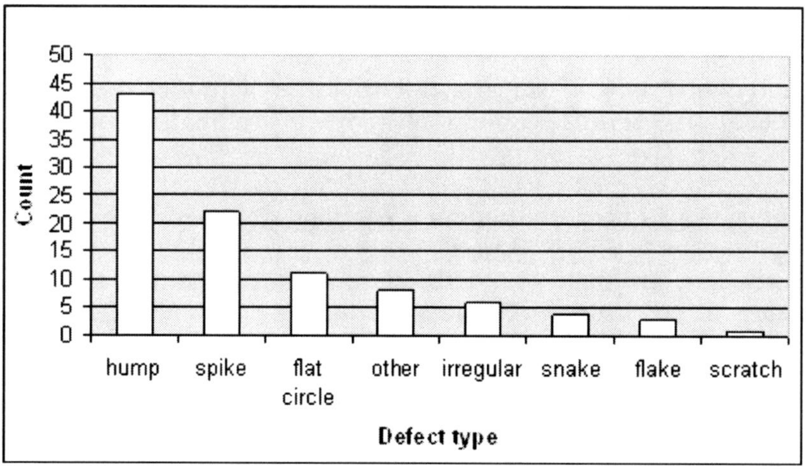

If comparison to past performance is possible, compare failure level per source and identify the source responsible for the increase in failure level. Find its cause and eliminate the problem.

If past performance per source of failure is unknown, there is no way to know which of the sources is responsible for the increased failing level. In this case, learning should be from this point on, and the team should confront the problem based on priority.

You may define the priority as confronting the dominant sources first (based on the Pareto Chart) or you may decide that it is preferable to confront sources that are easy to solve (low hanging fruits). The benefit in confronting the dominant defect is that it is possible to lower the failure level back to normal or even to a lower level than before (even if this is not the specific source that caused the increase in failure level).

The benefit in confronting the easy-to-solve defect (how do you know that?) is that it may contribute to the speed that you achieve results. However if this selected source is low in the Pareto Chart, the impact on the total number of failures will be low and the improvement will be insignificant.

Since a low level of failure is hard to analyze with statistics or experiments, it is harder to resolve. There should be intensive learning (for instance by lab analysis) of a few individual failures that truly represent the failure pattern.

Thorough learning and an attempt to tailor a model that explains the generation of the problem is more suitable for this kind of problem.

A few more words on a change as a problem

In this section, problem was defined as a change that is sensed in a parameter over time. Sometimes it is a real challenge to differentiate between harmless process **noise** and harmful **change.** Without proper definition of a target value, upper limit and lower limit for the selected parameter, any change in behavior will be hard to notice. The SPC (Statistical Process Control) addresses this and many computerized tools were developed to gain early alerts on process changes and prevent unnecessary loss.

There is no intention to examine SPC and other related subjects in this book, however it is highly recommended for the reader to have a reasonable knowledge of basic statistics in general and SPC in particular when dealing with processing issues.

Process Capability Problems

Is there a guarantee that our line will be free of failures just by avoiding any change? The answer is, no. Change over time is not the only reason for failures. In some situations, there is always a level of defective material in the background, or it appears that there is an increase in the level of failures at some point, but without an alert from the line on any noticeable change in performance. This section of the chapter addresses failures that are inherent to an existing process.

We know that process parameters that are checked in line have some correlation to end of line product performance. We also learned that any process parameter has some noise level that is responsible for the spread of the measured results. Therefore, targets and limits are defined for measured process parameters and SPC rules are applied for early detection and alert of a change in behavior over time.

One may think that for every parameter in the line, the target value and limits that were defined are optimal and once the process runs within these limits, no defective material is expected. This kind of optimal situation is graphically represented by figure 1-20.

Figure 1-20. Optimal distribution placement within process limits

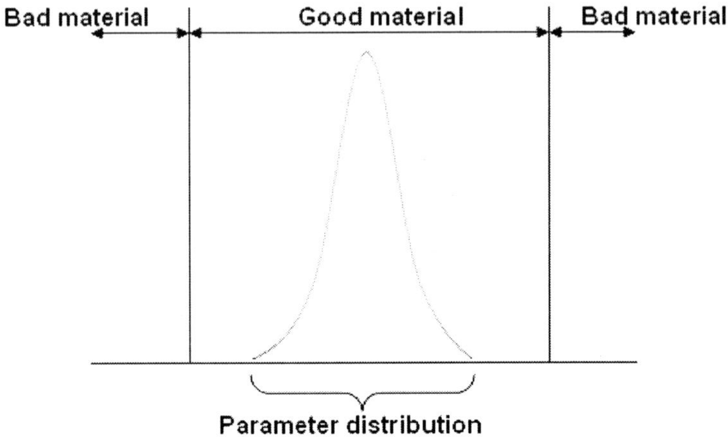

It is clear that if this processes parameter goes beyond or below distinct values, the result will be fatal to the end product.

Looking at the distribution of all taken measurements (over some time) with respect to its limits shows a perfect bell shape (normal) distribution with no outliers. It is placed exactly in the center point between the limits and has a very narrow distribution with respect to the process limits. All production material processed through that machine is far from the limits, and unless there is significant change in tool performance, we do not expect any problematic material from this process step.

How frequent is such an optimal situation in the process in real life? Rarely.
Several issues may impact this ideal picture.

- Limits placement (process window)
- Distribution width and shape
- Interdependency of process parameters
  - Process corner
  - Non-linear dependency (loss function)

Limits placement (process window)

Process working window is the tolerance to variation in a specific process parameter, without an adverse effect on product performance (either on functionality or reliability). A wider working window means a more robust process. In the ideal situation that was presented earlier, we considered the upper and lower limits as the exact borders of the working window.

The question is how were the target and spec limits for process parameters defined in the first place? In many cases, when developing a complicated process it is almost impossible to check the real impact of each process parameter in every process step on end of line results (or on any subsequent process parameter). So, sometimes target and spec limits reflect the actual tool performance on limited volume without knowing the real working window.

In this case we do not know the distribution placement with respect to the real limits. It could be that the tail of the distribution is already very close or even beyond the limit.

This effect is even more pronounced when shifting from the development stage to high volume manufacturing. More tools for the same process step may widen the actual distribution on the one hand, and widening the variety of products may narrow down the process window on the other (by having a higher chance to process sensitivity of a certain product). It is possible that our product is prone to failures within the predefined control limits as demonstrated in figure 1-21.

Figure 1-21. Limit placements are shifted in respect to; process working window.

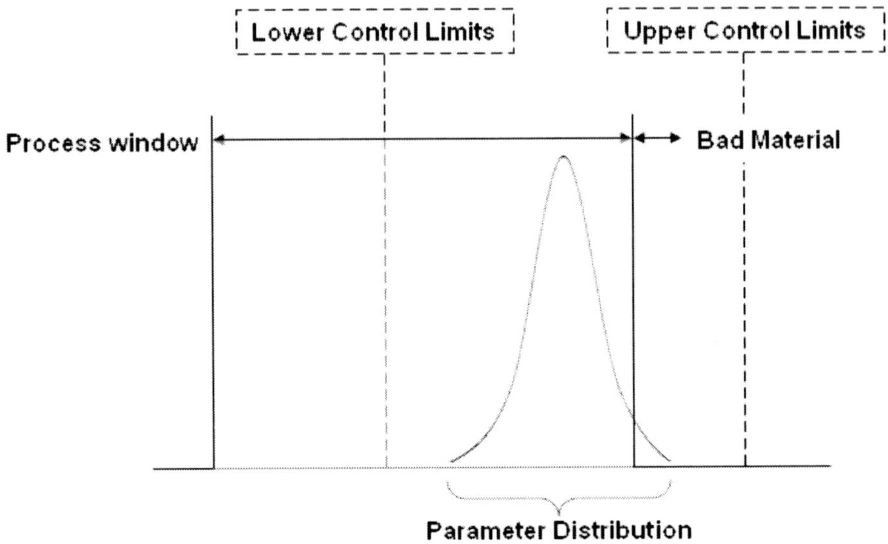

There is no issue with the distribution width in figure 1-21, however the target placement for this process parameter is not in its sweet point, and part of the distribution is outside of the working window. All material from the upper edge of the distribution will provide bad material. If the upper working window coincides with the edge of the distribution, we can say that the process in on a cliff. A small change in distribution placement or in spread may take the process over the cliff, resulting in significant loss.

If the target for this process parameter is placed in the middle of the shaded area and the limits move accordingly, then the related loss could be avoided (assuming the tool can preserve its satisfactory performance with the new target).

Distribution width and shape

Even when assuming that the defined limits reflect the actual working window, the distribution is not always so symmetric and narrow and some material near the upper or lower tail may be outside the critical limit.

Wide distribution

A process parameter that has an impact on (or correlation to) end product results could have a distribution that is too wide to keep all material healthy. Part of the distribution lies in an area that causes the material to fail. The situation could be that the distribution is centered in the working window as shown in figure 1-22 and material from both edges of distribution is failing, or the distribution is not centered and only one edge of the distribution is sticking out of the working window, causing the material to fail. In these cases, cause analysis will most probably focus on identification of the factors controlling the width of this process parameter distribution (while trying to narrow the distribution enough for proper performance). It may also find the actual reason that makes this process parameter critical to the product and reduces product sensitivity to this parameter. This means that we either try to fit the distribution to the working window or enlarge the working window to fit the distribution width.

Figure 1-22. Incapable process, parameter distribution is wider than working window

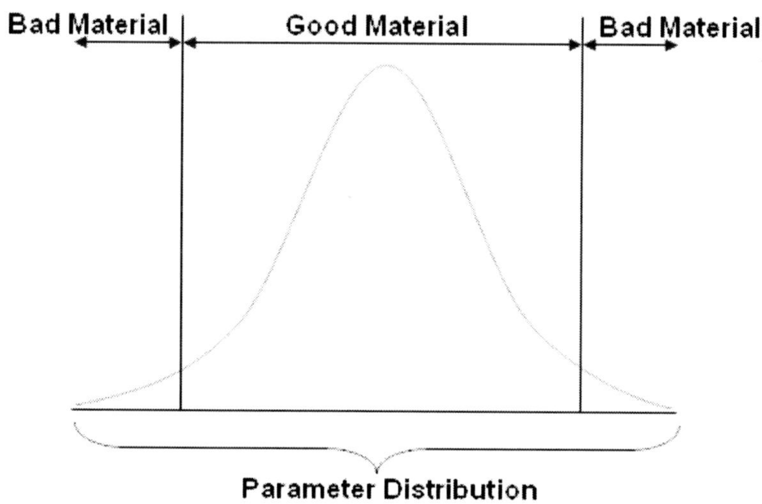

The issues related to the process capability (CP and CPK) are beyond of the scope of this book. The reader may find more about it in the Recommended Reading chapter.

Distorted distribution (skewed, bi or multi-modal, outliers)

The above example shows wide normal distribution. However very frequently we will find that the process parameters do not have such a symmetrical shape. If the concept of process noise is still fresh in our minds, we can understand that it is possible that the population will not follow the ideal shape of the expected Gaussian (bell shape) distribution.

Let's take an example where a tool has a normal behavior of slow deterioration after a certain period of stable performance. In this case, the distribution of the measured parameter will be skewed with a heavy tail as shown in figure 1-23. The stable period provides normal distribution, however once the deterioration starts, lower than usual readings are measured, causing a distortion in the distribution. If we allow the deterioration to live long enough, eventually some of the readings may be out of the defined lower limit.

Figure 1-23. Skewed distribution

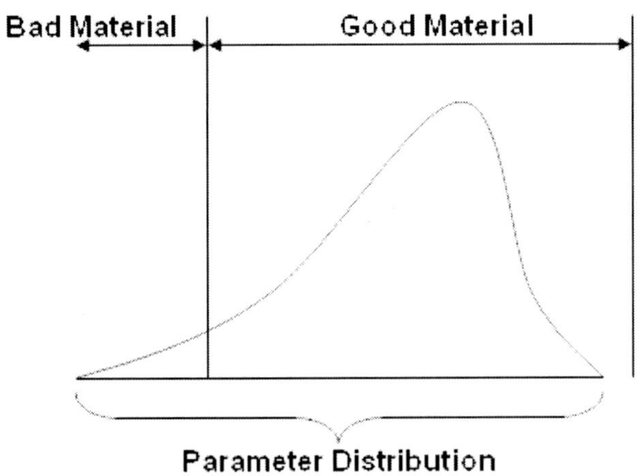

As explained above, in order to achieve a proper sampling, measurements are taken from different regions over the products, different locations within process tools, or from different process tools. The distribution shape of all readings is a result of the accumulation of all these sub-distributions. If the center (mode) of one or some of these sub-distributions is displaced from the center (mode) of the main distribution, the results will be bimodal or multimodal distribution. This situation is shown in figure 1-24, while some material from the shifted distribution is out of the allowed limit. It is important to understand the origin of the sub-distribution as the first step to correct the situation.

Figure 1-24. Bimodal distribution, with part of the distribution out of working window

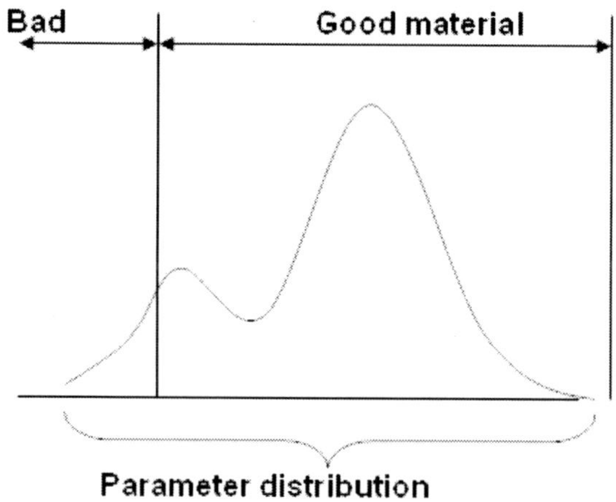

In some cases, the distribution has an almost perfect shape and it is well placed within the limits; however there are some points that appear totally out of the expected population (outliers), as shown in figure 1-25. Frequently enough, if there are very few points, there is a tendency to ignore these readings and filter it out of the calculations. However there is a potential risk in doing so. If this is an indication of a real problem that appears to be negligible, at some stage it can be inflated into a much bigger problem without noticing, due to the applied filtering.

Figure 1-25. Outliers, the outliers are away from the main distribution and out of working windows

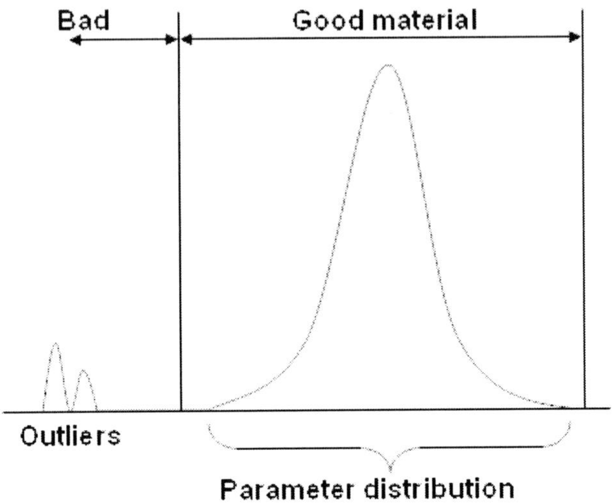

Interdependency of process parameters

The situation of having a problem with a specific process parameter with a known or detected direct impact on product performance (or on the performance of another critical parameter) is a relatively simple case (to learn, but not necessary to solve). The working window and proper limits for this process parameter are easy to identify, by learning the relevant results of the processed production material or by running a few experiments around the target value. The situation is more complicated in integrative process issues.

<u>Process corner</u>
End of line product performance or performance of later process steps are often impacted by a combination (integration) of several process steps. This may cause a certain parameter to perform well under some conditions of another parameter, but to provide bad results with different conditions of this other parameter. This situation is shown in figure 1-26. While checking the product performance according to the results of process parameter A, it appears to be fine in the entire range of results. This will be the same in the check for process parameter B. However, once low

results of Parameter A coincide with high results of Parameter B, the product fails.

Figure 1-26. Process corner, product performance dependency in two process parameters.

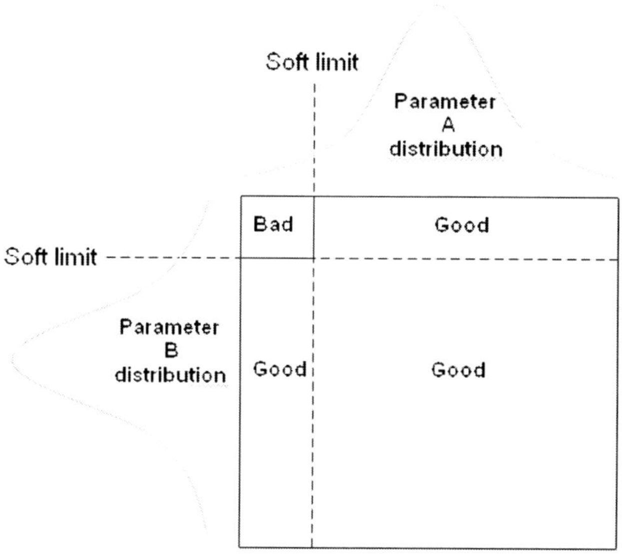

In this case, the analyst faces a double challenge. First, there is a need to understand that more than one process parameter is causing the failure, and second to identify those parameters and improve the situation so that no losses will occur.

Non-abrupt limits (loss function).

We may understand that the limits defined for controlling a certain process parameter behave like an on/off switch. In other words, when the measured results are within the limits, all material is healthy with perfect performance, and when this parameter is outside defined borders, all material is nonfunctional or bad.

Figure 1-27. Abrupt working window.

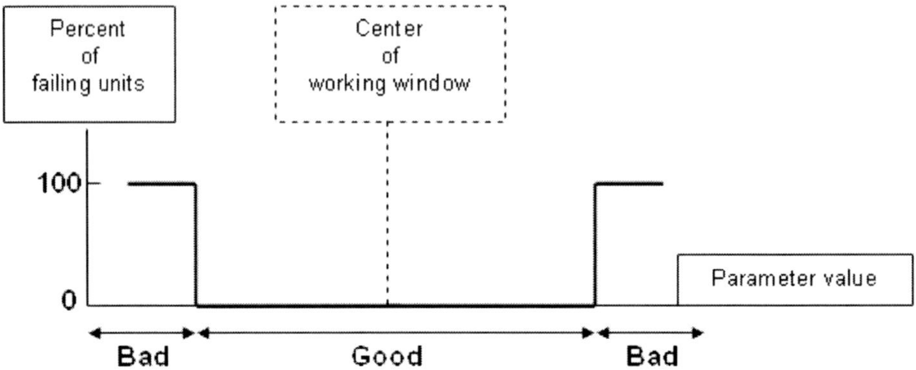

This situation is well represented in figure 1-27. As we move away from the center of the working window of a critical proccss parameter, there is no negative effect on the product until we cross a certain value. Once this value is crossed all material fails. The loss seems to be a step function.

However, as we already saw, there could be a process corner situation in which a certain process parameter value may provide good material at one time and bad material at another. In complex processes, there could be a situation in which product results are related to the interdependency of many parameters. In this case, we may find that a critical process parameter will have a different loss function.

Figure 1-28. Loss function

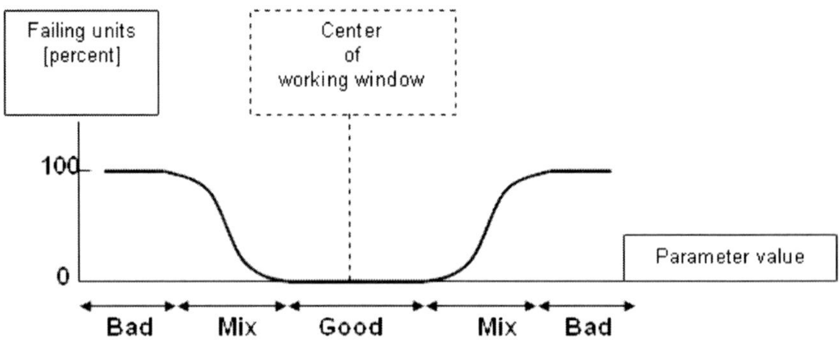

This situation is described in figure 1-28. As we move away from the center of the working window, there is a gradual increase in percentage of bad products. If the distribution of the process parameter is wide enough, part of the distribution will show massive failing (up to 100% above a certain value). We may experience a sharp increase in failure rate with only a small shift in a certain parameter, or we may see only slow deterioration in product health even when the measured parameter deviates significantly from the defined limits.

Overlapping the loss function and the actual parameter distribution can demonstrate clearly the problematic working window (Figure 1-29). When facing this kind of problem, it is difficult to understand all interdependencies that lead to this situation. The leaders should decide whether they would like to work on squeezing the distribution of this process parameter into a safe region (or into a region in which the loss is tolerable), or to try and make the product less sensitive to this parameter.

Figure 1-29. Process parameter distribution overlap with loss function

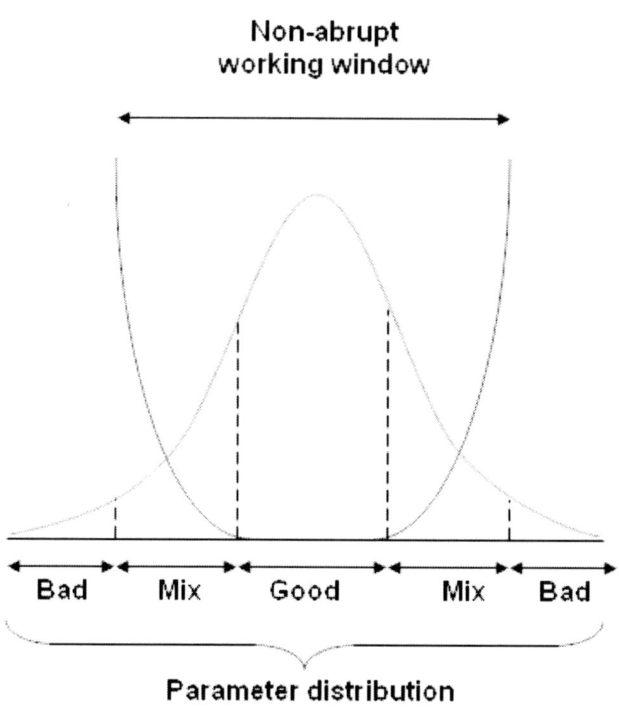

Poor process control coverage

In previous sections of this chapter, we discussed two situations. In the first one, a change was detected in a measured process parameter and the cause should be defined and solved to prevent any negative effect on end of line product or on later process steps. In the second, a negative effect is detected on end of line product or in late process step while it is attributed to the performance of earlier process step. In this case, a noticeable correlation between a measured parameter and the resulting problem is either known or could be found.

However, in some cases, failures occur and while trying to correlate these failures to any measured processes parameter, nothing is detected. It appears that there was no change in any process parameter and there are failures on well-characterized parameters with a well-established process window.

What could go wrong?

- o Poor sampling method
- o Monitor and product mismatching
- o Unrealized factor (internal, external)

Poor sampling method

When deciding to monitor a specific parameter in a certain process step, some decisions were made regarding the sampling. The decision is made while considering the typical tool characteristics and its impact on the manufactured product. The frequency and timing of measurement, material selection for monitoring, number and location of measurement sites, measuring tool and recording method are all included in this decision. And there is a lot of room for error.

Let's look at a few examples of sampling problems.

Case 1
There is one tool that consists of two processing stages. The tool designer decided that the first processing stage will have two

independent tracks, so as not to delay the second stage, which runs much faster. The processing sequence starts with the first item to be processed on the left track, the second item on the right track, the third on the left again, and so on. All items from both tracks will then continue to the second process stage.

The engineer decided wisely to sample items from the start, middle and end of each lot and instructed the operation techs accordingly. However, there are 25 items in the processing lot, so the measurements were always taken on items number 1, 13 and 25 in every lot. Obviously the right track of the first stage was never monitored. Imagine this: half of the line could be affected without knowing it.

Case 2

To achieve proper monitoring of the deposited layer's uniformity over the product (in a certain process step), the engineer decided to measure five points on every tested product. Top, bottom, center, left, and right points were measured. A new engineer was assigned to this tool and decided to save time spent on monitoring. He decided to reduce the number of measurement sites per item to three. He compared and found that the average of the right, center and left points matches exactly the average value of the five traditional points, while the std-dev appears slightly higher. Since he knew that this tool has typical non-uniformity from left to right, he decided to use these three points and was convinced that any deterioration in tool performance, either in deposition rate or uniformity performance, will be detected.

After a while, it evolved that this machine caused severe loss due to uniformity deterioration. The monitor failed to show it either in the average deposition rate or in std-dev results. There was even a slight improvement in the std-dev results.

It evolved that in this deposition tool, the product always kept the orientation of the previous process step when entering the machine. However, recently a change was made to the preceding process step and the material emerged from these process steps with 90 degree rotation. Nevertheless, the measurements taken after the deposition maintained the original absolute points over the product. Therefore the three measured points now represent the center line (top, center, and bottom) and failed to detect the change in machine's uniformity performance.

Case 3
A complicated and time-consuming monitor requiring evaluation was established to develop a new product. An engineer requested monitoring once per shift, with random selection of the lot by the operation tech. After a while it evolved that this monitor failed to detect the problem. Lots processed in this operation after the tool was idle for a while failed. The monitor was able to capture this phenomenon. However, the operation techs were free to select any lot during the shift. For efficiency, they concentrated a number of lots and ran them sequentially on this tool, taking the last lot that was processed for monitoring. None of the lots that were checked was processed immediately after the tool was idle.

Even if we say that some of the above examples should be anticipated, it is quite clear that sample size and sampling method have a significant impact on the ability to detect problems. We should keep in mind that sampling is based on previous characterization and learning with some assumptions, however if something is changed in the characteristics then the assumptions could be wrong. **Sampling by definition has blind spots.** Careful selection of a sampling method may minimize the blind spots, however when running root cause analysis, one should always suspect that a blind spot in sampling coverage is a potential explanation for an investigated event.

Monitor and product mismatching

In some cases, tool performance cannot be evaluated by direct measurement on the actual product. This can be for several reasons. The measurement technique may harm the product. The product shape, size or material does not fit the measuring tool. The analytical technique takes too long and will delay the manufacturing floor, and so on.

In these cases, monitoring is with a witness sample that fits the measurement technique and is not be as valuable as the product itself.

Initial learning verifies that there is a good correlation between measurements performed on this sample and the actual situation on a real product. Later, by monitoring the result on the witness sample, the tool owner can assume with high confidence that the tool is doing what it is supposed to do and the product passed with satisfactory results.

Still, there are several potential problems with this assumption.

- No change to tool performance, but the result of this treatment on the actual product was changed. The actual product progresses through the line while receiving the required treatment in every process step. Sometimes, variations in earlier process steps affect the results of a later process step. Monitoring samples that are not subjected to earlier process step treatment continue to produce normal results. The correlation between the monitor and the real product is lost. Since there is no indication of any problem by the monitor, the production material will continue to run and the change may only be detected at a later stage.

- Tool performance was changed. No change in monitor results. The change strongly affects the actual product, however the witness sample is not affected by this change (at all or to the same extent as the product). This can be attributed to inherent higher sensitivity of the actual product vs. lower sensitivity of the monitor to variations of the treatment, or it is possible that the selected measurement structure or monitor placement within the tool (location, position, orientation) are not affected by the change. The production material will continue to be processed through that tool with no indication of any problem.

- Change in monitor results or measuring tool. No change to tool performance. The assumption that was made earlier is that the witness sample (monitor) is not subjected to variations that will alter the treatment results. It was also assumed that the measuring tool is always accurate and free of errors, shifts and drifts.
What if the monitor starts to indicate a problem because of some change of monitoring vehicle or because of a change in the measuring tool? At best, the tool owner will put the machine on hold and identify the real cause of the problem. After identifying the problem, the tool owner will conclude

that production material was not affected. Apart from some downtime of the processing tool, no harm was done.
However, if the tool owner adjusts the processing tool to achieve satisfactory monitor results, the material will continue to run with satisfactory results on the monitor, but the actual production material will receive improper treatment and it will continue to be processed until the problem is detected at a later stage.

Unrealized factor (internal, external)

Imagine that you are responsible for running stable and mature technology. The process is well characterized and all critical parameters are running with excellent process capability in well established working windows. Unexpectedly, catastrophic failures start to appear.

When checking the failing material it looks as if they were monitored properly and all results are correct and fit the historical data. Failure analysis identifies the suspected operation causing the problem. Verification of all tool conditions, monitoring methods, machine components, and supplies still does not indicate any change.

What could go wrong? Well, a new player joined the game. A factor that did not exist or was inert up to now started to have impact on the product. It is possible that some specific process step will be identified as the source of the problem. However, this process step should not necessarily carry the blame. It is possible that nothing was changed in the treatment performed by this process step, and a new factor played a role in the failing mechanism.

This new factor could be **internal** or **external.**

If the factor is **internal**, the product characteristic is changed by the new factor (the product could be a real end of line product or the outcome of a certain process step).

An unrealized internal factor is usually related to a change in a certain condition that was previously considered as being inert to the involved process step, while it is not really so. This change could be introduced deliberately without realizing that it has an effect (such as change in product mix or change of chemical vendor), or it could be introduced unknowingly (change of a neighboring tool caused a change in the environment, lighting and other factors). This change intervenes in the treatment performed by this process step and alters the resulting output.

An unrealized factor could be attributed to a change in a previous treatment (incoming to the suspected process step) that interacts with the usual conditions of the later treatment to form different results. The effect on the production material appears to be related to the later process step.

It is also possible that it is related to a new condition that is subsequent to this process step. The new condition interacts with the product subsequent to the relevant process step and alters the results of the treatment later on.

If the factor is **external**, the product characteristic is not changed, however the product needs to withstand conditions or tests that it had not experienced previously. Once this external condition was introduced, the product failures start to appear. Under this new condition, a process step generating results that were found to be satisfactory up to now appears to perform inadequately and the material is failing.

The above situations are even more complicated when the new factor that was not realized earlier creates a new process corner (or enhances the sensitivity of the existing process corner), or changes the loss function. The challenge is first to recognize the fact that a new factor is involved, next to identify this factor, and last to establish adequate control over it.

Shift from source identification to cause understanding

In previous sections of the chapter, the discussion concentrated on events from the aspect of process control. The events were classified based on problem reflectance on process parameters. However, finding the tool or process step that is responsible for generation of bad material is **source identification** but we need to correct the problem and make the line productive and healthy. So, identification of the process step or process tool is just a starting point for a new type of cause analysis. The next step is to answer the question "What's wrong or went wrong in this system/tool that lead to the unexpected result?" or "What should be improved in this system/tool to achieve the expected results?" This section and some other parts of this book focus on this aspect of problem solving.

There are two major categories on this level of event analysis:

- o Events related to tool /system component malfunction
- o Events related to human behavior

Component malfunction

Wear out

Wear out is used here as general term to describe performance degradation or total failure of a tool or component as a result of service. There is no intention to distinguish between metallurgical failure modes such as fatigue, creep and erosion. However it is important to pay attention to the behavioral aspect of the failing component, because it may affect the way a solution or detection method is applied to prevent reoccurrence of the problem.

– Slow deterioration in a component without noticeable loss of performance that ends in sudden failure or damage (apply component change according to service time or volume of material processed through the tool or system)
– Slow change in a component with a noticeable related change in performance over time (apply component change or service once the detected change reaches a certain limit)
- Slow deterioration in precision or calibration (apply calibration or replacement based on volume or time as needed)
– Sudden failure of a component after stress or aggressive treatment (find the source of stress and eliminate it or design a component that can withstand this kind of stress)

Inherent flaw in component (incoming) or supplies (including a structural problem in a tool or component). One should keep in mind that the line is constantly changing. Raw material is processed and necessary supplies are fed into the line. Maintenance is performed on the machines and essential parts and kits are replaced. Even with thorough control over incoming material, there is no guarantee that occasionally some defective component or poor quality supply will not sneak into the production line and damage the products.

Another potential problem may exist when introducing a new tool or system into an existing process line. Usually, each component of the new tool is tested carefully and the quality of the tool's output results is verified. Still, there is a possibility that some latent flaw in the tool will show up at a later stage, when the tool starts to produce at full volume.

<u>Damaging treatment (poor PM) or conditions (hostile environment)</u>
We cannot assume that the activities performed on the tool or substances in contact with the tool are totally inert to it. There is potential damage to the tool, its components and its supply during processing, service, or even when idle. This could come from the tool itself, from the surrounding environment or by importing conditions that are incompatible with the tool during service or with the material to be processed. Corrosion, contamination, and erosion could be examples for this kind of problem.

<u>Working beyond a tool or component tolerance (optimal or recommended conditions)</u>
Sometimes a tool or component assigned for a certain operation is simply incapable of performing the job properly. This could be attributed to the tool design and its physical limitations or to one component within the tool. In many cases it will cause inadequate precision, repeatability, or uniformity in the output results instead of total failure. The result in these cases is failure or reliability problems related to higher process noise.

The conflict between a narrow process working window and the width or shape of critical process parameter distribution is in most cases related to this problem category. This is especially correct when trying to employ older process tools on newly designed products, while the new products require more precise control than the tool is built to provide.

Let's look at an actual example to clarify this situation:

Case #1
In a certain production line that ran without any problem for a while, a step function in std-dev of a certain process parameter was observed. The suspected machine was checked for the failing component and nothing was found. The indication was that something was changed after a specific maintenance activity involving pressure regulator replacement. The machine was taken down and the suspect regulator was replaced with a similar thoroughly calibrated one. This solution did not provide the adequate results, and the parameter continued to produce noisy results.

After detailed learning of the process/tool interactions, it was found that the pressure regulator needed to provide pressure of 2 PSI. The original regulator that was in use had 10 PSI full scale, however it was not available in stock at the time and the service tech replaced it with 200 PSI full scale regulator and tuned it to show around 2 PSI. This regulator has a poor ability to regulate pressure in the 1% level of its full scale. Naturally, replacing this 200 PSI regulator with another 200 PSI one could not address the problem.

Case #2
The department responsible for hard coating performed an excellent job for years. None of the customers ever complained about the coating thickness or early failures of any component coated in this machine. Recently a customer returned material with field failures after relatively short service. It was found that this component was the longest part coated in the machine. Due to the length of this part, some of it was beyond the optimal working zone of the coater and received a much thinner protection layer. This thin location was prone to early failure.

Human behavior failures

Even with the dominancy of process automation in modern technologies, there is enough room for human-related failures and indeed these problems frequently occur. Computers are not susceptible to tiredness and can assist in preventing human error, however programs are written by persons, data is fed to computers by persons, and a person can override the computer. Furthermore, a lot of process line activities are still performed or driven by persons. Routine and unscheduled service jobs are performed by persons.

This section discusses the basic reasons for human-related failures, from a situation that appears to be unavoidable by the involved person all the way down to a malicious act.

Problem created by lack of knowledge (information does not exist, is incorrect, or is not communicated)
An individual is required to perform a task and approaches it with all the good intentions to perform it in the best possible way. In the process, the individual is faced with something he or she does not know how to handle. Is it a problem? It is not, if the individual stops and asks for help.

The problem is when someone completed a task and unknowingly introduced an error. This person was fully aware of his actions every minute of the task but did not identify the gap in his knowledge.

The system that should prevent this kind of failure includes training that covers extensively every aspect of any task that a specific person is allowed to do in his or her job. There should be a written procedure describing in detail how a task should be performed. In tasks involving a significant chance of error or a potential high risk in the event of error, a novice should first see how this task is performed by an experienced person, then perform this job under supervision of the experienced person, and in the end, become certified to perform it by him or herself. Double verification is also recommended as a common procedure for this kind of task.

Human error: incorrect behavior or handling due to tiredness, distraction, or loss of concentration. An individual with adequate training, knowledge, and experience performs a task that is not new to him or her. Due to reasons related to physical or mental conditions in this exact situation, or due to abnormal surrounding conditions, the task was not performed as required. This could be related to loss of concentration, stress, or loss of sensitivity.

Negligence: a conscious decision to perform tasks contrary to requirements. Negligence occurs when someone performs an act without caring about the potential outcome. It is important to avoid confusion between risk taking and negligence. In risk taking, the person or team should consider the consequences of the act, and take necessary precautions to avoid a negative outcome, arrange measures for early detection of problem, and above all communicate the decision to others. The latter is contrary to negligence, when the person involved fails to inform or even tries to hide the problematic act that caused the problem.

Sabotage: deliberate creation of a problem, an act with intent to cause damage. Caution is required before concluding that something was caused by sabotage. The consequences could be devastating to individuals, groups or even companies if it is found to be true, but also if it ends in false accusation. If there is reason to believe that sabotage is the cause of an event, involve the top management as well as the legal department or authorities. The collected data and other action items may have judicial implications and must be handled by professionals. Keep in mind, most people come to work to do it right and there is usually a driving force behind different behavior.

When it is clear that damage is deliberate, you should find the driving force behind it. There are three typical reasons for deliberate damage.

Anger and frustration
Individuals that sabotage direct their anger towards an individual or system that they see as responsible for their bad feelings. The driving force here is more on the emotional level and therefore if the damage was mistakenly interpreted as unintentional, they may repeat it or talk about it to clarify their point (revenge).

During interviews, stay alert to relationships among the workers and try to detect a potential motivation for such an act. This could be a clash between an employee and his or her superior or colleagues, or frustration with the working place as a system.

Mental disturbance
This is a broad definition describing an emotionally-related driving force behind a deliberate act. Some cases of mental illness or borderline mental illness are expressed as vandalism. Since the rationale for the act is hard to follow, you may need professionals in this area to assist in or even lead the investigation.

There are other cases that are driven by mind rather than emotions. Some acts are driven by an alleged ideology or belief that justifies this kind of act. In this case this ideology or belief is often not limited to the workplace and learning about the individual's social life may provide the explanation for this act.

Competition

Competition immediately brings to mind an act by an external competitor. However, large-scale competition between companies is usually a potential explanation for a theft of critical information or items that carry information, but is unlikely to be related to local events or sabotage. Sometimes, competition between individuals and groups within the company could lead to a deliberate act with the intention of causing others to fail.

During interviews, look for the indicators that measure success or failure of groups and individuals. Check what sanctions are used for certain acquired performances (rewards and/or punishments). Is there an environment of bitter, rather than constructive competition?

Hackers are a special class of saboteurs, who may have any of the above characteristics. This could be classified as a competition (actually most hackers classify themselves as such). They are challenged by the security system (or any type of closed gate) and wish to compete with it. Some of them do not cause any harm when penetrating into an unauthorized area and simply enjoy the satisfaction of breaking in.

However, some hackers do not settle for this and cause real damage. Stealing and selling classified information is simply a criminal act that can be considered as industrial espionage. These acts can still be classified as competition.

Distribution of viruses, worms and Trojan horses, or deleting and altering information and system files are modern forms of vandalism. It can be classified as mental disturbance or anger and frustration, according to the motivation behind the act.

Four different stories about O-ring replacement

A number of tools are used to perform certain treatments on the process floor. This tool set is used in several process steps throughout the line. One of the process steps was changed recently and this change caused a more aggressive chemical attack on the tool's O-rings. It was decided to allocate one of the systems to run this process step and install a new type of O-ring that is compatible with this treatment. The maintenance procedures were changed to include the new type of O-ring. The O-ring supplier marked the outside package with a special mark for easy differentiation between the regular O-ring kit and the new one.

1. A well-trained maintenance person returned from a long vacation. He was asked to perform the required scheduled PM on several machines, including the one that was recently allocated to run the changed process step. Since this person was well trained on this kind of machine, nobody bothered to tell him that there was a change in the PM spec and there were special requirements for one of the machines. He performed the PM as required, however he used the regular kit, without knowing that a special kit is required.

2. A well-trained technician performed the PM. He took the required O-ring and fit it into its groove. While doing so, he was distracted by a phone call from his supervisor. The supervisor told him to complete this task ASAP, as he needs to take care of another tool in this shift. After being distracted in the middle of a delicate task and preoccupied with the thought of the new task, this person completed the required job. The system failed later on due to air leaking through this O-ring. Apparently a certain area of the O-ring was outside of its groove and when tightened it was pinched and distorted.

3. An experienced tech performed maintenance on the machine. During the work he realized that the special O-ring kit was not available. Due to a high demand he decided that the regular O-ring would survive long enough to support production until a new O-ring kit arrived. He installed the regular O-ring and returned the tool to production. The O-ring failed shortly after the PM and contaminated the material processed through this machine.

4. Due to delivery issues it was decided to use another supplier service as a second source for the special O-rings. After a while, it was found that kits with O-rings from this supplier tended to fail after short service. The supplier was astonished and claimed that he had never encountered this problem in any other manufacturing

site. A check showed that faulty O-rings had been placed in newly prepared kits. Investigation revealed that the person who prepared the kits was paid by the first supplier to include faulty O-rings with the intention of disqualifying the competition.

Chapter Summary

This chapter introduced the reader to types of events that could appear in the processing line. The event could be detected as a problem in process parameter behavior inline or as a product failure at a later stage (inline, end of line or field failure). The intention was to provide a basic understanding of potential reasons for problems appearing either in the process line or manufactured products.

Things to keep in mind:

To ensure a proper processing sequence of manufactured products in every required process step, critical process parameters are checked in line and at the end of line. A process parameter is checked or measured by predefined sampling and should reflect the required performance. The actual performance is an accumulation of all sources of process noise. To ease the follow-up of performance, the individual measurements are aggregated into summary statistics.

A problem can be detected as a change in a measured process parameter. This change may affect location or spread indicator, and it may affect some or all of the processed or measured material. A change event could be abrupt or gradual, and it could be bounded, continuous, or sporadic.

A problem in a product could be related to the fact that a critical process parameter or combination of independent process parameters is outside of the necessary working window. This is either due to the placement of the working window or related to the behavior of the process parameter/s.

A problem may exist when there is no apparent correlation of any measured process parameter with the detected symptom. This could be related to the fact that control over a critical factor affecting product performance is improperly sampled, insensitive, or totally missing. The latter usually occurs when this factor was not known to affect the product.

An event is usually initiated by an unexpected condition or action. In most cases an investigation will point to either human behavior or machine/system malfunction. It is important to understand the fundamental reason behind any identified unexpected act or malfunction in order to determine the most appropriate solution.

CHAPTER 2

The Sequence of Cause Analysis

The topics covered in this chapter are:

- The continuous cycle of cause analysis
- The problem definition funnel
- Problem characterization stage
- Model building and validation stage

The continuous cycle of cause analysis

Mr. Someone arrived home early this evening, opened the front door, switched on the light and took one step forward into total darkness. He scratched his head and thought to himself "I turned the light on but nothing happened. I didn't forget to pay the bill so it's most probably a burnt light-bulb or a power failure in the neighborhood".

Mr. Someone stepped back and looked around. All neighboring houses seemed to have pretty normal lighting. He stepped back in and holding onto the wall, he made his way into the kitchen and turned on the light. "Oh no, still in darkness," he mumbled to himself. He found his way to the main circuit board and the faint light that came in from outside was enough to see that one of the switches had tripped. He turned it on and sighed with relief, blinking his dazzled eyes in the sudden light.

Let's follow the sequence described in this short story.

- Mr. Someone faced a problem. Lights did not come on when he pressed the light-switch.
- Initial information (data) that he had (in mind) was that the light usually comes on when he presses the light-switch.
- He raised several potential explanations (hypotheses or models) for what could have caused the problem: 1. power failure in neighborhood; 2. burnt light bulb; 3. electricity disconnected because of late payment of the bill.
- He then checked if any of the above explanations is correct (verification or validation).
- Since none of these explanations were correct, he raised a new explanation and checked it. This time it was found to be correct (cause identification).

You may doubt whether this should be the final stage in Mr. Someone's investigation, since we do not know why the switch tripped. Well, I guess that this exact thought crossed Mr. Someone's mind... however, this is only a simplified example to demonstrate the cause analysis sequence and we cannot investigate it right now.

As demonstrated by this short story, the steps taken to identify the cause of a problem schematically are as follows:
Problem definition➔ data collection➔ hypothesizing (or generating models)➔ verification (or validation)➔ cause identification

A more conventional way to show this sequence is with a flow chart presented in figure 2-1.

Figure 2-1. Flow of root cause analysis

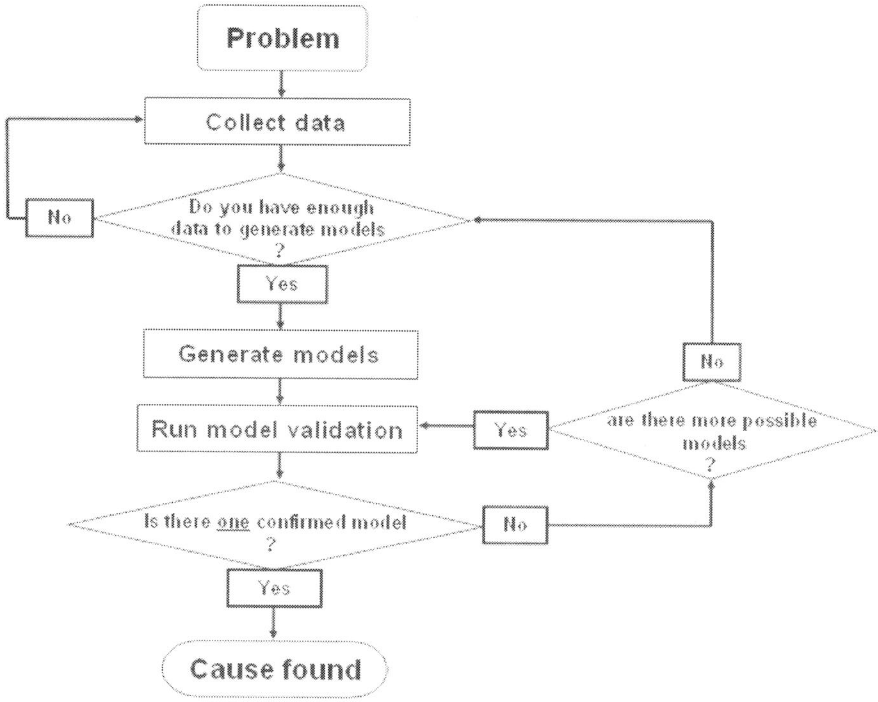

This cycle is common to many disciplines and appears in many textbooks dealing with failure analysis, event or incident investigation, cause analysis or whatever name exists to describe the search for the cause of an unusual event (unusual and not necessarily unwanted, as research and development tasks are similarly performed, and not necessary as a reaction to an unwanted event).

In the above sequence, the stages between detection of the initial problem and cause identification may be divided into different stages, which will be discussed in more detail in the next few chapters. The frame marked as Collect data aims to characterize the problem in more detail and hence it is the problem characterization stage, while the frames marked Generate model and Run model validation focus on building a potential explanation for problem generation and therefore these two are the modeling stage.

The problem definition funnel

Once an unusual event has occurred and is defined as a problem that needs to be solved, an individual or team are assigned to lead this effort (you). There may be some early information about the event, but it is most probably very brief and vague. This is the initial data that you have on hand.

It sounds nice and easy to state that it is necessary to define the problem, and once it is properly defined, the way is paved for cause identification. Well, it isn't. In most cases we know too little about the problem and we start with a very broad definition or general description of the **detected symptoms**.

As more data is accumulated and we learn more about the event, we focus our attention on the functions and conditions that are directly related to generation of the problem until we get to the bottom of the matter.

We can use the analogy of a funnel. We start with superficial knowledge and a broad definition of the problem, but as we delve deeper into the matter, the definition of the problem is narrowed down, until the problem definition is clear enough to be defined as a root cause.

So, even if we start with a certain definition of the problem, as we progress through the analysis we find ourselves constantly redefining the problem. Moving from one problem definition to another may require changing analytical tools, different data sources and the involvement of new key individuals. Nevertheless, it is necessary to have a clear understanding of the unexpected vs. the expected for every move that we make on our way to identifying the cause.

Let's take the practical example graphically represented in figure 2. Bad material started to appear at end-of-line.

1. The initial problem statement will most probably be something like **Material with high electrical resistance appears at the end-of-line**. It is expected (based on data) that all material is within spec limits. The unexpected situation is

that some of the material has out-of-spec results and is clearly outside of the normal distribution.

2. The next step is an attempt to identify the suspect module or process-step that is responsible for this event. The expectation is that the tools running the process will continue performing day in and day out and that all tools running any specific process will produce material within certain limits. The unexpected behavior is that on a certain date, one of the tools running a specific process-step starts to produce bad material while other tools on the same process-step do not. Once this is discovered, the problem may be redefined as **Process tool XX201 started to produce material with high electrical resistance on 1-Apr-200x.** At this stage, efficient action can be taken to contain the problem. We can stop running material through this tool and we can prepare a list of material that was processed by this machine from the day the problem was identified on this machine.

3. A new set of data analysis tools are used to understand what went wrong with XX201. The expectation was that the tool will match all parameters to its own history data and to other reference tools running this process step. The identified unexpected result is poor vacuum conditions in the process chamber caused by an air leak during deposition. The definition of the problem is narrowed down to **Leaky gate valve in XX201 after PM caused high electrical resistance in the end-of-line.**

4. The next step is to check the gate valve while expecting it to have a smooth surface for proper chamber sealing. The unexpected result is a **Scratch in gate-valve of XX201**.

5. And then **Poor cleaning procedure caused a scratch in the gate valve** and next **Misinterpretation of cleaning procedure caused scratches in gate valves** followed by **Poor training ...etc.**

Figure 2-2. Problem definition funnel

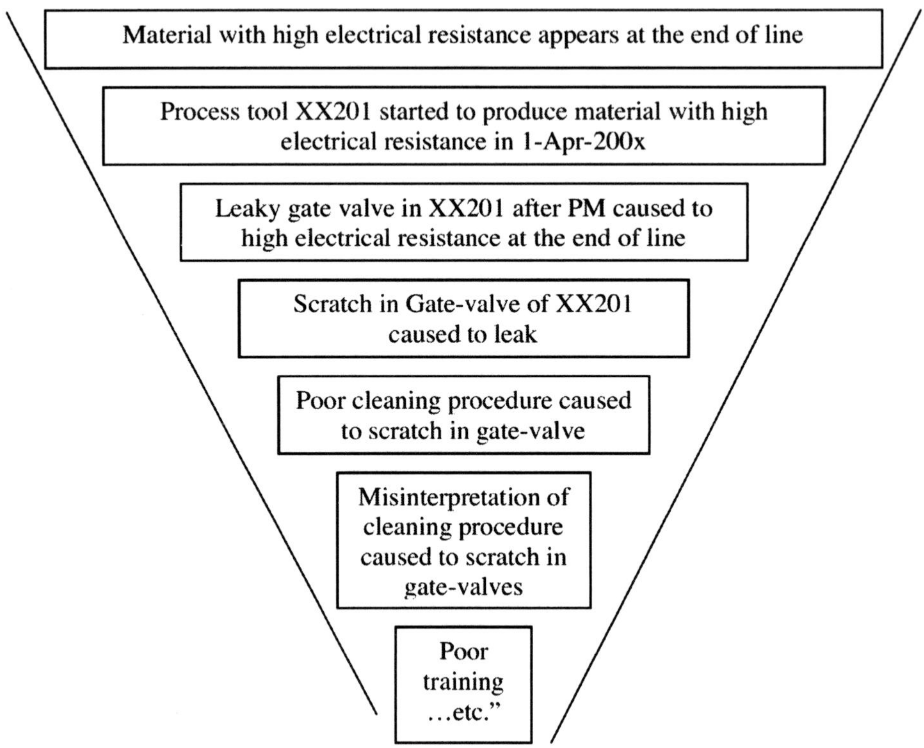

When is the right time to stop digging? If we dig deep enough we may start by investigating an airline event and end by trying to improve education in kindergarten, lecturing kids playing with Lego to "do things right the first time".

Deciding when to stop is based on judgment. The persons who are responsible should convince themselves (and others) that they have enough knowledge about the cause of the event for them to find a way to stop it or prevent it from re-occurring. In the example above, if the scratch in gate valve appeared only once and we have record of hundreds of flawless PMs (preventive maintenance), it may be sufficient to stop with identification and replacement of the defective gate valve. However with repetitive PM problems, it is necessary to understand the reason for poor PM performance.

In many cases the cause analysis will start with one leader and team and at a certain point, after problem redefinition, a new team will be assigned to complete the task. For example: a Q&R engineer will lead the investigation to the point where process tool XX201 is found to be the problematic tool, while the XX201 tool owner will lead the effort to figure out what went wrong with this machine.

Since root cause identification involves continuous problem redefinition, it may cause some confusion among people who are not deeply involved in the investigation process. To avoid confusion, save the initial problem definition (symptom description) as your problem statement and define the finer definition (deeper down the funnel) as your current understanding.

Problem characterization stage

When I was in Maui (Hawaii) several years ago, I bumped into a sign saying "Beware of the coconuts". I found this quite amusing. The person who wrote this took it quite for granted that coconuts fall downwards, but Isaac Newton found it surprising when he took a nap under the apple tree. When he found out to his surprise that the apples fell down, he started his analysis of gravity. Would he have started it just by seeing a sign "Beware of the coconuts"? Well, we cannot know that, but one thing is for sure, physics would have progressed quite differently without Isaac's personal definition of expected and unexpected events.

The core of root cause analysis is understanding why something behaves unexpectedly. Start every cause analysis by clarifying what you expected and what came out unexpected. Soon enough you'll learn that sometimes things that seem to be surprising are actually expected (however this could still be a problem that needs solving).

Let's use an example: You work in a factory that manufactures discrete electrical devices. The factory receives a huge order for precision resistors. You receive an alert from the testing floor that they have an unusually high amount of loss of products showing resistance values that are outside of the lower spec limit defined for this product. You are assigned to address this problem (meaning that you'll have to decide whether the line should be put on hold, what should be done with the suspect material, and how to solve the problem).

Your first task is to define the problem. It seems to be quite obvious, doesn't it? A higher number of faulty units at the end-of-line. Yes, but this is not enough.

What was the actual anticipated level of faulty units? Do we expect to have not even one failure? Do we expect a certain amount of failures? What is this amount? So, to better understand and define the problem, you need to have some knowledge about the usual performance of the line. Learning this may alter the direction you take to address the problem.
How? Let's look at two scenarios:

> Scenario No.1: Checking past data reveals that resistance values had very narrow normal distribution and based on this, no failure should occur. However, recent material shows abnormal distribution with a lot of material outside the lower spec limit. Obviously there is a significant change in the line behavior and thus root cause analysis should focus on finding the reason for this change and correcting it.

> Scenario no.2: Checking past data reveals that the resistance values have wide normal distribution and a small percentage of the material was always out of spec. Recently, due to the large order received from the customer, the volume through the line was increased and the same percentage of faulty units was reflected as a high number of units per week at the end-of-line. So, nothing actually changed in the line performance. However, now you have identified an opportunity to improve line performance and the root cause analysis should focus on narrowing the distribution of this parameter.

What is the difference in the way that we will deal with these two problems? In both cases we need root cause analysis. Here comes what I stated earlier: expected vs. unexpected. In the first case, we expected to receive normal behavior with no faults at all and the unexpected was that the line now has abnormal distribution and produces faulty material. We should now find the **specific source** that caused the bad material to deviate from our normal distribution.

In the second case, we define new expectations: we expect all manufactured material to be between the predefined spec limits; however the actual situation is that the process distribution was always too wide. We should now find **all sources** that affect the distribution width of this parameter and work on those that are either the most significant contributors to the noise or those that are easy to fix. Hopefully this would bring us to the expected target.

So, clarifying what you expected and what came out unexpected is not just a simple statement. It means to collect data and arrange it in a way that it will be quite clear how something deviates from expectation. You will see that "knowing what is expected" is interchangeable with "having a base-line", "learning past data", "using a reference", "running a benchmark" and other terms that intend to help us understand the problem based on comparison.

Model building and validation stage

You and your team start rolling scenarios (models) that may explain the problem. Your model may be generic and vague or it may be detailed and clear (depending on the data that you already have).

The model should fit existing data, but may predict other data that you do not currently have. Checking if a model predicts unknown data correctly is model validation. Since any validation will add new information (data) about the problem, the boundaries between model validations and data collection are blurred. The new data may affect your model as well (confirm, refute, tune, specify).

To make it more visual, we can imagine a cause analysis mill as shown in figure 2-3. The problem is fed in and data collection, model building and model validation are cycled to generate a confirmed model to explain the problem. This model is considered to be root cause identification.

Figure 2-3. Cause analysis mill

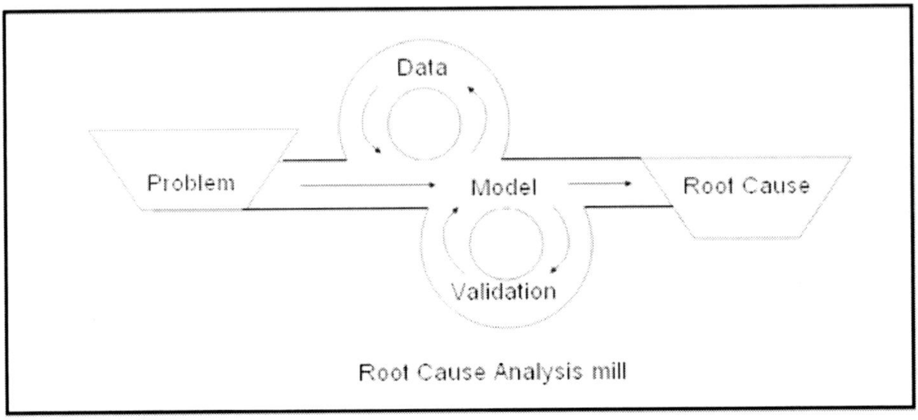

From time to time I face a challenge such as "We ran this sequence and identified the root cause, however when we applied our solution, it did not work. So, this sequence failed to find the root cause, didn't it?"

It was mentioned earlier that a model is validated by prediction and verification. A suggested solution is prediction. If this well-selected solution failed to provide the expected results it refutes the assumed model. Obviously this team is still within the cause analysis cycle.

Let's summarize this short chapter with a brief definition of each element in the cause analysis cycle.
The problem is an obvious unexpected behavior or outcome for an unknown reason.
The data is any information that relates to the problem.
The model or hypothesis is a potential explanation for creation or appearance of the problem.
Validation or verification is an action intended to confirm or refute a suggested model.
"Cause identification" is having a compelling explanation (model)for generation of the problem.

CHAPTER 3

Problem Characterization

Many textbooks that address problem solving emphasize that a well-phrased problem definition is crucial for achieving an optimal solution. This is appropriate when a team analyzes and selects the best solution to be implemented where the root cause is already known. At that stage, the problem definition may narrow down or even dictate the path that will be explored to find the solution, therefore proper problem definition is important.

However at the first stage of root cause analysis, there is no reason to spend too much time defining the problem. On the contrary, too much discussion may lead to premature interpretation of symptoms and speculations that could lead to wrong conclusions. Simply stick to the facts and name the event based on the initial symptom. This is important to realize, since your first attempt will be just to learn these symptoms. Without a deep study of the problem, the whole investigation could be based on shaky foundations. Gathering information and learning the symptoms to fully understand the nature of the problem is the definition of the problem.

In processing-related problems, extensive effort to understand the problem is invested by learning the existing statistical information. At the same time, the affected material should be studied directly by laboratory analysis or collection of field evidence.

This chapter provides an overview of problem characterization while perceiving the problematic material as a bunch of results that deviate from the expected. Lab analyses and field data collection will be discussed later in the Data Collection chapter.

The topics covered in this chapter are:

- Characterization and analysis of logged data
- The problem characterization sequence
- How to look into data
    - Learn the distribution
    - Look for a pattern
- Proper metrics
- Computerized data analysis techniques
    - Time-sequence based techniques
    - Comparison-based techniques
    - Correlation

Characterization and analysis of logged data

We are in the IT (information technology) era and indeed in process-based manufacturing sites, a huge amount of information is logged and stored every day in databases. As technology progresses, there are more systems connected to data-loggers with higher and higher sampling frequency (up to continuous real-time sampling).

Information may be in any style and form, such as numerical data, textual information, date/time records, images and graphs. For this reason IT and storage systems are extremely good business. As long as this information is just kept somewhere, it is good for nothing except for the bank account of the storage supplier. Using this data may change it from dumb-information to smart-knowledge. Usually this kind of data-logging is used as a watchdog, ensuring that everything is running as it should. SPC (statistical process control) is an example of this kind of watchdog system. If something wrong is detected, it will alert or even halt the tool or system to prevent further damage. Besides ensuring that everything behaves as expected while running the material through the line, the stored information can be used later on. This, either to optimize the processing system based on acquired information, or to analyze unexpected events. Naturally we are interested in discussing the aspects related to usage of data logging and monitoring results for investigation of unexpected events.

A process monitor that catches a problem in its immediate process step is usually easier to learn. The problematic tool (source of event) is known and the investigation should concentrate on finding the cause of the problem within this specific tool. So, after a brief problem characterization, attention is directed to model building. However, sometimes problematic material is identified only at a later time or even discovered in the end of line product. In such cases, the stored information is used extensively for problem characterization, even to the extent that it may identify the source (process step or tool) that generates (or generated) the problematic material.

Problem characterization sequence

Problem characterization may be described as a workflow with a few steps leading from initial problem detection down to a well-characterized problem, and even to source identification.

The basic work flow of a problem characterization consists of the following steps:
Symptom detection ➔ Initial problem characterization ➔ Metrics definition ➔ Refined problem characterization ➔ Usage of analytical tools/techniques ➔ Potential source identification.

A brief description of each step is provided first, while further elaboration appears later.

Symptom detection
When unexpected behavior is detected, it provides a motivation for investigation. At this stage not much is known, beside the process parameter that sensed the problem and the material in which this problem was detected. It is quite usual to name the event at this stage, based on the detected symptom. One may argue whether or not this nickname is a proper problem statement, but in any case, at this stage a problem statement is no more than a simple description of the detected symptoms and any interpretation of the facts should be avoided.

Initial characterization
Initial learning is performed on the material that was pointed out by the detected symptom. It is necessary to identify the material sharing that symptom, learn the amount of material involved, and

check whether other symptoms or phenomena accompany this problem.

The affected material is compared with the material that is not affected by the detected symptoms. It is necessary to learn what is expected from the very fundamental level up, and to understand the unexpected in the same way. In other words, the differences in the distribution between the bad and good material should be learned, and the source of these differences should be understood by looking into the raw data of the affected material as well as the good material.

You should ask yourself questions such as: Are differences related to some readings or is it an entire shift of affected material? Is there any affinity to a specific product or certain type of material? Does the affected material tend to show a repetitive pattern or appearance (such as repeating a bad location on affected products and repeating an order or arrangement of problematic material)?

Metric definition

A metric is a quantitative measure, used for evaluating the quality standard of the material of interest. A metric is an aggregation of individual readings into a summary level, using a single representative statistic. It could be that the routine metrics used for line follow-up is not sensitive enough or sufficient to properly detect all affected material of a detected event. When investigating an event, the selected metric should be able to differentiate the material of interest from other material (good and bad) that is not related to the same event or problem by its characteristic phenomena. The intention is to select the most appropriate metric to best represent the problem based on the initial characterization.

When selecting a metric you should ask yourself: What is the phenomenon that represents the problem? What statistic will best show it? What can blur the clarity of the statistic? How can I avoid it? Is this avoidance going to affect the quality or sensitivity of this metric?

Refined characterization

Based on selected metric, the processed material can be rechecked. The affected material is more accurately defined and it is possible to distinguish between bad and good material. Good material is differentiated from bad material by comparing the results within a defined limit (success criterion) based on the selected metric.

You may find that some of the material that was not flagged in the initial alert actually carries the same symptoms but with lesser effect. It is also possible that some material that was initially identified as having the same problem actually suffers from a different problem. Naturally, when the exact material that is involved in an event is known, the extent and timing of the problem can be better appreciated.

As well as more precise identification of problematic material, it is rather important to pay attention to or even look for repetitive patterns in the appearance of affected material (lot sequence, material arrangement). By pattern, I mean an observed regularity of any kind, such as a certain repetitive order or timing, an affinity to a certain location or position, or a repetitive shape or symmetry on a product.

This could be extremely helpful, and may point to a potential source of an event, or even provide a good hint of the cause of a problem.

Running analytical tools/techniques

With a correct list of good and bad material, knowledge of the problem time frame, and the unique appearance (pattern) characterizing the problem, one can run a set of statistical techniques that may point to the correct process step, tool or system either involved in or causing a problematic event.

Potential source identification

If proper techniques or tools are employed on well-characterized and properly selected material, the source of the problem may often be identified with high confidence. The problem may be contained by stopping this source (tool or system) from causing further damage. The team may now shift the attention to cause identification within the identified process step, tool or system.

The above problem-characterization flow could be performed more than once. As more recent material related to the same event is detected, it should be incorporated into the analysis and another iteration of a characterization cycle could take place. It could be repeated in a very fast cycle during an ongoing urgent event, or it could be performed easily and thoroughly in a bounded event.

There are several issues that need further discussion of this characterization flow. How to look into the data and what to look for when doing so? How to select proper metrics to reflect a problem? What kind of analytical technique can assist in the investigation?

How to look into data?

We have already addressed the issues related to process noise, sampling, and process window. So, it is not new that the measured process parameter is aggregated into statistics to facilitate follow-up of process performance. Therefore, a problem is more often detected on aggregations than on raw data. So the first step for evaluating the material is to learn the distribution of the raw data.

Learn the distribution

When concerned about process parameter performance, it is common to follow statistics that indicate central tendency (location) and statistics that indicate dispersion (spread) of measured results. The central tendency is usually indicated by mean or median, while the dispersion is most frequently indicated by StdDev or range.

In perfectly normal distribution – mean, mode and median are the same. In perfectly normal distribution, 6 Sigma is very close to range. **In data analysis during event investigation, do not assume a perfectly normal distribution.** The most useful tool for investigating a distribution shape or comparing several distributions is the probability plot (also known as normal-plot or prob-plot). (Figure 3-1)

Figure 3-1. Normal probability plot of normally distributed 250 reading

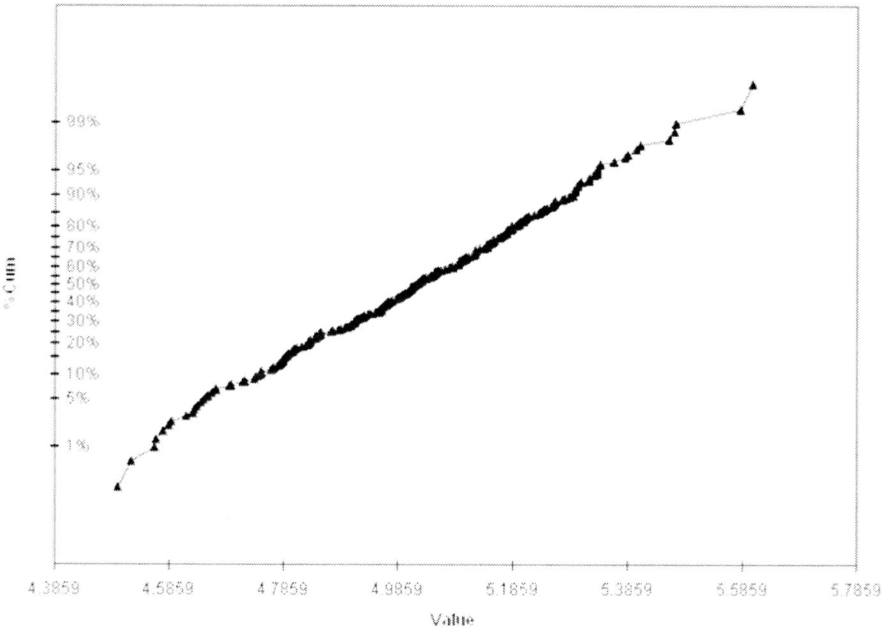

A perfectly normal distribution appears on a normal plot with all points in a straight line. The X-axis indicates the actual value of each individual reading and the Y-axis indicates the respected cumulative probability of the reading. A quick look tells what the distribution looks like in respect to normal distribution, what the dispersion is, what the highest and lowest readings are, and what the median is (50% point).

As mentioned above, the philosophy of basic problem characterization is to understand the unexpected by knowing the expected. So, in most cases two or more distributions should be compared, such as comparing the performance of several machines, or comparing more recent performance to an earlier period. The prob-plot displays it all by placing several distributions on the same plot (as shown in figure 3-2).

Figure 3-2. Comparison of two data sets using normal-plot

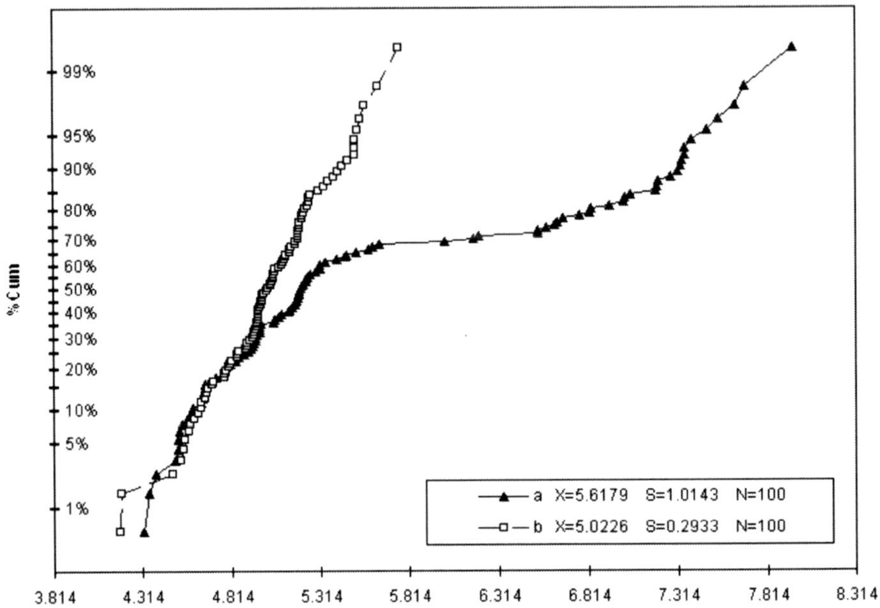

When looking into this prob-plot (Figure 3-2) it is obvious that one of the tools (***b***) shows healthy behavior with normal distribution. However tool ***a*** behaves strangely. The distribution is broken into two distinct regions, each characterized by a different slope. The tool appears to have bimodal distribution. It is clear that some of the readings of this tool reflect a different kind of processed material. When there is such a difference in performance you may wonder: Are the high readings coming from all products processed through the machine? Is it that part of the population affected? Does the machine continue to provide bad material? And so on. So, obviously it should be learned where these readings are coming from.

<u>Look for time/sequence/order effects</u>

This information cannot be learnt from the distribution shape. Another method for looking into the same data is needed. If the material is arranged in the order that the measurements were taken in the relevant process step, more information about the problem will be visible (Figure 3-3).

Figure 3-3. Trend chart of readings by tool

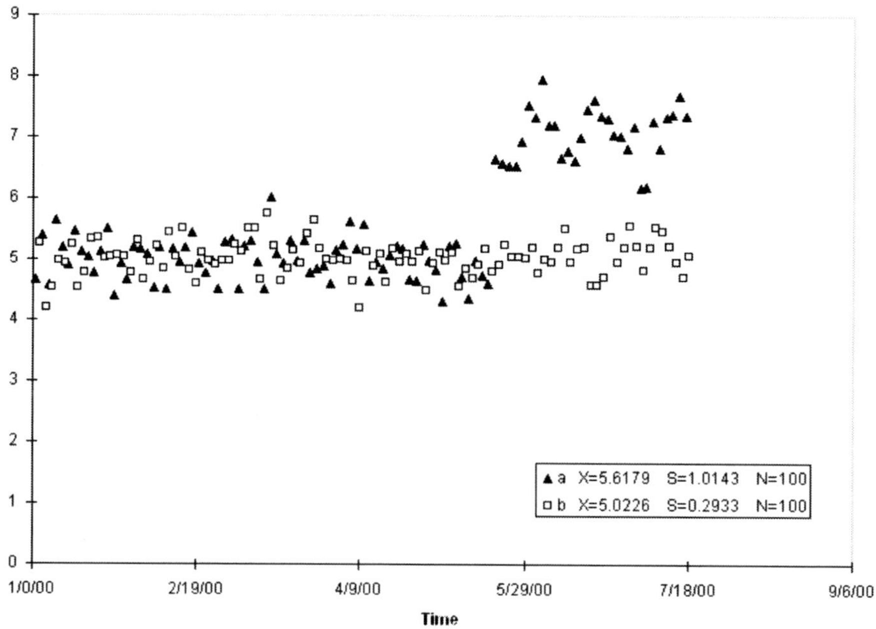

It is clear that the tools had similar performance for some time. However at a certain point, something changed in tool *a*. Now, it is appropriate to ask what exactly happened to tool *a* just before the change.

A strange distribution shape such as bimodality, multimodality, and tails could be related to time or sequence, but it could also be caused by other effects.

Let's picture a situation in which a certain product should be covered by specific thickness of a certain layer. To ensure uniform coverage of the entire product surface, three individual readings are taken on every checked product. What would be the result if one of the two tools employed for this operation lost its ability to provide uniform coverage?

Figure 3-4. Trend chart of readings (separated) by measurement-site and tool

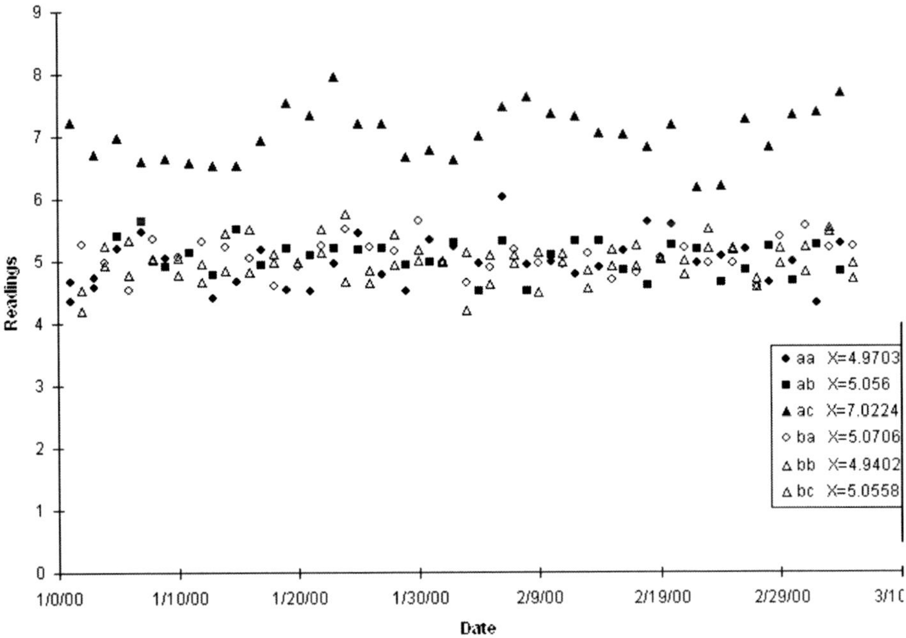

The trend chart in figure 3-4 shows the individual measurement sites on each machine. One can see that sites *c* in tool *a* (denoted by *ac* in the legend) provide consistently higher readings, while this non-uniformity does not exist for tool *b*. So, only by looking at the individual results in a certain way, can one learn that the strange distribution in tool *a* is related to a specific measurement site.

If you do not exhaust learning of the distribution and strive to understand the real reason for its shape, you may fool yourself that you are doing the right things to correct a problem, while in reality you may be making matters even worse. How come?

Simpson's paradox

A large corporation had two manufacturing sites that used the same process and manufactured the same set of products. There was a complaint that products coming from site X showed a higher failure rate in a certain quality test performed prior to shipment to the customer. The results of site X showed that almost 6% of the products failed the test, while the failure level of site Y was less than half. A prob-plot showing the results of all tested products (Figure3.5) was sent to site X, with a request to improve the situation to at least the level of site Y. An audit identified several relevant differences between the two sites. As a result, site X immediately implemented the procedures of site Y. The situation became even worse. What went wrong?

Figure 3-5. Normal plot comparing performance of the two sites

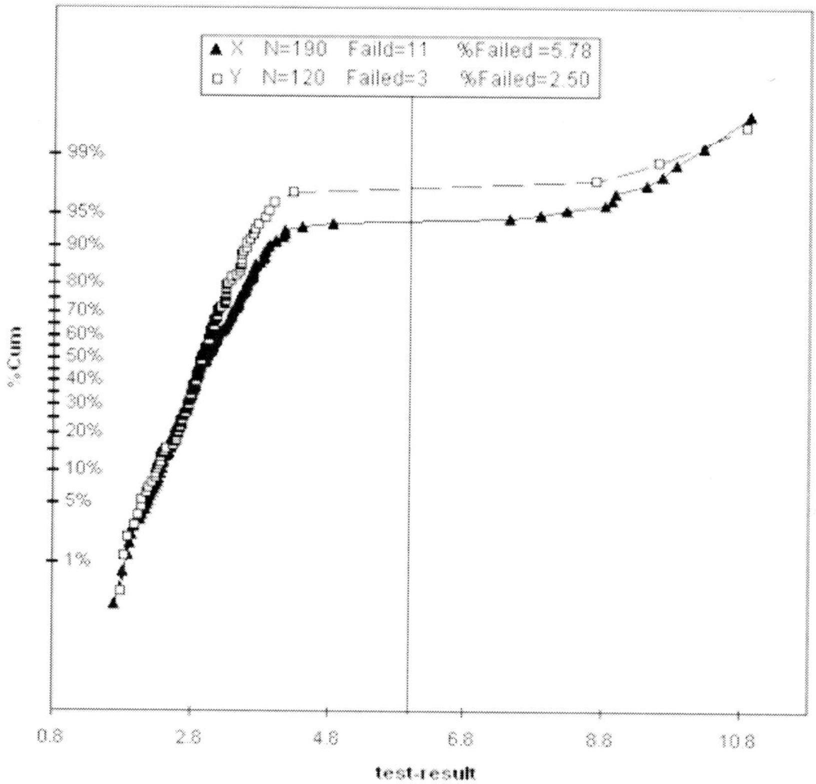

Further in depth analysis revealed that the two sites are running the same process and the same two products. However, site X carried most of the loading of product A which is more prone to failure in this specific test, while site Y produced more of product B, which is less sensitive to this test. As demonstrated in the table below (Figure 3.6) site X was actually the better site on both products.

Figure 3-6. Comparison table of failure rate per site per product

	Site X			Site Y		
	Number of units	Number of failed units	Failed units [%]	Number of units	Number of failed units	Failed units [%]
Product A	160	11	6.8	20	2	10.0
Product B	30	0	0.0	100	1	1.0
Total	190	11	5.8	120	3	2.5

The heavy loading of the sensitive product made the better site look worse. So it is not surprising that the changes adopted by site X to bring it to the same level as site Y made the situation even worse.

So now you know. Not only do you need to know **how** the distribution looks, it is also extremely important to fully understand **why** it looks that way.

Look for patterns

Learning the distribution is one aspect of learning the data while looking into details. Another important thing to look for when checking the unexpected results is the consistency in behavior, or in other words, the pattern. An observed pattern that is unique to the problem in hand is a stamp that can be used in every stage of event investigation.

In problem characterization -
An observed pattern will provide clear differentiation between good and bad material, thus making the next data analysis steps (metric definition and running analytical tools) more accurate and significant.

In model building -
Trying to explain an observed pattern may limit the possible models or even point to potential sources that may generate such a pattern.

In model validation -
An ability to manipulate an observed pattern deliberately by in-line experiments (either by tool manipulation or by product

manipulation) can provide the necessary indication or even proof that certain tools or process-steps are generating the problem or involved in problem generation.

When trying to observe a pattern, look for repetition in shape, order, location, and timing. Do this on any level, item-to-item, lot-to-lot, and load-to-load.

Shape –
Concentrate effort in understanding the shape. What are the physical differences between the regions that form the shape? What are the potential reasons that cause such a shape to appear? What can be done to a tool, process, or product to make a shape look different or to disappear. For example, if a certain effect is repeatedly shown on the top part of a product, is it possible to change product orientation between process steps and find the one that causes this effect?

Order and location –
If repeating the order or tendency of a specific location to show an effect is observed, this could be employed to learn the effect.
Try to explain how such a repeating order or specific location can be generated. For example, if the sequence shows that every other product is affected, then it is more likely for a treatment that processes the material alternately to be involved rather than a successive or bulk treatment.
Look for ways to change the order or placement between consecutive process steps and check the source of this effect. This manipulation may lead to the one process step responsible for the observed effect.

Timing –
Repetition of effect appearance over time implies that unusual reoccurring situations and conditions are involved. Was there any treatment, event, occasion, or person common to all incidents?
It is more likely to identify these conditions when the next event can be anticipated and monitored closely. It is easier to validate that a fix or a change is producing the predicted effect when the next occurrence is known and can be monitored.

It is essential and useful to look for a pattern. A pattern is a characteristic symptom. It should be learned thoroughly and used in model building and validation stages.

Proper metrics

So, the material that was flagged by the symptoms was thoroughly learned. There is a better understanding how it looks and why it looks that way. Based on this information, it is now necessary to define more precise statistical criterion that may differentiate between bad and good material. This statistical criterion or metric will serve two main purposes. The first purpose is to recheck all material (within the suspected period) using this metric for finer identification of affected material. As mentioned earlier in this chapter, you may find that some material that was not caught initially is actually affected, or that material with similar symptoms is related to yet another problem. The second purpose is to run analytical techniques that may point to the source of the problem. Why it is suspected that the initial metrics was not good enough? And, what is a better metric?

The symptoms were first indicated by predefined criteria that aimed to control the process line. As explained in an earlier chapter, material being processed is sampled and raw data is aggregated to facilitate this task. It is quite typical for symptoms to be detected first on aggregations such as lot average or lot StdDev. It is commonly seen, after initial characterization, that this kind of aggregation is too rough, and the material that was initially detected is only the tip of the iceberg.

Let's look at an example. A critical product is plated by a thin uniform coating layer. The layer is required to have certain uniformity. To ensure that this is the case, several measurements are taken on each product. Performance is followed up by looking into the mean and StdDev of each tested product. A problem was detected when a few affected products had readings with very high values that removed the product average and StdDev from the specification limit. The problem was found to affect one or two measurement sites that were high, while other sites on a bad product were normal. Further checking revealed that a bad product was only flagged by the average if the readings were way out of limit. Other affected products with readings slightly above the limit provided average results within the spec limits and a problem was not detected.

Note that it may be decided later that the latter products are good enough for shipment to the customer. However, for the purpose of RCA, these products are affected by the same event, and should be added to the list of affected products. So, a more accurate list of affected and healthy products is required.
How can this be done?

First it is necessary to **define the limit** beyond which the material is considered bad. If the distribution of the affected measurement sites is distinct from the distribution of good sites, this is relatively easy. The limit is in the middle of the gap between the distributions. (See figure 3-7)

Figure 3-7. The good material and the bad material have two distinct distributions.

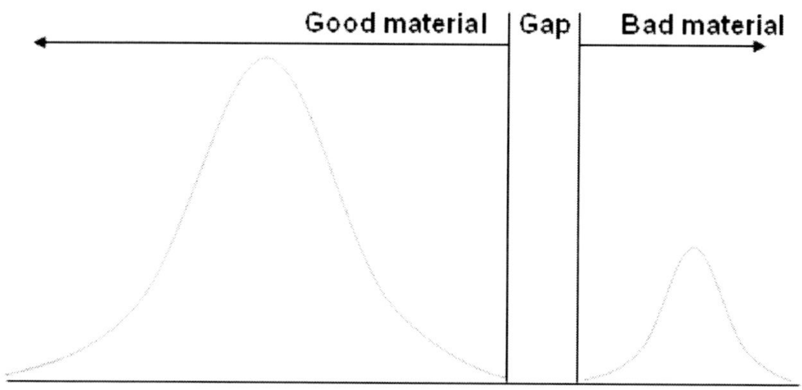

A situation with an overlap in the distributions of bad and good sites is more problematic (bimodality where the lower tail of bad points overlaps with the higher tail of normal points). In this case, it is necessary to define the overlap region between the distributions and to restrict the definition of bad material to products with values that are higher than this region, and to define good material as products where all points are below the region. Products with values within the region should be defined as material in question (see figure 3-8).

Figure 3-8. Overlap of the distribution of good and bad material

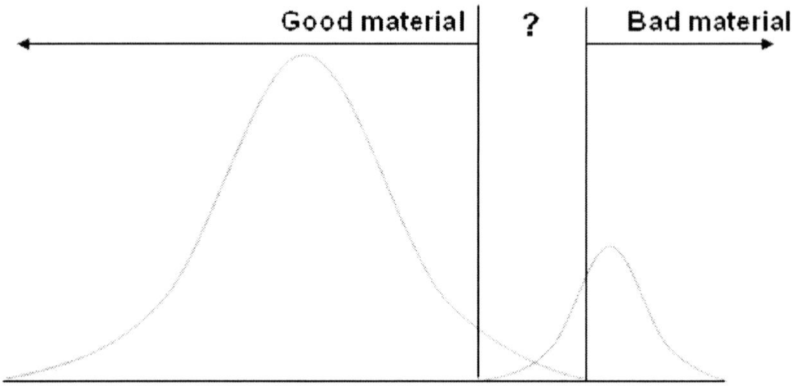

During investigation, the analysis should rely only on the purely bad and purely good products. Once the source of the event is found, it will be possible to judge which materials from the list in question are bad products and which are good.

The next step is to **define a metric** that will relate the material to this limit, and then recheck all material and identify any product that shares the problematic characteristic. In our example, since only a few points from the ones measured on bad products are affected, it already said that mean (average) cannot be counted as good metrics. However, if the maximum value [Max] of the measured sites on every product is checked against the limit, every product with at least one problematic point will be identified. So, the product's Max value appears to be a proper metric in this case.

From the above example, it is clear that at the end of the metric selection process, two goals should be achieved. One is the statistic that best reflect the problem (this is the metric to be used) and the other is the limit that should be used for this metric. For proper metric selection, it is necessary to look at the phenomenon that was highlighted by problem characterization and ask "What kind of statistic can demonstrate it best?"

<u>Metric selection (imaginary case study)</u>
For better understanding of considerations made during metric selection, an event that affects an imaginary manufacturing line is discussed next.

To ensure proper performance of a certain process parameter, the material quality is verified by a sampling plan that consists of five items per lot and five individual readings per item. A lot is considered as good if the lot-mean (lot average) provides values between 9 and11 (target =10), and the lot StdDev should be less than 1. A limit for individual reading was not defined (and was not tracked either) but it is known that a result above 13 degrades the product performance.

A representative good lot appears in fig. 3-9 with lot mean = 10.24 and lot StdDev = 0.43

Figure 3-9. Typical good lot sampling results.

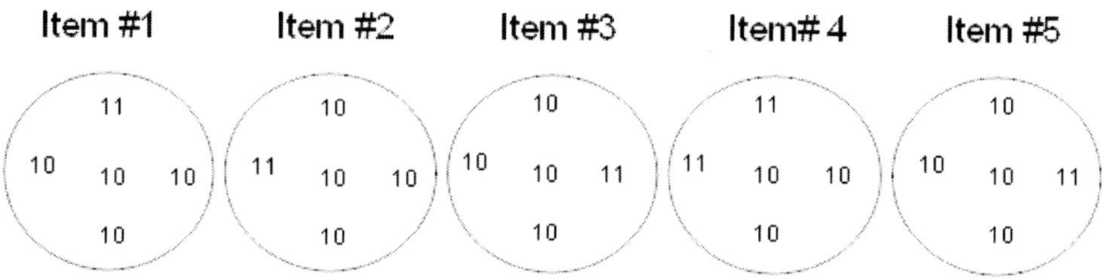

From time to time strange lots with results like those in figure 3-10 appeared in line. This kind of lot was flagged since both lot mean and lot StdDev were higher than usual (lot mean = 11.24; lot StdDev = 1.83). So it seems as if either lot mean or lot StdDev can be used to differentiate between bad and good lots. Obviously lot median will not provide a good indication for bad lots because most of the readings have normal values.

Figure 3-10. Typical bad lot sampling results.

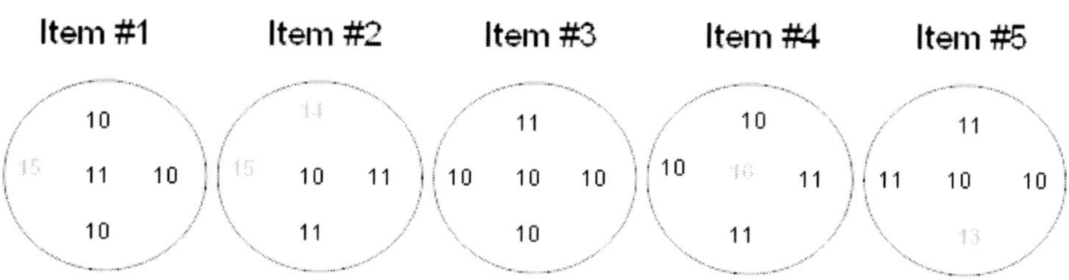

Further checking of lots flagged by lot mean (and lot std) showed several lots like the one in figure 3-11. According to the measurement equipment expert, this kind of readings is a measurement error. It should be ignored and this lot is actually a good one. So now it is necessary to either filter out the invalid results before calculating the lot average or to find better metrics to represent the problem.

Figure 3-11. Lot with several invalid (false) readings

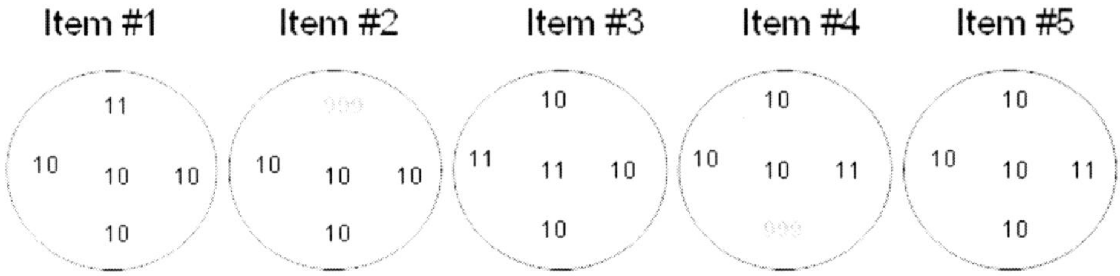

Other unusual lots were identified. On these lots the lot mean did not indicate any problem. However the lot StdDev was high. When checking one of the lots (as shown in figure 3-12) it was found that this lot is related to the same problem, however some of the readings were higher than usual while others were lower than usual. Results on this lot were lot mean = 10.32 and lot StdDev = 1.86. Obviously, lot mean is not a proper metric to identify all bad lots. Is lot StdDev a good enough metric?

Figure 3-12. Lot with high and low bad readings

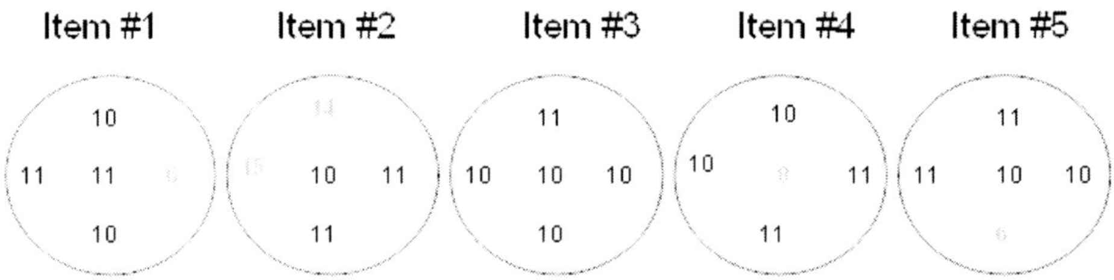

Thorough checking of other lots in the suspected time frame identified a few lots like the one in figure 3-13, where lot mean = 10.72 and lot StdDev = 0.97. In this case, it is clear that a lot with bad readings was totally missed. The engineer was faced with a requirement to catch any lot with bad points, so a better metric was necessary.

Figure 3-13. Lot with few bad points

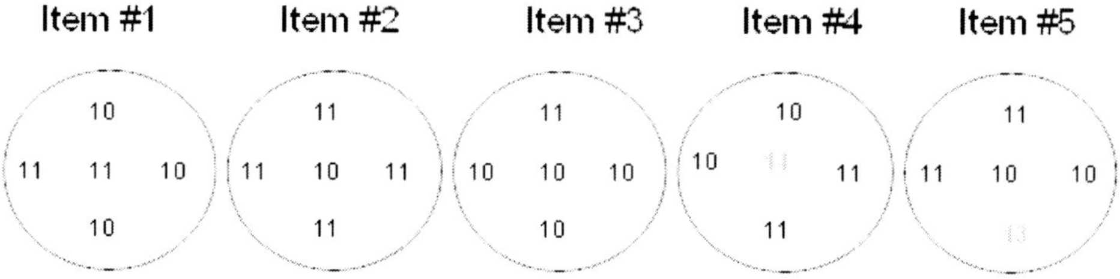

The metric that was found appropriate is number (or percent) of points beyond limits, while beyond limits is defined as any valid reading (<999) above 13 or below 7. Healthy lots should provide 0, while bad lots are those that have any value greater than 0.

The above case demonstrates the selection process of a metric for optimum identification of problematic material. As mentioned above, metric selection for event investigation is performed on a case by case basis. Several common metrics are discussed below.

Single aggregation metrics

Single aggregation may be loosely defined as summary level statistics providing one representative value from multiple individual readings.

Location (central tendency) metrics

- Average (mean): Impacted by outliers or tail in distribution. Used to learn a problem characterized by a shift of results while data is free of irrelevant outliers or tail (when data is perfectly clean or there is a proper way to filter out irrelevant data).

- Median: Insensitive to outliers or tail. Used to learn a problem characterized by a shift of population while data is contaminated by irrelevant outliers or tail in distribution.

Dispersion (spread) metrics

- Standard deviation: Provides information on variation, however impacted by outliers or tail in distribution. Used to learn a problem characterized by sensitivity to variation with no significant shift (of average values).

- Range: Provides information on spread but is very sensitive to outliers. Used to learn a problem characterized by strong sensitivity to difference between extremes and data is clean of irrelevant outliers.

- Robust Sigma: Provides information on variation, while ignoring tail or outliers. Calculation is based on inter-quartile range. Used to learn a problem characterized by overall spread change when data is contaminated by irrelevant outliers or tail. It is also used to define the limits of the distribution (in cases of outliers, tail, and overlapping distributions).

<u>Outliers and tail metrics</u>

- Min or Max: Provides information on extreme values of a given data set. Used to learn a material with a problem characterized by even a single reading beyond a certain limit. Practice it when you know that all the readings are relevant.

- Percent (or number) of points out of limit: Provides information on the number of affected readings in relation to the limit. Used to learn a problem characterized by an alternating number of points beyond a certain limit.

<u>Double aggregation metrics</u>

Double aggregation may be defined as a summary level statistic of another summary level statistic. This aims to provide one representative value to highlight an effect that cannot be demonstrated by a single aggregation.

In some cases, a single aggregation will not be sufficient to indicate which lot is related to an event and which is related to yet another event.

If a machine repeatedly provides the same unsatisfactory results over a product (poor uniformity over a product), but generates this problem consistently on every product being processed, we can say that the problem is characterized by sub-level variation, but not with upper-level variation.

If the machine fluctuates from product to product but the uniformity over the product is not affected, then we have a problem with upper-level variation, but not with sub-level variation.

Obviously, single aggregation will tell us that there is a problem in spread; however any single aggregation will be unable to tell if the problem is characterized by upper level fluctuations or by a lower level problem.

Double aggregation aims to provide an indication of the contribution of a certain level independently of the other. The two bad lots in figure 3-14 demonstrate the need for a double aggregation metric.

Figure 3-14. The need for double aggregation metric

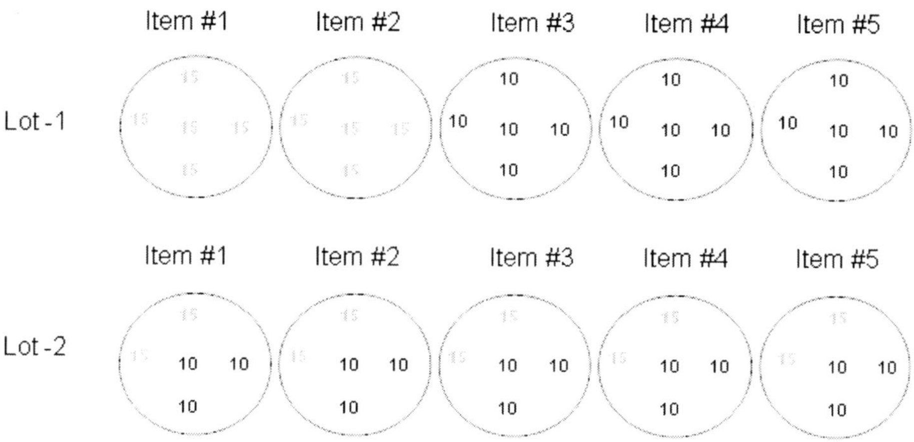

The two lots in figure 3-14 clearly demonstrate that in both lots, 10 out of the 25 readings have an abnormal value of 15, and 15 out of the 25 readings have normal values of 10. Nevertheless, these two lots do not have the same problem. Lot 1 is characterized by good and bad items, while on the bad items, all readings are bad. Lot 2 is characterized by several readings that are bad on each and every item.

What single aggregation metric can differentiate between these two lots? None.

Lot average, lot StdDev, % out of limit, and others will all provide identical values for both lots (lot average = 12, lot StdDev = 2.5, % OOL = 40%). Obviously, another kind of metric is necessary.

Lot mean of item StdDev (or within item uniformity)
This metric provides information on the dominance of item (product) uniformity in the contribution to lot spread. It is used to learn a problem characterized by sensitivity to lower level variation (within item), while upper level variation (item-to-item) is irrelevant.

In the example in figure 3-14 for comparing within item uniformity between the lots, the StdDev for each item should first be calculated and then the average StdDev results should be calculated for each lot.

Lot StdDev of item mean (or item-to-item uniformity)
This metric provides information on how a difference between items (products) is dominant in the contribution to lot spread. It is used to learn a problem characterized by sensitivity to upper-level variation (item-to-item), while sub-level variation is irrelevant (within item).

Figure 3-14 demonstrates comparison of item-to-item uniformity between the lots. The mean for each item should first be calculated and then the StdDev (of means) should be calculated for each lot.

Let's assume that in a typical good lot all readings are 10, and perform the above calculations for a good lot and for the two lots in figure 3-14.

Figure 3-15.

	Lot mean of item StdDev (within item spread)	Lot StdDev of item mean (item-to-item spread)
Good lot	0	0
Lot 1	0	2.74
Lot 2	2.74	0

The calculations summarized in figure 3.15 reveal that a good lot is characterized by perfect uniformity on every item as well as perfect repetition of performance from item- to-item. Both within-item, and item-to-item calculation produce 0.

Lot 1 has perfect uniformity on each and every item; therefore it provides 0 in within item calculation. However, Lot 2 has poor uniformity performance on every item and therefore it provides high (2.74) within item value. On the other hand, Lot 1 has poor repetition performance from item-to-item and therefore it provides high item-to-item value (2.74), while Lot 2, with perfect repetition provides 0.

So, when single aggregation fails to provide a proper metric to differentiate between different event characteristics, double aggregation should be considered.

Ad-hoc metrics

In some situations, direct use of measured values will not be sufficient to represent the problem. The noise of a level that we are not concerned about could mask the signal that we are interested in checking. In such cases, the proper metric should be an outcome of a certain calculation or manipulation of the measured values that highlight the problematic phenomenon. For example, let's take a situation where several products are arranged in a row along the furnace in every run. A certain layer is deposited over the products' surface. Due to the different conditions along the furnace, each product receives a different layer thickness on average and this is not counted as a problem. However, non-uniformity within the product is crucial and it appears that every product coming out of this furnace provides unsatisfactory results. The engineer assigned to solve the within-product uniformity problem could not use the product's StdDev as a way of measuring the uniformity. Higher deposition thickness produced higher within-product StdDev, while products with lower thickness produced lower StdDev. The engineer needed to achieve within-product uniformity metric independent of product thickness. This was achieved by expressing the within-product uniformity (StdDev) as a percentage of the product's thickness ((product StdDev/product ave)*100). Since the engineer normalized the within-product uniformity results, the product-to-product thickness or load-to-load variation was no longer a concern. The engineer could now run experiments in a much shorter time by lowering the total thickness and comparing the uniformity performance.

From the above, it is clear that unlike the limited number of metrics used for process control, there is a richer choice of metrics employed for event analyses and the choice of the proper metric is made on a case-by-case basis.

In addition to metrics definition, it was mentioned earlier that the other goal is to define the limit or line that differentiates between good and bad (expected and unexpected) material. The question that one should ask is "What is the limit that correctly judges the material?" The limit, or limits, will be placed at or beyond the edge of good material distribution.

This limit, or limits, can be defined on the basis of a known value (hard limit) beyond which the product is degraded significantly, or it can be defined by learning the statistics of material that is known to be good.

When working on problem characterization, we may define initial limits based on raw data, and continue to learn the problem until a proper metric that better reflects the problem is defined. This will require recalculating a new limit according to this newly defined metric. Naturally, another iteration of checking all material in a suspected period is needed to differentiate between good and bad material.

Analytical techniques

The metric that best reflect the problem was found and the limit (or limits) to differentiate between good and bad material was also defined. We are now able to define purely bad and purely good material. How can differentiation between purely good material and purely bad material help us?

Learning the results of a process monitor or parameter that is measured at or immediately after its relevant process step, may provide a better understanding of the problem in this process step. But somehow, all of the trouble around problem characterization described above does not appear to be very important to cause analysis when the process step, and even the problematic tool, are already known.

Indeed, process characterization has special importance in the cases where the problem is detected on a process parameter that is after the affecting process step or even detected on an end-of-line test result. In this case, the results of characterization steps are further employed to provide better understanding of the problem, or even to identify the related process step or machine causing the problem. This is performed by employing analytical tools or techniques.

What are these analytical techniques and how they can assist in the investigation?

The analytical tools/techniques are computer programs (usually employing statistical routines) using already collected (known) information to provide relevant information that was unknown. This new information provides more understanding about an event.

If proper analytical techniques or tools are employed on well selected and characterized material, the source of the problem may often be identified with high confidence. The problem may be contained by stopping this source from causing more damage (take it down or avoid using it). The team may shift its attention to the identified process step and concentrate on RCA of the specific process step, tool, or system.

Better understanding of the nature of the problem may also help in building a model to describe creation of the problem, thus helping to identify the problematic system or even point to a potential cause.

The analytical techniques can be separated into three major categories: time-sequence based techniques; comparison-based techniques; and correlations.

Time-sequence based techniques

These analyses attempt to conclude the source of a problem based on the timing or sequence of running the material through the line in each process step. In general, there is a tendency to keep a process line linear. This means that the amount of start material entering the line per unit time should be equal to the amount of material emerging from the end of line. Naturally, all process steps need to support it, by running the material at the required pace. If a certain process step is very slow, production material will pile up in this operation and this process step dictates the production pace from this point on (a fleet cruises at the speed of its slowest vessel).

In order to overcome this, process steps with a long processing duration per production lot will require running of more machines in parallel. FIFO (first in, first out) is a favorable method of managing production material to avoid long delays of production lots in any process step. However, even with the described effort, there are always some slow to advance and fast to advance production lots, and there is a change in the order of the lots from one process step to another. These imperfections in line linearity can be used for cause analysis. Shall we intentionally introduce some randomization in material sequence?

Alignment to problem initiation (or ending)

As in any dynamic system, process tools or systems are less prone to failures in a steady-state situation. However, changes are a potential trigger for problem generation. So when observing an abrupt change in a certain test performance, effort should be invested in finding a treatment or change that coincides with the observed change in every process step. The trend chart of the appropriate metric is drawn for each process step and the exact date of problem initiation is marked according to the first production lot to show the problematic effect. Each tool owner is required to check their tool or system for any treatment that was performed or for any unusual event detected in the respected time or when running the first affected production lot.

Alignment in the appearance of problematic production material with a known change in tool or process step (such as maintenance activity) may provide a good indication of the source of the problem. Saw-tooth pattern is the most obvious situation addressed by this kind of analysis. The repetitive step change makes it easier to identify a common treatment that repeatedly triggers the problem.
If the problem is reflected as gradual change and the exact time of problem initiation is unknown, an approximate time frame may be defined to look for a change or treatment initiating the problem. However, this frequently provides too many results and any real one will be hard to distinguish. Do not discard this option too early, as having a long list of suspected causes is something to start with.

Problem time span

A certain process step caused a problem for a short time (bounded event) and all affected lots related to this event were processed during this period. If we assume some mix in lot order from one process step to another, the time-span between the first affected lot to the last one will be shorter in this process step than in any other process step. So time-span comparison between process steps (from first to last problematic lot in the respected process step) may provide an indication of the source of a problem. However be careful with it, since it may also provide misleading results.

Time-series analysis techniques

The rationale that problematic lots tend to condense (in order) at the problematic process step may be further employed for source-of-event identification.

The situation could be that from a certain point onwards, a specific process step may deteriorate and start to produce material with higher and higher (or lower and lower) values. A problematic tool could also start to produce bad lots in a consecutive order with little or no good material in between. Keep in mind that these values are discovered only at a later stage of the process and the source of the problem (the problematic process step) is unknown.

Time-series analysis techniques are used extensively by brokers to distinguish between significant market changes in (trend) and fluctuation related to normal market noise. Techniques based on time-series analysis may be employed for search and identification of a process step that is responsible for a certain trend pattern, providing this trend pattern is faded by the random change of lots order in neighboring process steps. Let's follow the logic behind such technique (developed by Matt Bousek and David Miller, Intel corp.)

When following typical process parameter measurements according to the sequence of running the production lots, one would expect the results to randomly fluctuate around the target level. This up and down fluctuation will cause a certain lot-to-lot delta. Under normal circumstances, the distribution of these deltas is kept stable over time.

Figure 3-16 demonstrates a time-trend of few consecutive lot results of related process parameter. (To simplify the example, the readings alternate between two discrete values).

Figure 3-16. Trend of process parameter as reflected in a process step

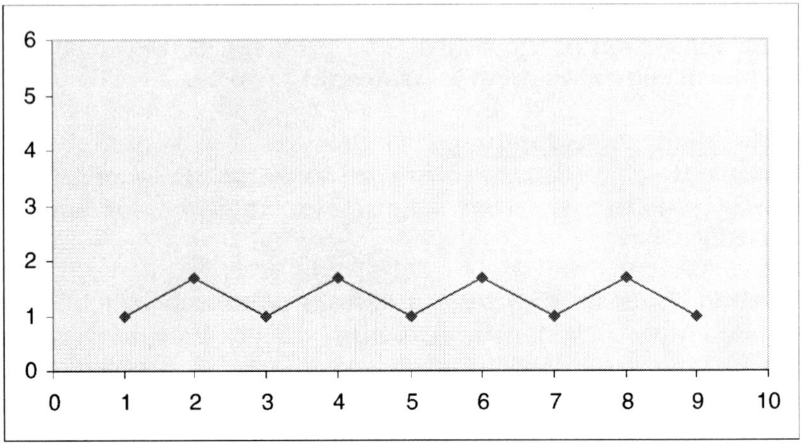

Calculating the sum of absolute difference between each neighboring pair, divided by the number of pairs, produces a certain value (mean of absolute deltas).

$(|(1.7-1)|+|(1-1.7)|+|(1.7-1)|+|(1-1.7)|+|(1.7-1)|+|(1-1.7)|+|(1.7-1)|+|(1-1.7)|)\ /\ 8 = 0.7$

Now let's consider that at certain time, this process-step started to show degradation in machine performance and this is reflected on the measured process parameter. Instead of fluctuating around a certain level, points will show a monotonic shift (as shown in figure 3-17) in the respected process step.

Figure 3-17. Trend of nine consecutive lots in problematic process step

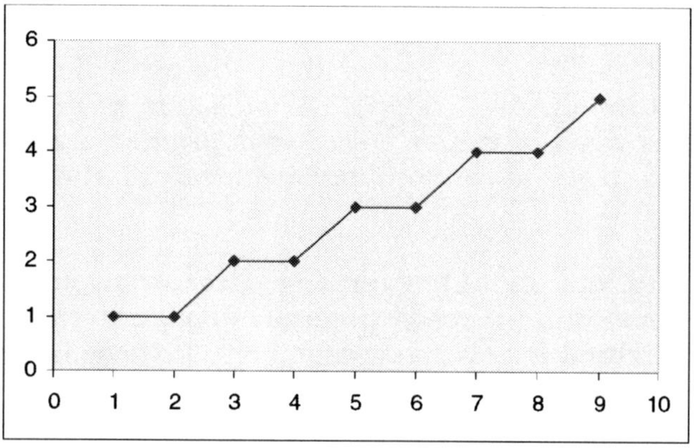

The same calculation (mean of absolute deltas) produces a value of 0.5. $(|(1-1)|+|(2-1)|+|(2-2)|+|(3-2)|+|(3-3)|+|(4-3)|+|(4-4)|+|(5-4)|) / 8 = 0.5$

The lot order of the same nine lots is disturbed when the material moves from this process step to the next one, and then further mixed on the flowing steps, until the order is fully randomized. We can also assume that the change in lot order occurs between earlier process steps and the problematic one. Now, if the same set of nine values is plotted according to the order in a different process step, it will show a situation like the one demonstrated in figure 3-18

Figure 3-18. Trend of the nine lots in a different process step

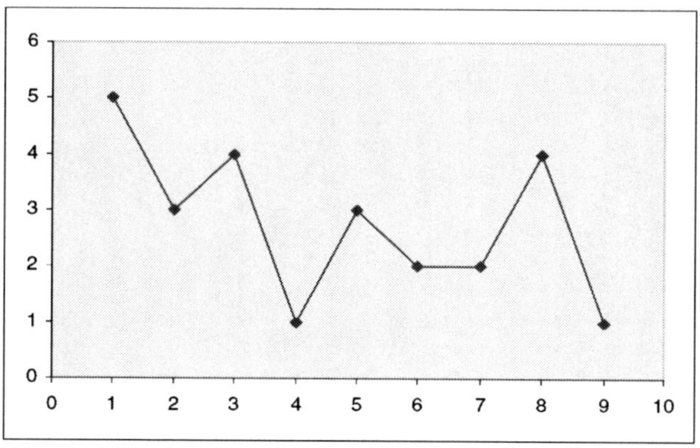

The mean of absolute deltas produces the value of 1.75.

(|(3-5)|+|(4-3)|+|(1-4)|+|(3-1)|+|(2-3)|+|(2-2)|+|(4-2)|+|(1-4)|) / 8 = 1.75

This number is significantly higher than the one calculated for the up-trending situation. And indeed, the situation of gradual change (up or down) for a set of values will always produce a lower mean of absolute deltas than a random arrangement of the same set of values.

The same set of lots should be arranged according to sequence of running the material in every process step, and the calculation should be performed for every process step. If there is a significant minimum in a specific region along the process, which gradually moves up away from this region, it could be a very good indication that this region of the process line is highly likely to be the one manipulating this process parameter.

If the data is sorted according to the order of process steps and plotted on a graph, the many individual points (as the number of process steps for which you are calculating) will fluctuate around it, but the schematic graph shape will be as demonstrated in figure 3-19.

Figure 3-19. Schematic representation of a plot indicating a specific process region to control the process-parameter

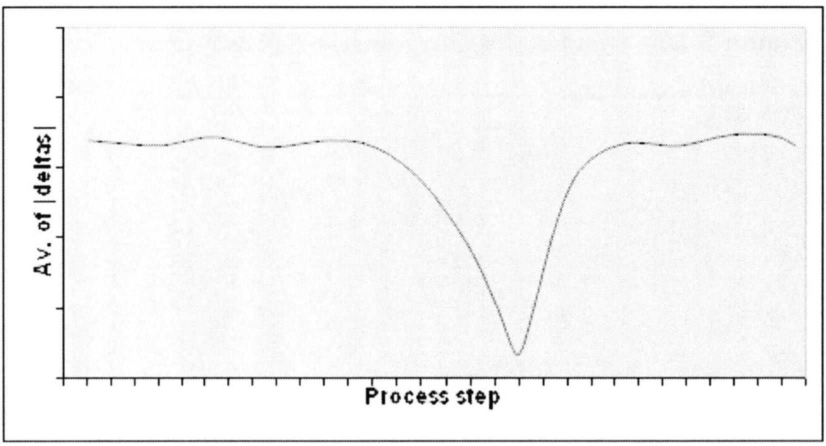

You may argue that such a small amount of lots is randomly rearranged along the line (especially if the line consists of many

process steps) in an order that will provide low values again. That is indeed true. In a small number of lots you may find that the signal to noise ratio is way too large to provide a useful indication.

If you wonder whether this technique is capable of detecting a step function that occurred in a certain process, and not only gradual deterioration, the answer is yes. Why? This is rather simple.

In step function, the process-parameter results fluctuate around a certain level and then jump (up or down) to fluctuate around a different level. As shown in figure 3-20, there are several small deltas before the step, several small deltas after the step, and a single large delta of the step.

Figure 3-20. Step function in process parameter as reflected in causing process step

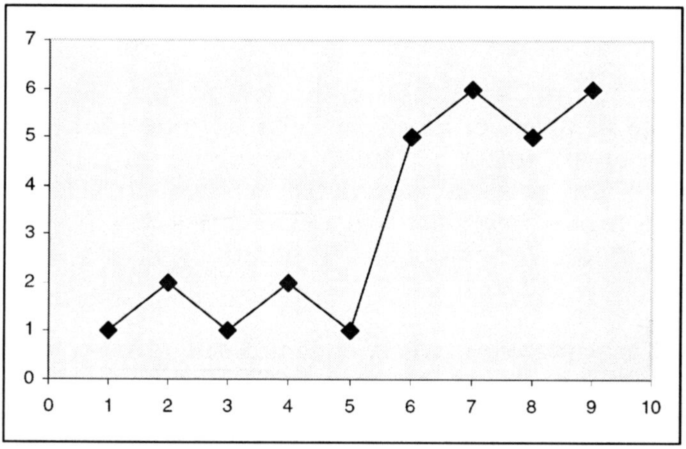

$(|(2-1)|+|(1-2)|+|(2-1)|+|(1-2)|+|(5-1)|+|(6-5)|+|(5-6)|+|(6-5)|)$ / 8 = 1.37

As the material moves away from this process step to the next one (or maybe as it was arranged in a previous process step), there was slight change in lot order. Figure 3-21 shows that in this other process step, all lots kept the same order, except for the one that is marked. Due to this change, there are three large deltas in this arrangement.

Figure 3-21. Disturbed order of lots with blurring step function

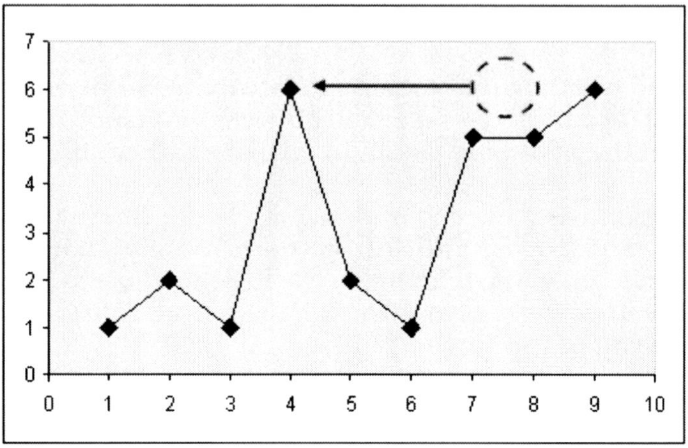

(|(2-1)|+|(1-2)|+|(6-1)|+|(2-6)|+|(1-2)|+|(5-1)|+|(5-5)|+|(6-5)|) / 8 = 2.12

The difference in mean of absolute delta is quite obvious, and the step function arrangement produces the minimum value. Note that if the step in the process parameter is small in relation to the normal noise (again low signal to noise ratio) this may affect the clarity of the signal. Too many lots in the analysis may also obscure the signal.

So, in event investigation, when a significant number of lots with problematic results appear in a late process stage or at the end-of-line, it makes sense to try time-series based analysis. However, if the line is perfectly linear, most of these techniques will not do much good.

Comparison-based techniques

This kind of analysis attempts to provide an understanding of the reason for a problem by comparing groups of bad and good material, or by trying to track the source of the bad material.

Commonality study (common treatment identification)

It was mentioned earlier that production material is introduced into the manufacturing line according to the line's production capacity. This means that in an ideal situation, the average amount of lots processed in a time unit is equal in each process step. However, not every machine in every process step is capable of running material through it at the same pace, therefore process steps with slow-to-produce tools employ more tools in parallel to meet the necessary pace.

Let's assume that there are several machines working in parallel in a certain process-step, and one of them is problematic. This leads to a mix of bad and good material emerging from this process step. However, this situation was not noticed in-line, and it was only apparent that some of the production was bad at the end-of-line. If we take all of the material processed in this time frame and check it in every processed step employing more than one machine, we may find one or more process steps that show that all bad material was processed through one machine out of several that were in use. This may indicate that this machine is the one that is most likely to cause the problem.

Let's follow the rationale behind this by following the material moved through the process steps in a simplified process line (Figures 3-22 to 3-25)

Figure 3-22. Simplified process line

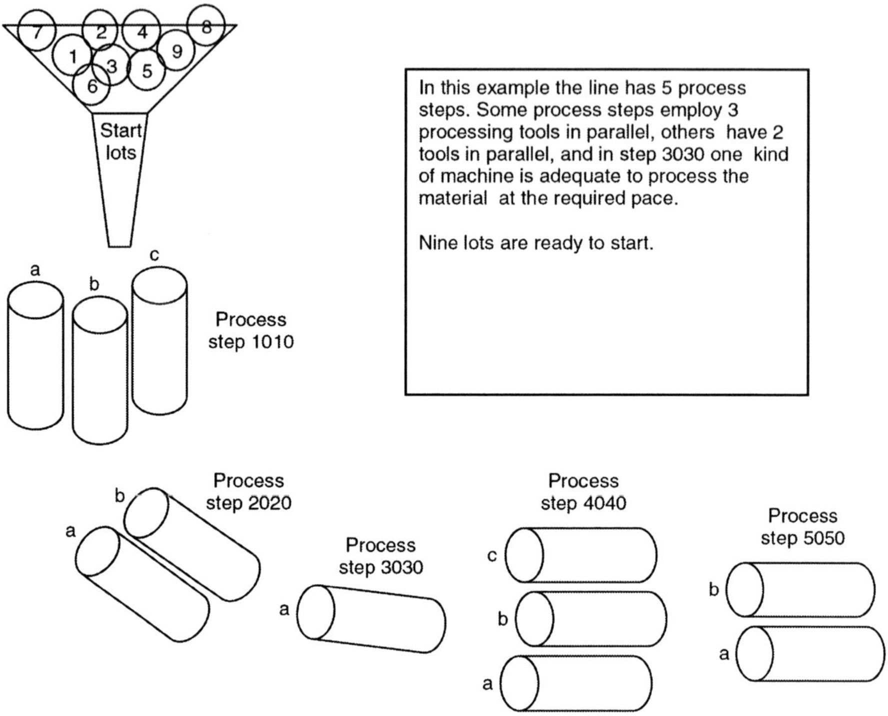

Figure 3-23. Material progression through a linear process line with two bad lots

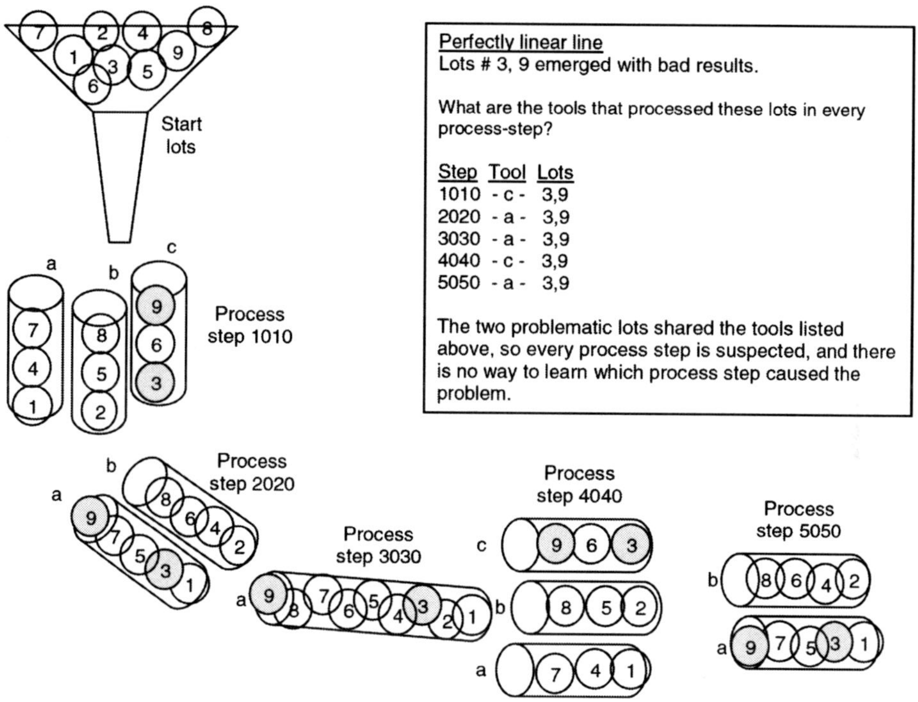

Figure 3-24. Material progression through linear process line with three bad lots

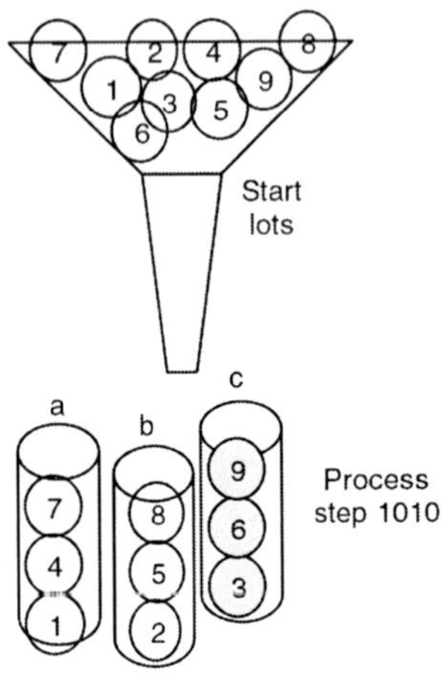

<u>Perfectly linear line</u>
Lots # 3, 6, 9 emerged with bad results.

What are the tools that processed these lots in every process step?

Step	Tool	Lots	Tool	Lots
1010	- c -	3,6,9		
2020	- a -	3,9	- b -	6
3030	- a -	3,6,9		
4040	- c -	3,6,9		
5050	- a -	3,9	- b -	6

The three problematic lots shared the same tool in 3 out of 5 process steps. So, we can assume that these process steps and the respected tools are more likely to cause the problem.

One can speculate that in process step 3030 there are several good lots in between the bad lots and this makes this process step less likely to cause the problem.

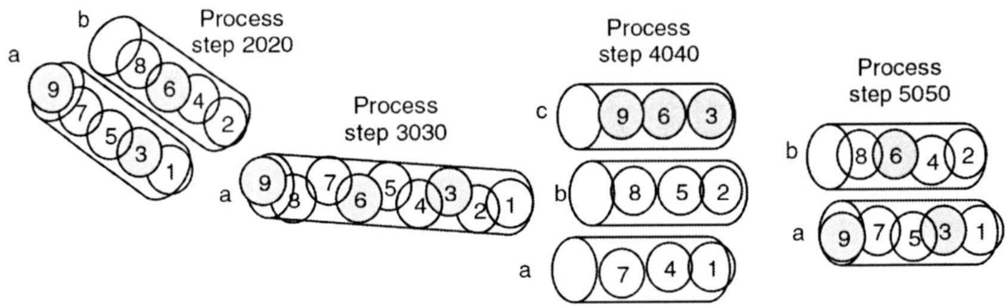

Figure 3-25. Lots progression in random order through a process line with three bad lots

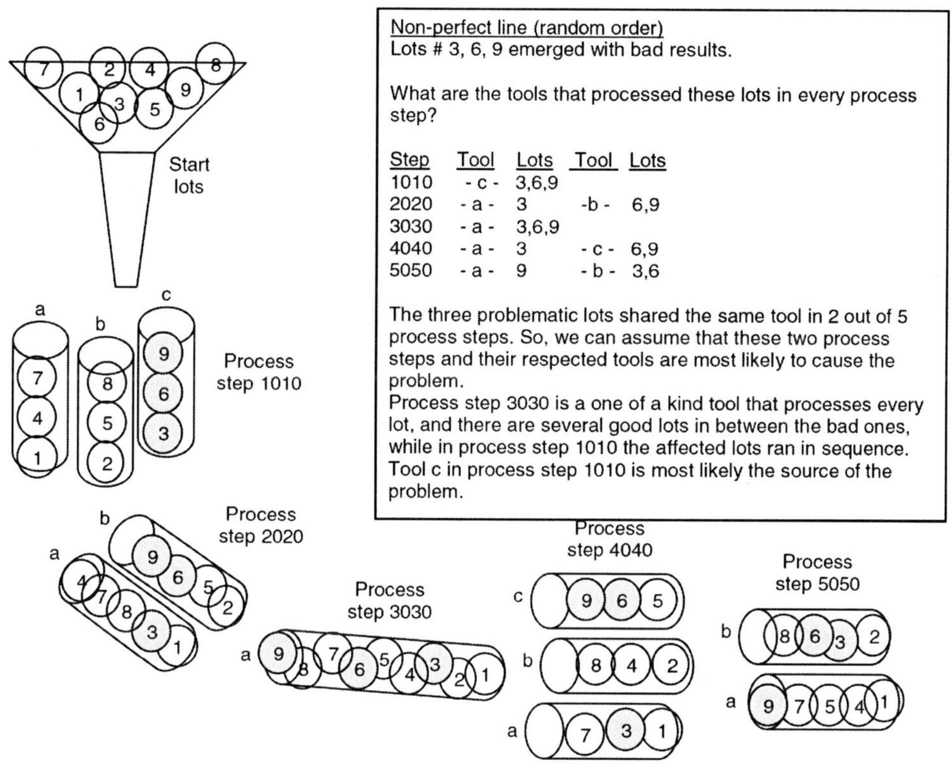

Non-perfect line (random order)
Lots # 3, 6, 9 emerged with bad results.

What are the tools that processed these lots in every process step?

Step	Tool	Lots	Tool	Lots
1010	- c -	3,6,9		
2020	- a -	3	-b -	6,9
3030	- a -	3,6,9		
4040	- a -	3	- c -	6,9
5050	- a -	9	- b -	3,6

The three problematic lots shared the same tool in 2 out of 5 process steps. So, we can assume that these two process steps and their respected tools are most likely to cause the problem.
Process step 3030 is a one of a kind tool that processes every lot, and there are several good lots in between the bad ones, while in process step 1010 the affected lots ran in sequence. Tool c in process step 1010 is most likely the source of the problem.

Commonality study is a good way to identify suspected process steps and tools. However, for this technique to be effective there are several requirements. There should be more than one tool per process step and the line should have some randomization in lot order between one process step and the next.

There are several typical pitfalls that may cause commonality study to fail.
- If the problem is not well characterized and the marked bad material is actually a mix of relevant material with some material unrelated to this specific event, the commonality will fail to provide adequate results.
- If the number of lots (or products) used for the study is too small, it may provide too many alerts and not much will be gained by the analysis.

- When a machine is capable of running the entire load without being a line constraint of a certain process-step, this process step may employ only a one of a kind machine. Since all of the material is running through this one of a kind machine, this tool will always appear to be common to all bad lots. Naturally, it is not possible to say that this indicates that this machine is problematic, or to say that this machine is OK.
- A short term dedication of a tool to run a specific process step will cause it to indicate this tool as problematic, causing a false alert by making it temporarily a one of a kind tool.

Good vs. bad

A different treatment in a certain process step may have led to different results in immediate monitoring of this process step. However, this difference in results was too small to observe at the time of the event. This problem remained unnoticed until products reached a later process step or even until the end-of-line. By comparing a group of bad production lots (or products) to a group of good production lots (or products) these small differences could be detected. The intention of the technique is to place two distinct groups against each other and compare (statistically) the entire test results (monitors) that were taken in-line in every process step. The comparison results may then be ranked according to level of significance. A process parameter that is found to be significantly different between the two groups may indicate that this parameter has something to do with the problem. This check could provide a significant indication of the source of the problem and may help in developing the model of failure.

This comparison is usually performed on output parameters or tests, but it may be even more beneficial to enlarge the scope of comparison between the groups beyond this. Clearly, it is more convenient to use process parameters that can be tested statistically and to rank the findings according to a significance test, however sometimes the answer exists in parameters that are not easy to compare statistically. So, it is also suggested to compare other factors that may affect the processed material, such as timing-related effects, maintenance issues and loading effect.

Some examples for good versus bad comparison may provide surprising results. These include tool input parameters, delay times between process steps, recorded running time (day vs. night hours), manufacturing shift on duty, time from last set-up, time (or count) from last maintenance activity and position of material in tool.

A detected difference in monitor results may point to a specific process step, but it also raises an effect that could assist in model development.

Any signal that is detected by GVB analysis should be used cautiously and further confirmation, either by experiment or by other means, is suggested. As in any tool, there are potential pitfalls that may cause detection of false signals.

- If the list of one (or both) of the groups is too short, you may suspect that the detected signal is not necessarily correct and it is just related to the small sampling.
- If the two groups were not processed in the same time frame, there may be irrelevant detected differences that are related to the natural line variations over time.
- If the two groups were selected in a way that each group is processed through a different set of machines, it may provide a false alert related to natural machine-to-machine variation.

Correlation

The rationale in controlling the process parameters lies in the dependency between the performances of these in-line process parameters and the end-of-line product results. Interdependency is also typical between the in-line process parameters in different process steps. Learning these dependencies may provide a valuable understanding of which parameter could cause what effect on other process or product parameter.

Knowing the interrelations between different process parameters and the ability to draw conclusions based on it, is a strong tool in event investigation. The ability to point out specific parameters that have an impact on the behavior of a certain product or structure can direct the analysis towards the correct reason of the failure. This learning is especially valuable when trying to tailor a model to an unexpected event, but may also be performed as part of problem characterization.

The good vs. bad technique compares two distinct groups and tries to conclude suspected process steps or process parameters. A correlation may be performed on the entire material (mix of good and bad) and provide an understanding of interdependencies in process parameters.

When investigating change in a certain variable (process parameter), it is often obvious that there is a related change in another variable (another process parameter). It is remarked that there is a correlation between these parameters. The level of interrelation may either be illustrated by drawing a scatter chart (as seen below) or quantified by statistical methods to produce **a correlation coefficient**. Perfect correlation is marked by 1, perfect inverse correlation is marked by -1, and no correlation is marked by 0.

In real life, it is quite rare to see two process parameters that are perfectly correlated to each other as shown in figure 3-26.

Figure 3-26. Perfect correlation

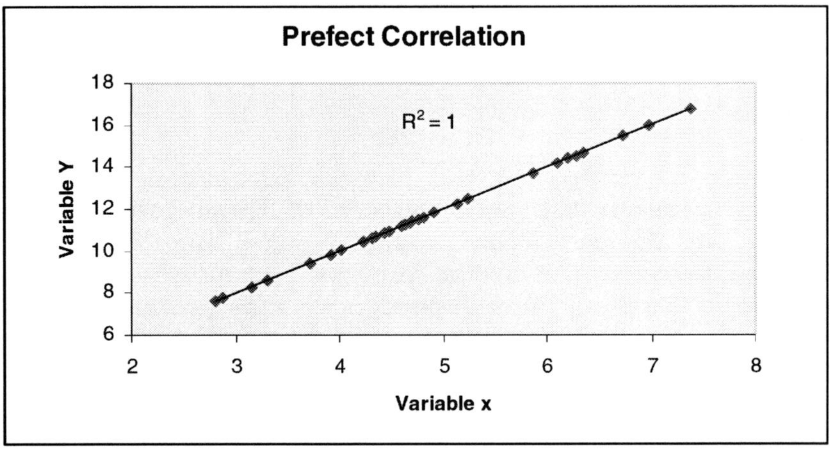

It is more likely to see the correlation demonstrated in figure 3-27. The points are not aligned in a perfect row and are more scattered. Still, it is quite easy to see that there is some interrelation between these process parameters.

Figure 3-27. Typical correlation between process parameters.

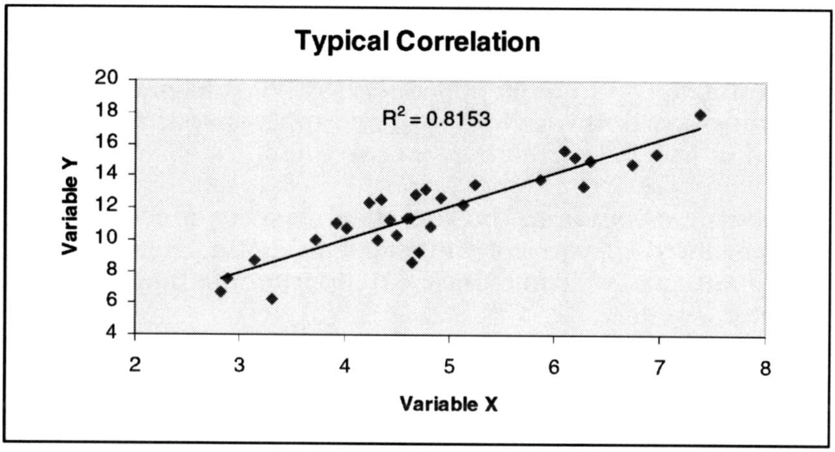

Obviously there are many cases where there is no correlation, as demonstrated in figure 3-28.

Figure 3-28. No correlation between process parameters

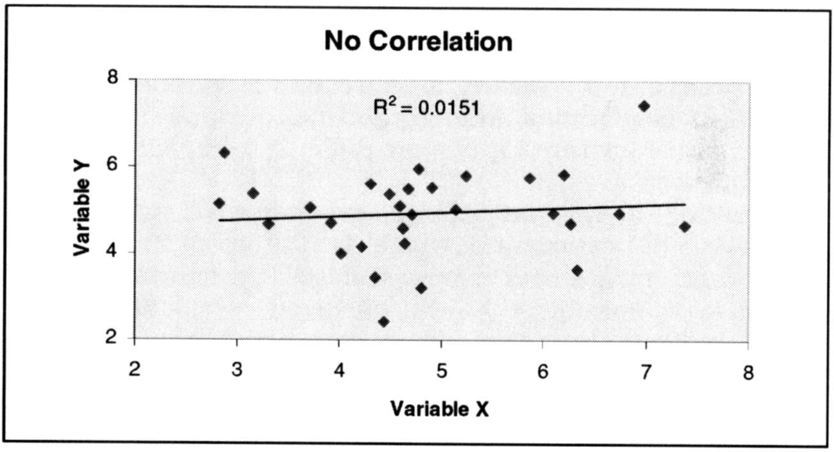

You probably observed that **correlation coefficient (R^2)** is marked on each one of the above graphs, providing a quantitative indication of the level of correlation. Be careful not to use a correlation coefficient as the only indication for interrelations between process parameters. Sometimes even a single outlier that is not relevant to the problem may distort the calculation and alter the correlation coefficient result. In some other cases, you may observe that there is a correlation for part of the population, while the correlation coefficient will be blind to it. The interrelation between process parameters does not necessarily need a simple linear correlation; you may miss an odd shape dependency if you do not look at the shape of your chart. Always look at the graph's shape. Your eyes are pretty good in judging correlation, so use them.

In the following discussion, the statistical aspects of correlation will not be considered. If you are interested in getting deeper into the statistics, you are welcome pick an appropriate book from the bibliography.

The discussion covers the relevancy of correlation to cause analysis and the way to treat an observed correlation. Therefore, here, as in other parts of the book, I will not adhere to statistically correct terminology and I will allow myself freer use of statistically reserved wording.

During problem characterization or when building a potential model in RCA, we often would like to understand how the process parameter connects between them, or how they impact one another. It is always important to know what is expected and what comes unexpected, either by having an expert opinion on the discussed matter, or preferably by having a reference correlation on good or past material. Sometimes interrelation is obvious and easy to understand, and sometimes it is more difficult to explain.

When observing a correlation one may wonder: which of the parameters is the cause and which is the result? Maybe both parameters are results and are modulated by another dominant parameter? Is it possible that the observed correlation does not necessarily indicate interdependency between these parameters? There is no simple rule for a yes or no answer to these questions. However, the need to explain the observed correlation forces us to think about possible reasons for dependency (or loss of dependency), thus deepening our understanding of the issue under investigation.

There are a few scenarios we can think about when dealing with correlation in RCA.

- Two parameters that showed correlation in the past (or on reference material) cease to show this correlation on the problematic material.

- Two process parameters that are not expected to show dependency, show correlation.

- Correlation is expected and still exists, but it is not the same correlation observed on reference material.

<u>Two parameters that showed correlation in the past (or on reference material) cease to show this correlation on the problematic material</u>
When a variable is a direct measure (or a direct indication) of one process parameter that impacts the other, we define the first as the modulator and the second as the modulated parameter, or in other words, the first is the cause and the second is the result.

When we have an understanding that this kind of relation exists between two parameters, and the correlation is lost or weakened, we may suspect the involvement of a third parameter. This third parameter may also modulate the resulting parameter, and it becomes more dominant on the problematic material.

Now here is a tricky question:
Could two process parameters that have no correlation with each other both show correlation to yet another parameter?
The answer is yes. Let's discuss an actual example. Narrow resistors are defined in a process line and measured at the end-of-line. There is a strong correlation between the resistance and the cross-sectional area. The cross-sectional area is defined by the width of the line (one process step) and the height of the layer (another process step). There is no correlation (and there is no reason for one) between the metal thickness (height) and the line width. However, when correlating the end-of-line resistance to either of the above process parameters, correlation will be shown for both.

Any increase in the variation of one parameter will degrade the correlation quality of the other parameter to the end-of-line resistance. So, when looking at a change that could be caused by several process parameters, suspect the one that shows improved correlation.

We may think that if an observed dependency exists for a certain process window, it will continue to be kept away from this window. However, the process window could be on a cliff. This means that a small shift will cause a catastrophic change. The process moved away from a region with dependency to a point of no dependency – the process is lost. It may be related to a recorded process change or due to some failure that caused parameter deviation from its original set point.

You may find that interdependency between the two parameters only supposedly exists. The detected correlation is nothing but a false indication. The loss of correlation is related to the change in one parameter and this is meaningless to the other. These parameters never had any real dependency between them.
Obviously an example is needed in this case.

Let's take a situation where there is center to edge non-uniformity in thickness of metal deposited over a product surface, and this was always the case. The reason is the shape and position of the metal target within the deposition tool in respect to the product. The thickness in the product center is thinner than this layer at the edge.

In a later process step, the product is sprayed by two nozzles located at a certain distance from each other. Since there is an overlapping in the coverage between the nozzles, the sprayed layer is thicker in the overlap region (center of product). Since both tools generate center to edge non-uniformity, a correlation between the metal thickness and sprayed material will be observed.

A change in metal uniformity was recently observed and there is an effort to understand this effect. Naturally the correlation with the spraying tool is lost. Does this loss of correlation have any relevancy to problem investigation? Of course not! The spraying tool uniformity has no impact on the metal deposition, nor is it impacted by it. The correlation that was originally observed was nothing but artifact.

<u>Two process parameters that are not expected to have dependency, show correlation.</u>
If you find a real correlation that was unknown, it could be extremely important to the cause analysis. When trying to tailor a

model to the problem creation, the newly observed factor should be included. This could be a key finding to achieve progress.

When there is a very noisy process parameter that usually strongly modulates another parameter, it could blur the ability to observe an existing dependency to other parameters. If, for some reason the noise level in the known modulator was restrained, or there is an increase in the fluctuation of another modulator, the hidden correlation may appear.

If an unexpected correlation appears, extra care is needed. Again it could be that the newly identified correlation is an artifact. Coincidental occurrence or appearance of an effect with a similar stamp may fool you into believing that a real correlation exists, while there is no real dependency.

Let's look at an example of coincidence in occurrence. Say, for some reason, there is a continuous improvement in end-of-line yield results, and recently there was a trend up in metal resistance. When studying a plot of yield vs. metal resistance, one may see the correlation and wrongly conclude that the improvement in yield is related to the change in metal resistance.

The coincidence in appearance is also possible. For example, the order of running material through a machine may impact the measured results. The first product to be processed in a sequence will produce a result that is slightly different than the last to be processed. Since the production lots tend to keep their order throughout the line, this effect may have a similar impact on production of several process steps. These process steps may show correlation, while there is no real dependency between them.

Correlation is expected and still exists, but it is not the same correlation observed on reference material.

While saying that the correlation is not the same, there are a number of possible changes. The first one is a simple loss of correlation quality in relation to the reference. It was mentioned earlier that if all points are in line, this is perfect correlation ($R^2=1$). As more points are scattered around the correlation, quality is lost. This kind of situation was covered earlier when correlation loss was discussed, but there is one more important point to add.

If a certain dependency was observed between parameters for a certain range, the same dependency is not necessarily kept beyond (above or below) this range.

Check carefully whether the range of new results (problematic population) is wider than or away from your reference population. The same situation exists if results tend to get wild on one parameter, while these fluctuations have a lesser effect on the other.

There are two more possible changes in correlation that are worth mentioning. In the next two cases, it will be apparent that perfect correlation is kept ($R^2=1$), however something was changed with respect to reference.

Change in correlation slope

A possible change in process parameter dependency is the difference in correlation slope (as shown in figure 3-29). This problem can be rather annoying and may indicate a profound property change in the process.

Figure 3-29. Change in correlation – slope change

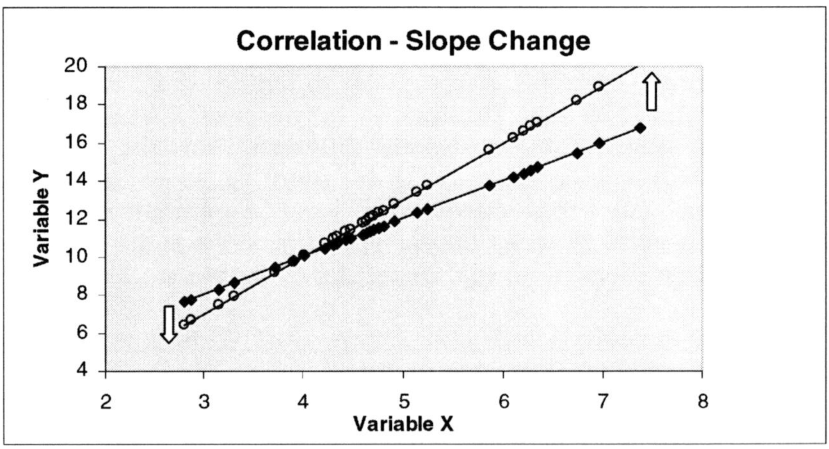

Slope change means that one parameter that used to show a certain amount of change in response to a change in another parameter now provides a different amount of change.

You need to look for a parameter that can dictate the amount of change in the altered parameter. The dependency between variable

Y and variable X may be impacted by another variable (Z). This other variable may be either a condition or property that alters the X to Y dependency.

Let's look at a real life example:
A certain process step aims to remove part of a pre-deposited layer to an exact thickness. By knowing the removal rate and the initial layer thickness on the arrived product, the engineer could dial the exact time required for the tool to do the job.

One day the calculations went wrong. When plotting the correlation between the removing time and the removed layer, it appeared that the correlation had a different slope. The removal rate was changed. There was nothing in the machine that could explain this change. It emerged later that the engineer responsible for layer deposition had set his tool to a new pressure level. The deposited material has a higher density, and became harder to remove. The removal rate decreased accordingly, and this was the reason for the change that was observed in correlation slope.

Correlation shift
As demonstrated in figure 3-30, there is no doubt that the dependency between the variables has the same quality as judged by the spread of points around the correlation line. The slope was not changed either. However, the entire correlation is shifted down.

Figure 3-30. Change in correlation – shift

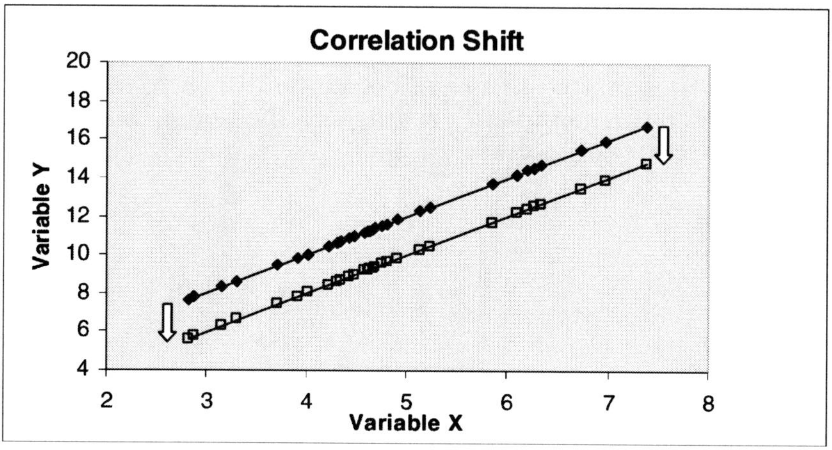

This problem is typical in calibration variation. If a component is replaced in a process tool, or a structural change was performed on a machine, the interdependency could be maintained, but this kind of shift will be observed.

When you see such a change, check the conditions. It is quite usual to see a correlation shift after tool maintenance, or as a machine-to-machine difference.

Was the same tool set in use? Was there any change in the process tool conditions? Do not exclude the test equipment or testing conditions as another potential reason for the shift.

Important note about shift:
Sometimes things are not exactly as they seem. You may identify a certain change as a correlation shift while it is actually a change in slope. How come?

We usually check the correlation for a certain process window. We may not have any results or indication of what is happening with material that is far above or below this window.

When we have two populations with different slopes, at some point the two linear correlations will cross each other. This cross point could be far away from our typical working window and cannot be seen in our results. As a result, the two populations will appear to us as shifted from each other, while the change in slope is so small that it is totally ignored. So, be careful with shifts.

In this short discussion about correlation, I attempted to reveal some of the issues related to use of correlation in RCA. It should be clear that it is not a complete coverage of the issue, and there is much more to learn about correlation.

Chapter Summary

Before summarizing the Problem Characterization chapter, I would like to note something important:

Data analysis needs skills, tools and experience for proper handling. Useful information could be hidden under a large pile of numbers and characters. If the problem is characterized by a skillful person, you are more than halfway to success in event investigation.

I find it rather important and appropriate to refer any reader who is interested in in-depth learning of data-analysis to the Engineering Statistics Handbook **http://www.itl.nist.gov/div898/handbook**. This is a free downloadable treasure.

The chapter that you have just completed provides a brief overview of the basic way of thinking in the problem characterization stage. It emphasizes the importance of in-depth learning of the detected symptoms. Proper characterization will not only prevent the investigation from going in the wrong direction, but it may lead to the source of the problem and even assist in problem modeling.

Things to keep in mind:

Problem characterization is important and is a combined effort of computerized data analysis, physical lab analysis, and field data learning.

Computerized data analysis is thorough learning of an event by comparing the unexpected with the expected.

Initial problem definition for cause analysis is made by stating the basic facts of observed symptoms.

Initial characterization involves learning of all sources of noise, involved material distribution, and all characteristic symptoms. These are necessary to drive the investigation in the right direction.

Proper metric selection with correct limits is required to identify the involved material. This will prevent improper material from reaching the customer and waste of money in further unnecessary processing. Cause analysis will enable a clear definition of related and unrelated material to support the source identification with analytical techniques.

Proper usage of the analytical tools and techniques may lead to the source of problem identification. Rerun analytical tools if new material is available to reinforce findings. Rerun analytical tools if the distinction between related and unrelated material was refined.

CHAPTER 4

Model Building

This chapter will lead you though the model-building process. You will learn that a complete model has three elements and that progress in event investigation is achieved by learning each of these elements. This learning process involves inclusive and exhaustive investigation by arranging information in hierarchical trees.

The following topics will be covered in this chapter:

- Cause and effect rationale
- Conditions tree
- Building a conditions tree
- Sequential vs. coincidental effect
- The three elements of a complete model
- Properties tree
- Building a properties tree
- Raising a scenario
- Working with modeling trees
- Navigating in modeling trees
    - Segmentation
    - Categorization
- Practical example
- Running the team to build the trees

Model building: things are not always as they seem

"I went into the room and there she was, lying on the floor with all this blood around. I saw this young man kneeling right next to her holding a bloody knife; he dropped it when I came in and ..."

Many stories start like this, and then the very intelligent detective / lawyer / reporter with his or her unusual insight, and against all odds, provides a brilliant explanation that shows that things are not always as they seem. The hero risks his neck to gather the required critical evidence, and drinks gallons of coffee during sleepless nights, until at the last minute, all the pieces fit together into remarkably surprising and convincing story.

Even if the above description sounds like a cliché, it is also relevant to our routine cause analysis tasks. As we defined in the introduction, the model or hypothesis is a potential explanation for problem creation / appearance. The task of building a detailed model usually requires numerous iterations. Intelligent use of the data collected between these iterations is the proper way to progress to the most accurate model. This in turn will help to apply a proper solution to the problem.

If model building is the best compass to direct us from one level to the next in the problem definition funnel, how can we build a model? What is considered to be a good model in processing the problem? How can it help in root cause identification?

Cause and effect rationale

The basic rationale behind traditional model building is the belief that if we provide a complete set of identical conditions for an ideal system, we will repeatedly achieve the same results. If something comes out with an unexpected result, we need to find out what change in the conditions caused it. Any unexpected result is an **effect** and any condition that generates it is a **cause**. If the change in conditions was unexpected, it is an effect in itself and should have a cause as well. This perpetual **cause and effect** cycle may continue until we decide that there is sufficient understanding to satisfy our needs. This rationale is demonstrated in figure 4-1.

Figure 4-1. Cause and effect rationale used for problem investigation

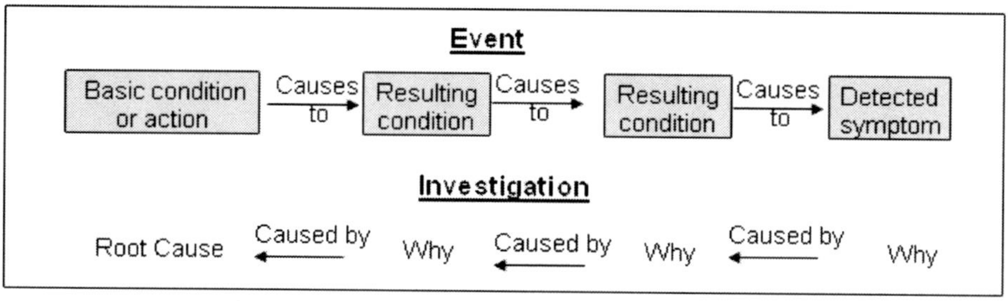

The above rationale is used extensively in many disciplines that conduct root cause investigations. The usual way of running it is by using some flavor of a **hierarchically arranged tree** that graphically displays the relation between each effect level and all of its potential causing conditions.

Conditions tree

The conditions tree is a hierarchically arranged tree that aims to show all possible conditions necessary to provide the desired outcome, and then use it to identify the stems (conditions) leading to the undesired result.

The example in figure 4-2 represents a simple conditions tree built for investigating a change in CVD (chemical vapor deposition) tool performance. The tool should deposit a layer with a certain deposition rate, however there was an unexpected change and the tool started to produce a lower deposition rate.

Figure 4-2. Schematic conditions tree for investigating low deposition rate in a simple CVD (chemical vapor deposition) system.

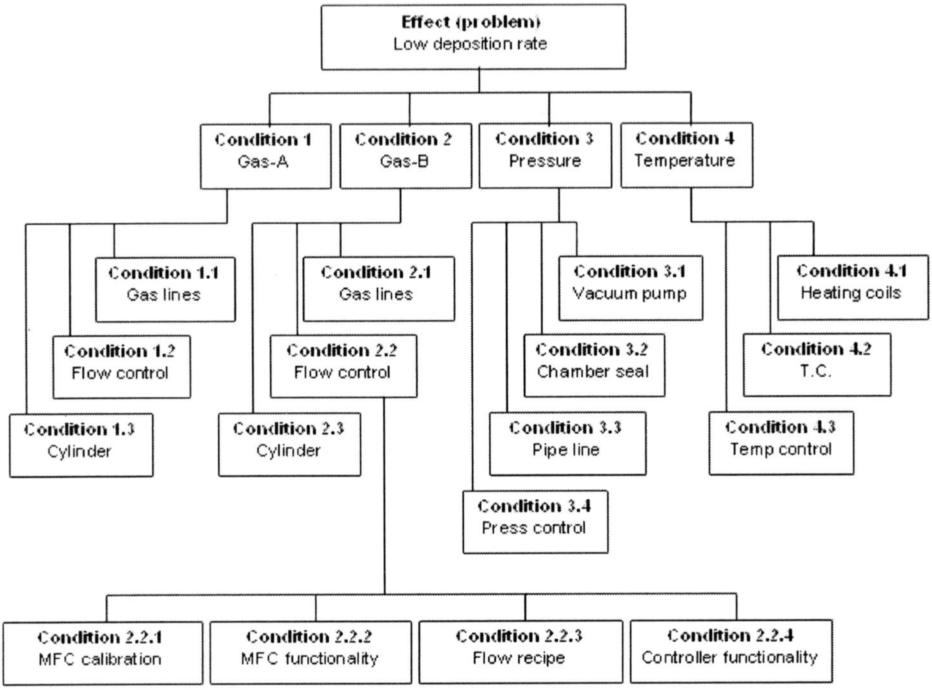

The first branching level defines the condition required by the tool/chamber for depositing a layer. In this case, this is two gas modules, a pressure control system and a temperature control system. The next level breaks each condition into the basic components or functions in the tool that support this condition. The level below breaks each component or function into sub-components or sub-functions. In the example, only one branch is shown.

How is this conditions tree constructed?

Building a conditions tree

Mapping requires a team that knows the system or process that should be analyzed. The unexpected effect (detected symptom) should first be presented to the team. Next, it would be wise to bind the problem within certain boundaries (based on initial information gathered in the problem characterization stage).

This will focus the team on the system or on the process segment that is known to cause the problem. For example, the leading person will say "The earliest suspected process-step is X and the latest suspected process-step is Y" (let the team challenge that), or "The origin of the problem is in the water-supply system".

For the defined system or process segment, the team members should suggest (or prepare offline) all the conditions and actions that are needed to achieve **proper results** (normal situation), and arrange it on a tree diagram. The purpose in arranging the conditions tree is to suggest and verify any **possible change** (altered, added, or missed) in these conditions or actions that may lead to the problematic result.

To ensure that every level of the conditions tree has a manageable number of stems, it is sometimes necessary to group several conditions together. If there are too many suspected process steps (in the suspected segment) it would be wise to group several process steps into a process module. The tree will start with fewer branches (modules) at first level, and each module will have several related process steps. Similarly, if the problem is related to a major system with many sub-components, it is recommended to group several sub-components into functional assembly.

So, the team starts with the problem (detected symptom) at the top box of the tree and continues to list any major condition that is needed to support the expected outcome. These major conditions are the first branching level. It then picks one of the main branches and starts to list its sub-conditions. The team repeats this sequence to achieve the most complete map. It is rather important to be as inclusive as possible at any branch level. If, at a later stage, a condition is found to be forgotten, add it to the proper branch level.

Keep in mind that conditions here is a generic term describing one element from a set needed to support the level above it in the tree hierarchy. To help you with inclusiveness and to cover all aspects of conditions in any branch, think whether all **S.Co.T.T** (supplies, components, treatments, and timing) are listed.

Supplies: any supply that is needed to support the tool or process, either during processing or when idle. Since the product itself enters the tool during processing, it can also be considered as a supply.

Components: any part or component that serves any function in the system. Think about shape, functionality, position, and condition of any part or sub-system related to the processing tool.

Treatments: all actions necessary for proper processing or/and system maintenance. This includes handling and transportation, loading and unloading sequence, process parameters set points (recipe) and actual, idle conditions, maintenance procedures and activities, and environment.

Timing: All timing or delay issues before, after, or during a required action. This includes duration of sequence or step, delay times, and proper timing of parallel events.

Keep in mind that once you write a certain stem, it may be necessary to rethink the S.Co.T.T under this stem. For instance, you may mark the D.I. water supply as a potential cause of the event, but once you do this, you have to keep in mind that the system supplying the D.I. water requires supplies, components and treatment to function properly. If you try and cover all of the branches thoroughly, you'll end up with a huge and detailed conditions tree. So, don't be too involved with many small leaves. Try to find ways to cut upper level branches. Start to check what the data in hand can tell about the initial tree. Can it eliminate certain branches right away? Can it point strongly to a certain direction? Can the team suggest data items (existing or to be collected) to differentiate between branches?

If the answer is yes, list them. These are the potential key data items that will lead to the correct branches.

Sequential vs. coincidental events

The cause and effect rationale employed for building a conditions tree diagram assumes direct and immediate relation between symptoms detected on the system or structure under investigation and conditions causing it. The basic idea is that a fundamental change or cause led to certain effect and this effect caused another effect and the sequence of the events eventually ended in a noticeable effect that was detected and defined as a problem. By going from a detected effect (symptom) backwards, one would assume that this sequence could be identified in reverse order, reaching the fundamental reason that initiated the sequence. One can say that this event is a **sequential event.**

In a sequential event, there are hidden events within the event sequence that could not be noticed at the time of occurrence, but the cause and effect chain still continued toward the noticeable end result. There could also be a situation where the sequence of events is interrupted, stopped, or detected at an earlier stage before causing the problematic end results, by barriers that should either detect (monitor) or block (interlock) the event sequence. If these measures are missing, ignored, bypassed, or implemented inefficiently, they are counted as a contributing factor that should be emphasized during the event investigation summary. However, these are not part of the cause and effect sequence, they just failed to stop or detect the sequence of events. Therefore, when checking the sequential problem, there will be one route that will follow the cause and effect sequence from the condition that initiates the problem all the way up to the end result. Even though there are some other parallel routes that indicate contributing factors that failed to interfere with the problematic sequence, this problem is still counted as a sequential problem.

The above conditions tree method works fine in many cases, especially when focusing on a specific system or component. But will it be sufficient to help in any or most of the cause identification tasks in the processing industry?

The answer is, no. In some cases, several independent conditions coincided together to generate the problem. This kind of problem can be defined as a **coincidental event**.

In the coincidental event, the independent causing conditions are aligned in time or space to form the problem. The challenge in analyzing a coincidental event is doubled. The investigating individual or team should first reach the understanding that the problem is initiated by independent conditions, and then identify these conditions and characterize the exact situation with these conditions that lead to creation of the problem. The process corner problem that was described in the problem sources and classification chapter is probably the most obvious example of a coincidental problem. In many cases, an intermittent problem is also related to a coincidental event, and the conditions that are aligned to form the problem should be identified. As well as this integrative effect (coincidental problem), there are problems that are detected at a later stage with no known connection to any immediate source or cause.

Using the conditions tree to try and investigate the conditions causing the problem may cause the team to wander around without knowing where to look or without thinking that the problem is related to a combination of few independent conditions. In these cases (at the start of the investigation) it appears that there are either a **huge number of potential explanations for the problem** or **not even one possible intelligent explanation.** An attempt to generate a cause and effect diagram (Ishikawa or fishbone diagram) or conditions tree diagram may provide wild results in this situation. There could be so many branches in the tree that it will never be fruitful. In many cases, the demand to show potential models right away makes the short cut to cause identification longer. The team is busy generating an irrelevant chart and working on irrelevant data collection instead of focusing on the effort in finding key information required to achieve real progress in cause analysis. Using the conditions tree in the same way it is used for a sequential problem could be frustrating. When investigating any branch, it seems as if every condition by itself is OK. Everything that is within normal variation and similar performance in the past produced good results. The notion that a coincidental problem is involved should result from a different way of thinking.

If a conditions tree describing all conditions is not sufficient, what else can be done to assist cause identification?

The three elements of a complete model

In the discussion, we may call the failed or analyzed object an IUI (item under investigation). This could be a real end-of-line product or a monitor, structure, defect, component, or system.

When dealing with this IUI one may realize that:

1. There are process steps, resources, and actions that are needed to produce it, or as described earlier in more a generic term: conditions.

2. Certain internal properties or characteristics are required for this IUI to be functional. If the IUI is a complex system it may have a few smaller components; each should have some characteristics and properties in itself. Note that if the IUI is a defect, being functional means having properties that can distract the normal functionality of the product or a system in which this defect is embedded.

3. The IUI externalizes detectable or measurable behavior. This is usually how a problem is detected.

When thinking this way, we can say that a problem with an IUI is generated by the conditions needed to produce it, which create (or alter) its internal properties or functionality, and this in turn causes the detected or sensed behavior.
A good model is one that describes it all: the conditions that existed (or were changed) in the system, the impact of these conditions on the internal character of the item being investigated, and how this reflects on the resulting behavior. These three elements of a complete model are demonstrated in figure 4-3.

Figure 4-3. The three elements of a complete model.

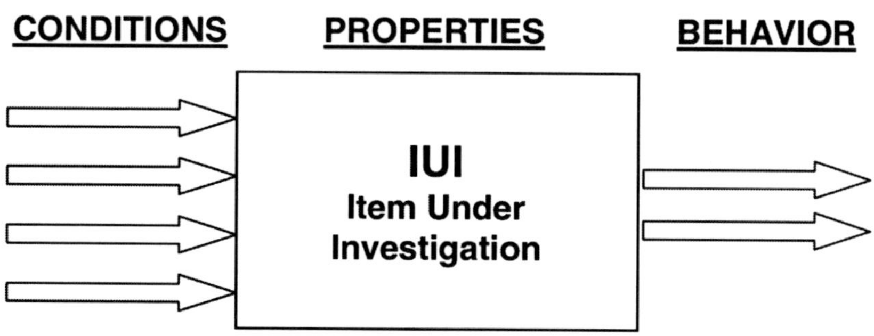

But more important to us is that learning every one of the above three elements could promote understanding of the others. Identifying the problematic resource (learning the inputs) may provide understanding of the product's failure mechanism.

Localizing and understanding the flaw within the product (learning what is going within) may point to the problematic resource or process step that caused it. Thorough learning of the product behavior or its measurable properties (learning the outputs) may help in understanding the flaw within it and/or the conditions that created it.

Let's look at a very old and solid example that shows how learning IUI properties can teach us about the conditions that were needed to create it.

One day King Hiero approached Archimedes and said, "I gave the goldsmith 1 kg of gold and asked him to make the most beautiful crown that ever existed. The goldsmith made a golden wreath, and indeed it is the most beautiful crown I have ever seen. The goldsmith said that he used all the gold and nothing was left. However, I suspect that he took some of the gold for himself and used some silver to build the crown. Please take this crown, check it, do not harm it in any way, and let me know if the goldsmith was honest with me."
Archimedes could not go to the goldsmith and investigate him or check his tools. He could also not cut out any part of the crown to melt it for checking. But, he knew that 1 kg of gold has the same volume whether in the shape of a gold bar or a crown. So he took an equal weight of pure gold, placed it in a tub of water and marked the water level. Then he took the crown and placed it in the same tub and checked whether the water level reached the exact level of the gold bar. Thus Archimedes identified and used two properties of the crown (IUI) that could teach him about the supplies (conditions).

It is quite obvious that when we discussed the conditions tree earlier, we emphasized our attention to the conditions but neglected the other two elements that are critical to cause identification.
How can we use the other elements in cause identification?

Properties tree

As well as the tree discussed earlier, which is based on conditions (conditions tree), there is another kind of tree that could be useful for cause analysis. This is the properties tree, which is based on the inner characteristic / properties / behavior observed in an IUI. This IUI could be a familiar object showing unusual problematic behavior, or a phenomenon without any reference for comparison. The difference in these two basic situations is meaningful and will affect your approach when developing a properties tree. This issue will be discussed later in more detail.

The basic intention is to map the inner components, functions and properties of the item that provided the unexpected results. Isolating and learning the component and/or property that was altered may point to the process step or module within the process line that generated it. The next step is to go back and build a conditions tree to find out what went wrong in this process step. Often, understanding the flaw in a certain component or property of the IUI indicates that an integrative (coincidental) effect is involved, while this is very hard to realize with a conditions tree.

Let's look at a practical example that clarifies this idea.
A problem was detected at the end-of-line in a semiconductor manufacturing site. An electrical structure called a contact chain, which used to have a certain typical resistance value, started to show higher than usual resistance. This electrical structure is not an actual functional product but it indicates a problem in the line that is hard to detect in the actual product. The contact chain structure is formed together with the actual product during processing; however it requires construction of only part of the process steps in the total process flow.

Figure 4-4 shows a cross section of a contact chain. The chain is made up of a repeated arrangement of metal lines, contacts (holes filled with metal), and silicide (a metal and silicon compound) lines. Resistance is measured by probes touching the two ends of the contact chain. During this resistance measurement, electrical current flows along the metal line and down the contact, continues through the silicide line and up the next contact into the next metal line, and so on. Naturally any problem in the process line that alters the properties of this path's components will affect contact chain resistance.

Figure 4-4. Cross section of a typical contact chain

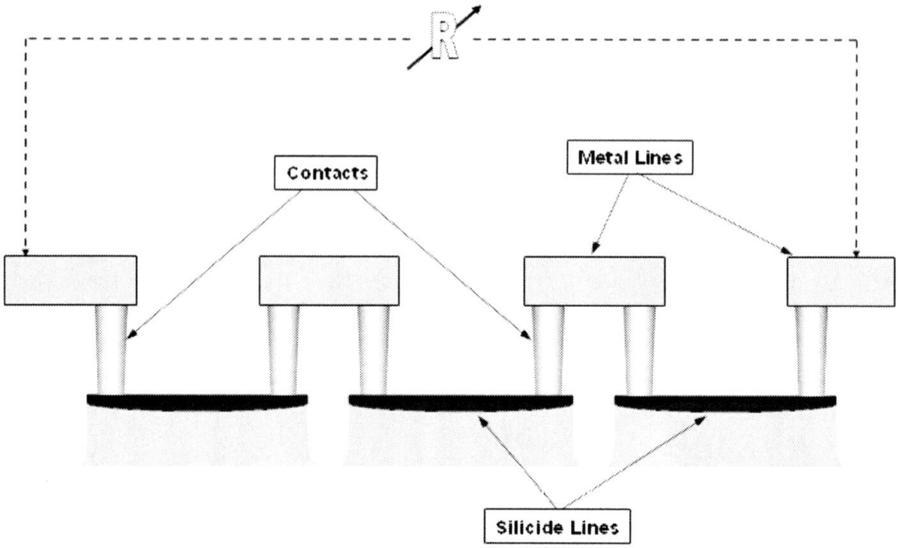

Even if less than the full process flow is required to construct the contact chain, there is still a significant number of process steps that could affect it. Hence building a detailed condition tree with all the involved process steps will be exhausting and time-consuming. Instead let's use this structure as our IUI and build a properties tree for it. For the purpose of this discussion, we assume that it has already been confirmed that the problem is real and not a measurement error.

A closer look into one link of the contact chain is shown in figure 4.5. The intention behind this zoom-in on one link is to direct our thinking towards the most basic required elements for its proper functionality.

Figure 4-5. Basic elements of a link in the contact chain

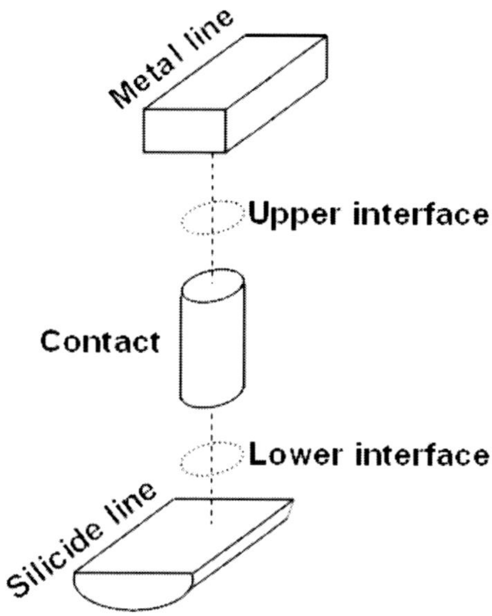

The basic elements that are needed for maintaining the required low resistance are: metal line properties, interface of metal-to-contact characteristics, contact properties, contact-to-silicide interface, and silicide line properties.

It is now possible, and even recommended, to physically study an affected structure and compare it to a good reference structure. However, it is rather important to continue to build a properties tree by specifying the required properties for each basic element. First, the next stage of the properties tree could suggest a different physical analysis technique instead of the one initially suggested. Second, even if the physical analysis points to a certain basic element as the source of the problem, it may not provide sufficient explanation for the cause of the problem.

The properties tree in figure 4-6 is an example of a tree that started to be developed for the contact chain event.

Figure 4-6. Contact chain properties tree

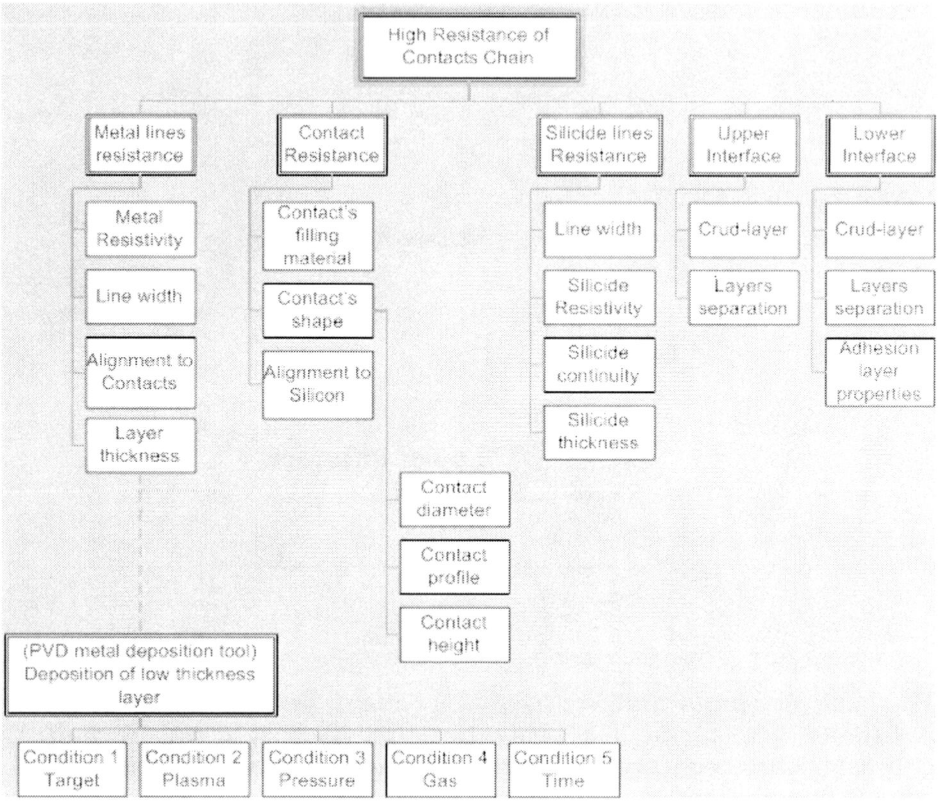

When looking at this tree, we can see that the failing item (contact chain structure) requires certain properties and could be affected by certain effects. A specific branch or property does not necessarily need to be related to a specific tool or process step. Analyzing the item itself or its behavior may point to the property or component within the product that failed. This could direct us to the conditions that caused it.

It is usual to structure and use the properties tree by first suggesting all the properties required to achieve a properly functioning item for each element, converting it into a possible problematic situation, and finally suggesting all potential causes (scenarios) that could generate this situation. In the example, the metal-to-contact interface should provide low ohmic contact. The inverted situation is to have high resistive (or even capacitive) contact behavior that could be caused by layer separation or by the presence of a crud layer in the interface. If a crud layer is confirmed by the physical analysis, then the team may require potential explanations for formation of the crud layer in this interface.

However, in this example, a thinning in metal line thickness was isolated as the problem in the contact chain event. The metal thickness is defined by a PVD metal-deposition tool. The next step is to draw a conditions tree for this process step, while the problem is narrowed down to a deposition of a low thickness layer.

When studying this tree, it is obvious that knowledge in the process flow, process tools and interrelations between the process and IUI is a basic requirement for the job. And indeed, the combined effort of a knowledgeable team is required to build and use a property tree.

Building a properties tree

Similar to condition tree building, it all starts with stating the unexpected vs. the expected. Describe how a problem is detected and what the known symptoms are. The initial problem statement is the same as in the top box of the condition tree. This is where the similarity between the trees ends. Unlike the conditions tree that has an easy-to-follow structure (because of its natural building blocks), the properties tree has a structure that is less natural and easy to follow. So it could take several iterations of building and re-building the tree before you decide that you have a property tree that satisfies your needs.

The first step is to decide about the IUI which, by analyzing its properties, will help you to understand the event. Study the data that was collected so far in the problem characterization stage, and check which items this data dealt with. Is it a system or tool? Does the system show problematic system behavior or is it a problematic product (a product could be a real end-of-line product or another physical outcome of a certain operation)? If it is a product, is the problem related to a specific structure or defect in this product?

Keep in mind that the IUI could be anything that has properties that can be learned and provide information relevant to the event or problem. In other words, the IUI could be a structure or defect in the product, the product itself, a certain component within a system, or the entire system. So there is no single correct tree. It is important to keep in mind that there could be more than one possible IUI in a single event, and it is acceptable or even desirable to practice more than one property tree for analyzing a problem. As a rule of thumb, exhaust learning of the properties of the most basic problematic element within a system, before confronting learning of a larger or more complex system.

After selecting the IUI that needs to be investigated, start to identify its branching levels. Here you may face one of the two possible situations that were mentioned earlier.

a. The selected IUI is an affected structure or component and you are able to know its required properties. This could be by comparing it to a similar healthy item or by having previous knowledge or experience with the same structure or component.

b. The selected IUI is a defect or phenomenon for which there is no previous knowledge or reference to compare it to.

IUI with known required properties

As demonstrated in the latter example, it is expected that the object (IUI) will function in a certain way or demonstrate an expected behavior as it should carry certain required characteristics and properties.

Start with identification of each property that this item (IUI) should carry for proper behavior and list these as branches in the tree. Arrange the tree by placing the most basic properties at the first level branching and any sub-property under its respective basic property. Try to be inclusive and exhaustive in every branching level.

Think about **structural properties** and **functional properties.** Note that a functional property may or may not correspond with a real physical substance in the IUI (for example, an interface is counted as a functional component, but it is not a real physical component of the structure.

Stop.
Is there a way to learn about the situation of each property within the properties tree that was just mapped (by existing data, direct checking, lab analysis, or experimentation)?

Then, invert the way of thinking and identify potential ways to alter each property (or the one that was identified as problematic) to produce the observed symptoms. The way of thinking should be something like, "If I want to create the observed symptom, this characteristic or property should change to, or must have a..."

Stop. Think again.
Is there a way to directly verify or negate the existence of any suggested disturbances on an affected IUI?

Then, suggest ways to generate the described disturbances, or the one that was already identified. Think about possible **action, interaction, reaction, intervention** that could result in such disturbances.

Finally, list any potential reason that may enable this situation to occur.

You may find that in any of the above stages there could be a situation where the investigation points to a certain property directly related to a specific tool or process step, and from this point on you should continue with conditions tree development.

IUI that is a strange phenomenon
When the problem is a phenomenon with no expected characteristics or properties with which it can be compared, the situation is less straightforward. It is necessary to start collecting and learning any property, characteristic and behavior accompanying the observed phenomenon.

The best guide that leads from one branching level to the next is listening to your own voice, in other words, the most basic and simple question in mind.

The question, "I wonder if every apple always falls downwards?" can be translated into: Option A: apples can only fall downwards; and Option B: apples may fall in any direction. I guess some of you would like to add the option that apples may float in space. Oh yeah, but that is smart to say when you know about gravitation and already saw objects floating in a space-shuttle. I'm not sure if this would have been considered before Newton reached his conclusions.

Stop.
Do you have any way to confirm or deny any of the suggested branches?

Once you present this question with its options, you are in better shape to ask the next questions and present the next set of options.

Sub-option A:
A1. Something pulls the apples downwards; A2. Something pushes the apples from above; A3. Some inner property (sense) of the apples lets them find the shortest way to mother earth.

Stop. Yes, again.
Can you find a way ...?

Once you have exhausted study of the IUI by questioning and learning the potential options, the next step is to suggest all possible origins that fit the observed properties and/or raise scenarios that provide a reasonable explanation for the appearance of the problem.

As in the previous case, you may find that during this learning process, a certain branch of the properties tree points to a specific tool or process step that may require the development of a conditions tree. In this case, from this point on you may work either on both trees in parallel or concentrate on the resources in one of the options.

This last method of properties tree development may seem a bit ambiguous at this point. Towards the end of this chapter you'll see a more practical example that demonstrates how this properties tree is used to investigate an event that involves an unfamiliar defect.

When working with a properties tree, you are free to skip or add branching levels, or reshape the tree to fit new findings until you find the best way to arrange the properties in a logical hierarchical way. You may use the guidelines that were presented earlier, but feel free to arrange the hierarchy of the properties tree in any appropriate way. The properties should help in following the course of the investigation and clarifying the rationale behind the data collection tasks. Remember that the purpose of the trees is to help you and your team running the investigation, and it should not be a Must Do task to satisfy the management. If you are progressing rapidly from one stage to another, do not bother to complete stems in upper levels just for the sake of completeness. You can build a solid model by running all the way down from top to bottom.

It has already been said that building a model should include all three elements: what goes into the product; what is going on within the product; and what is reflected out of the product. However, just identifying certain conditions or properties within a tree cannot yet be considered as a full model or cause identification. As you have probably observed, the last stage of property development involves suggesting a detailed explanation for generating observed properties (or a change of properties) by raising scenarios. What should this scenario look like?

Raising a scenario

A scenario is a story that uses the known facts to provide a viable explanation of how certain conditions may lead to the observed results. There could be more than one scenario for a given set of known facts.

The questions that the scenario should answer (in whole or in part) are:
What is the unusual phenomenon behind the observed symptoms?
What actions/reaction/interaction could lead to this phenomenon?
What are the required conditions or sequence of events that enabled the above?
What are the possible reasons for the existence of these conditions?

Building these scenarios is not always simple and requires the involvement of knowledgeable persons that are able to interpret the collected information and draw conclusions about the event. The scenario may come from a key person with knowledge in one discipline relevant to the event (such as chemistry, physics, material science, and electrical engineering). However, in more complicated situations it may require integrative effort to explain a combination of multidisciplinary effects that were required to generate a problem.

The scenario should be raised as part of the investigation when enough facts or data were collected to support it. At some point, the possible scenarios may or should appear as bottom level branches in the conditions or properties tree. The team may study it and try to find a way to confirm one or another scenario by collecting more information.

You may argue that scenario is interchangeable with model, and in a way you are right. The basic difference in my mind is that an initial model can be a very generic or loose explanation as a stem in the first level branching, while scenario is a detailed model that may answer the question described above.

Working with modeling trees

The conditions and properties trees are fundamental tools for achieving development of a full model or raising scenario. What is the way to work with these trees?

There are two basic methods for working with a hierarchical tree.

Method 1. Invest effort in thorough mapping of all conditions and then work on checking all the conditions one by one, in parallel when there are available human resources, or in sequence if there are only limited human resources.

When thinking this way, it is easily apparent that if we have three levels of conditions with an average of four conditions on each level, we may need to investigate 64 conditions (see figure 4-5). Naturally, mapping a complex problem requires extensive effort and in depth knowledge of all components and conditions of the system under investigation.

Figure 4-7. Running investigation by full tree development

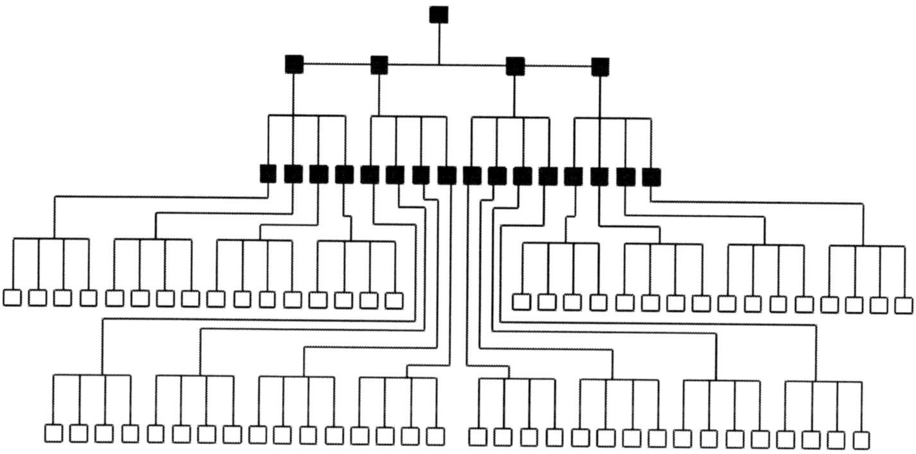

As thorough as it is sounds, this kind of investigation may be either very slow or requires generous resources to go over all branches of the suspected conditions.

Method 2. Map the upper level and find a way (data) to direct to the problematic branch or branches. Break the problematic branch into its sub-components and find a way to isolate the problematic sub-branch or branches. Repeat this until the root cause is found. This method is shown in figure 4-6

Figure 4-8. Running investigation by branch isolation

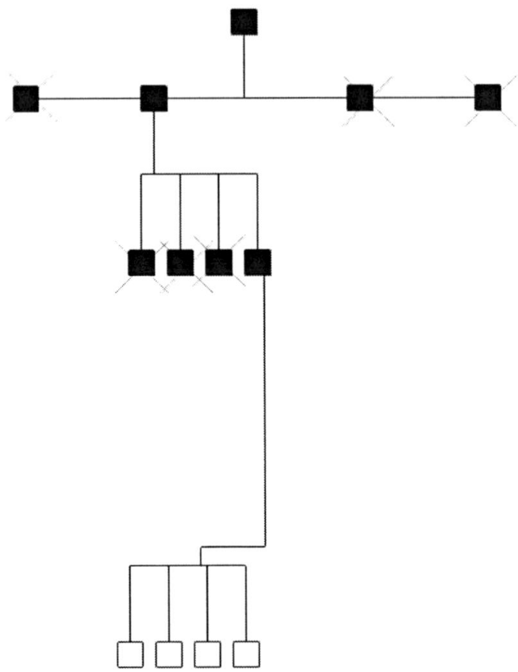

It seems as if this method is more efficient. It does not require the intensive work of mapping as before and may focus the resources on the most probable cause of the problem; hence it will be a faster route to cause identification. On the other hand, it appears to be a less comprehensive method and may cause some essential factors to be overlooked.

What is the best approach between these options? As expected, the reader will say, map thoroughly as in Method 1 and work to isolate the branches and sub-branches as in Method 2. Yes, this is a good way of thinking. You will learn that while taking care of the line problem, it is more typical to work in the second mode, because it is usual to have enough data or ways of collecting data to confirm or deny branches. However, when investigating complex systems with many possible directions and a limited amount of data to direct the investigation, there is a greater tendency to invest in thorough mapping and learn more about all potential sources of failure.

Navigating in modeling trees

Picture your modeling tree as a maze. You enter it from the main entrance (the initial symptom that you defined as a problem), and you need to find your way to the treasure (root cause). You step into the hallway and face several doors (branches of the tree). On each door there is a sign telling you what is behind this door. However, you have to find a hint (data item) that will tell you what door to select to lead you towards the treasure.

To make life easier, in this game you have the luxury of building several mazes (several trees), borrowing data items found in one maze and using them to open the right door in the other. How can this be done?

The two techniques that may help reduce the number of possible directions or potential models for checking are **segmentation** and **categorization**.

Segmentation

The purpose of segmentation is to cut down the number of suspected process steps or sub-components within a system involved in problem creation. Successful segmentation will narrow down the investigation to fewer models by cutting out process steps, systems, or components that are not involved in creating the problem. The effort in segmentation is to find and learn data items that can differentiate between segments (process steps or functional components) by telling if the problem source **is there** or **not there**. Wise selection of data items to collect will cut out irrelevant segments piece by piece, until isolating the segment that is identified as the most probable source of the problem.

This methodology works nicely with the conditions tree, since segments are natural building blocks required to build the problematic IUI. When running a segmentation process you will try to:
- Narrow down the number of suspect **process steps** into fewer steps or even to the one process step that caused the problem.

Example: If a visible defect is found at a late stage of the process, a visual check after every process step could find the earliest process step in the flow to exhibit this defect. Once this is found, all subsequent process steps are no longer suspect.

- Reduce the number of **suspected components** within a system or tool that caused the problem.

Example: When turning the key in your car ignition, the starter spins but the engine only coughs. There are two main suspect segments: the fuel system and electrical ignition system. Each of these two segments could cause the problem and each contains many sub-components. The best way to confront the problem is by understanding which of these two major segments is causing the problem. Checking whether there is a spark in the cable leading to the spark plugs could verify the functionality of most of the electrical system. If a spark fails to appear at the end of the cable, it is necessary to continue to isolate the component (smaller segment) within the electrical system causing the failure. If there is a nice and healthy spark, one should suspect that the problem lies in either the fuel system or in a small number of electrical components behind the cable.

Categorization

The purpose of categorization is to cut down the number of possible models by grouping one or more possible models (branches) that share similar characteristics. The intention is to find and verify the existence of a unique problem characteristic or phenomenon common to a group of models, and negate its existence in another group of models. The effort in categorization is to find and study a data item that differentiates between categories (groups of models) by telling what the problem **is** or **is not**.

Unlike segmentation, in categorization there is no natural separation into process steps or system/tool sub-components. The person or team running the analysis needs to identify one property (relevant to the problem in hand) that is expected to appear in one group of models, but cannot appear in another group of models. It is then required to find a way to confirm or deny the existence of this property. If a data item reflecting the property shows the existence of this property, then it is confirmed that this group of models is involved in creating the problem. The other models that are not related to this property (outside of this category) are not valid models for the cause of the problem.

Wise categorization may isolate one or more models most probably involved in creating the problem. Unlike segmentation, a certain model (or branch) could appear in more than one category during the analysis, since different properties may connect models in different ways. This means that it is possible to select a property or characteristic that groups previously eliminated branches with models that are still possible into one category, to confirm or deny other groups of branches that do not share this property.

You may perform categorization upwards. In other words, you already have numerous suggested models and checking each one of them will take time and effort. Try to include several models with something in common under one category, and group other models under another category. Once you have found a way to eliminate a certain category, you will reduce all the models in this category.

You may perform categorization downwards. In other words, you do not have any models yet, but by relying on a known or previously identified characteristic or property, you may limit the investigation to fewer potential models. Thus you avoid the need to build the full branching related to the category already denied by the exact same property. Continue with this attitude and try to find a way to re-divide the suspected category into sub-categories by another characteristic to further reduce the number of potential models.

Example: A certain process flow involves several identical metal layers to be deposited over a product. A step down in metal sheet resistance was observed in electrical tests at the end-of-line. This change can be related to inherent properties of the metallic material, or to the physical dimensions (thickness) of the layer. As an affected product was cross-sectioned previously, it is already known that the layer thickness and width meets the requirements and so models related to improper dimensions can be eliminated (elimination by downward categorization).

Since the metallic layer properties are suspected as the cause of the problem, several potential models that may affect the metal properties were suggested. It has already been mentioned that during processing, several metal levels are formed with the same tool set.

The electrical property of each metal level is defined initially during the metal deposition step. After all metal layers have been placed over the product, a heat treatment step defines the final properties of the full stack. The models that could impact the metal properties were separated into these two main categories. One category is metal deposition effect and the other is thermal treatment effect. As there is a two to three week delay between the deposition of the first metal level and the last one on the same product, it was decided to use this characteristic to find out which category is responsible for the detected change. Trend charts that arrange the production material according to metal deposition date for each metal level were prepared. If the problem is in metal deposition, then the date of the change will be the same in each trend in each metal level. However if the problem is related to the thermal treatment common to all metal levels, the same trends will show that the last metal deposition operation started to generate problematic material two to three weeks earlier to the first metal level. One data item - event start date comparison between metal layers- could distinguish between the two categories. This is elimination by upward categorization.

As we can see, in both **segmentation** and **categorization**, there is an attempt to break the number of potential models into fewer groups (each one covering several potential models), rather than to develop a full list of every possible model. This could be with multiple models or with no model.

However, as mentioned earlier, there is a fundamental difference between the two. In segmentation, natural groups already exist and you are trying to isolate the problem by breaking it into smaller and smaller segments. In categorization, natural groups do not exist and the team needs to be creative and generate groups based on problem behavior or characteristics.

The first stage of working on an event does not necessarily include any detailed model building. It is more likely that you'll try to cut out chunks of potential sources and concentrate on getting closer to the source of a problem with each cut. Think about Michelangelo describing his work, saying that the statue was inside the stone, he just needed to carve out the unnecessary material to reveal it.

Detailed models can only be generated and worked with when you are close enough to the source of the problem.

Conditions and properties trees should not be a stagnant process only performed once for root cause analysis. It is an iterative process. Look into it, correct it, change it and rebuild it, as new data and more understanding is entering the picture. Remember that data is intended to differentiate between branches of the tree, and trees are intended to help in progress to cause analysis. At a certain time, you may combine several trees into one tree for a clearer picture, and at other times you may find the need to separate a large tree into smaller trees.

Once you have eliminated a model or category from your tree, cancel open actions that are related to the respective models. This will save valuable resources and time and prevent frustration. No worker wants to feel that they were important enough to be asked for the data but nobody cared to inform them that this data is no longer needed.

Practical example

In lines that manufacture sensitive products, it was found that at the end-of-line many small particles cause product failures by affecting the properties of a deposited metal layer. The expectation is for a clean continuous metal layer and the unexpected situation is that a certain type of defect degrades the quality of the metal layer on affected products.

For this investigation, it was decided to select a proper IUI and to develop a properties tree for it. It can be said that the IUI is the product, or the metal layer, but it is also fair to say that the IUI are the particles found to disturb the deposited metal layer. Let's follow the progress made using the properties tree in figure 4-7, using study of the defects as the IUI.

The first branching level was related to the relative position of the particle with respect to the deposited metal layer. This could be over the layer, under the layer, within the layer, or other.

Figure 4-9. Property tree of defect that causes degradation in metal layer performance

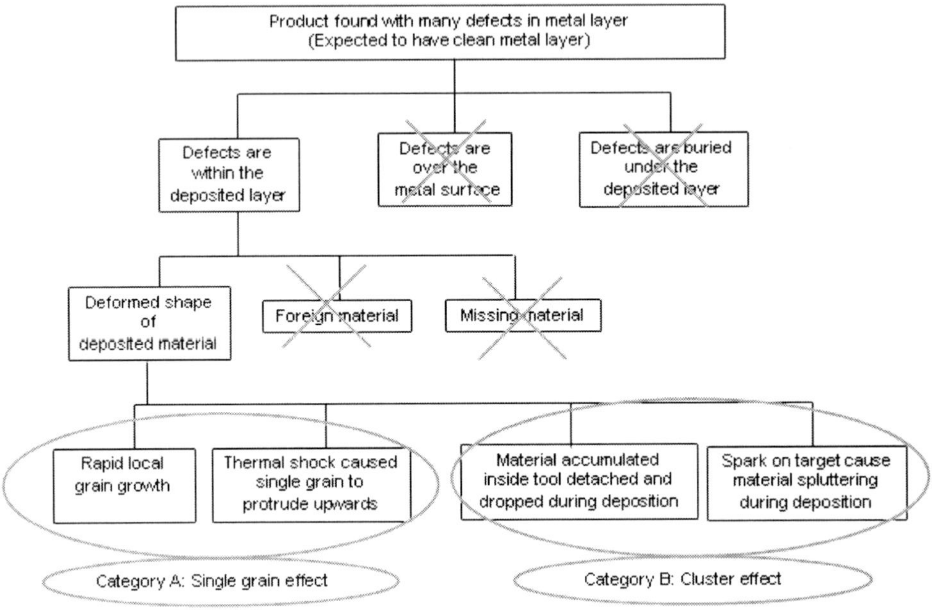

By cutting a representative defect and looking at it sideways (in a cross section) it was obvious that the defect is embedded within the metal layer. The option that the metal layer wraps it from above or the particle lies just over the metal layer were eliminated.

This may lead to the conclusion that the defect occurred during the metal deposition process step and the investigation effort could be redirected towards building a conditions tree for this metal deposition tool. However, as we will see, this could be a misleading conclusion. It was decided to continue working on the properties tree and to progress in understanding the defect properties.

The next question about the properties is related to its content. If the defect is within the metal layer, what is it made of? Is it foreign material? Is it a void or discontinuity in the metal layer? Or, is it simply a deformation of the same kind of metal? The elemental analysis showed that the defect is made of the same material as the metal layer. At this stage, the team started to raise theoretical hypotheses of how local deformation with an extra amount of metal could occur. You may have doubts whether the four suggested scenarios are a full list of all possible models. And rightly so. There should always be another option (either real or in your mind) in any level of the tree. This is simply because we may not cover all potential explanations (models), either because of missing knowledge or because of lack of imagination. Keep in mind that a missing property or model may be added at any later stage if found to be necessary.

After suggesting several models, it was apparent that these models could be categorized into two major groups based on expected defect property: one group of models generating single metal grain defects, and one group of models forming a cluster of grain defects. Several representative defects were checked and it was found that all of them are made of a single grain. Since groups of models already listed on the properties tree were separated into these two categories, the tree was rearranged to reflect it (see figure 4-8). As explained earlier, this is counted as upward categorization.

Figure 4-10. The property tree after updating the hierarchy to reflect model categorization

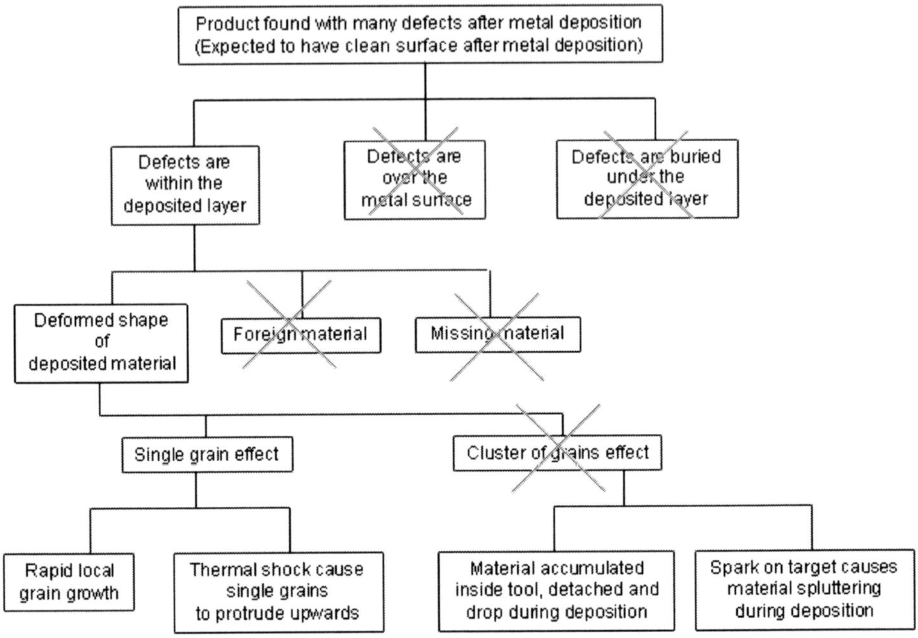

A model that was not raised previously is now suggested: defects created by mechanical damage inside the tool land over the product surface during deposition. This kind of defect is expected to appear as a cluster of grains. As it was already found that the problem is related to a single grain, this model has no importance at this stage. However, it is possible to capture this model and place it under the cluster of grains effect category.

The tendency at this stage is to point again toward the metal deposition tool and to start investigating the tool's conditions. However, according to one of the team members, there are several subsequent process steps that imply aggressive thermal shock to the product, and according to the tree this could be a potential explanation for the problem. The team decided to inspect the metal layer immediately after metal deposition, and then after each subsequent thermal cycle (segmentation).

It was found the metal layer is nice and clean after deposition, but excessive thermal shock in a later process step is the reason for the problem. This later tool was found to have a malfunction in its cooling system, causing the product to experience thermal shock.

This example is a simple demonstration of how a properties tree is used to achieve progress in root cause analysis. Proper selection of what data to look for and which properties to check enabled fast progress in the investigation and prevented wrong conclusions and unnecessary work.

In this section, you learned that model building involves iterative actions of building maps of the unknown territories involved in problem creation. We call these maps conditions trees and properties trees. To facilitate navigation and speed up the way to cause identification, you have learned the segmentation and categorization vehicles. It is now clear that the key data item, which you constantly need to look for, will help you in segmentation or categorization. You also need a proper team to suggest and achieve it.

Run a team to build the tree

It's time to assemble the team! How do you select the team members? There are two main approaches to work on model suggestion. The way you select a team depends on the approach you choose.

1. Model suggestion: brainstorming session with a large number of participants

This method goes hand-in-hand with the brief problem statement described above. The basic idea is to acquire a wide spread of viewpoints, therefore a wide range of skills and knowledge levels are welcome to participate in model suggestion. So potentially at this stage, the expert will sit next to a person who has no knowledge in the specific subject. You may want to warn the experts ahead of time not to filter any raised idea or disqualify its validity at this stage. The ideas generated by this kind of team are usually so dispersed and generic that it is actually no more than a wild guessing game. I have seen this time and again, and in many cases it was performed to please the management by generating a fancy cause and effect diagram (Ishikawa or fishbone diagram) the size of a whale, with enough investigation directions to keep the entire factory busy for a year. In some cases, experts who are especially needed for the next analysis stages find these sessions inefficient and exhausting and therefore they quit the team with frustration at an early stage.

2. Model suggestion: expert team
When presenting the problem and related facts collected so far to a group of knowledgeable persons, one may achieve a limited amount of models. In most cases, this method is preferable, since there is a greater chance that this team will point to the most probable direction and will usually raise ways to validate the suggested model. Careful and wise selection of complementary skills and expertise may enhance the model suggestion stage.

You may combine these two approaches into one, starting with brainstorming and then filtering the outcome with a smaller team of experts. In the processing industry, I usually recommend the second approach.

<u>Identify knowledgeable resources</u>
As you probably noticed, I believe that the best way to progress is by assembling a team with a range of expertise, knowledge, experience, and abilities to generate intelligent ideas that will be translated into a finite number of models. This group should be first identified by the team leader (problem owner) and then assembled for suggestions. The team leader may approach the core members he already knows and ask them to suggest other potential contributors to this task.

A typical team for the model building task should include:

- Someone with the best knowledge in component, structure, or system of interest (such as tool owner, process engineer, equipment engineer, tool designer or developer, or test engineer). The role of this person at this stage is to describe the affected tool, components or structure and provide details about the conditions required for running everything in normal mode. It would be even better if this person is able to describe the expected results if these conditions are altered.

- Someone with the best integrative knowledge on overall material or system flow (integration engineer, process engineer, test engineer, reliability engineer).This person should be proficient in the interactions between the suspect material and other operations or systems (previous and later operations).

- Someone who is most familiar with the regular operation of the tool (experienced tool or system operator, experience service staff). This person should know the actual day-by-day operation, use or handling and potential sources for errors in operation or mishandling during regular operation or maintenance activities. If it is known who was in charge of the system during the event, you may want to interview this person. However, it would be wise to avoid involving this person in the model building stage. He or she may describe the usual way of operation, but may be reluctant to describe shortcuts and work-arounds under the circumstances.

- Independent viewer (coach / consultant / independent witness) (experienced and unbiased person with technical understanding of the issues under investigation) Apart from the usual expected contribution of model suggestion, it is expected that this person will carefully observe the team work and alert the leader of deviations from a desirable outcome, such as missing functions in the team, loss of focus (rat-holing), conflicting situations (accountability vs. blame; reluctance to provide incriminating information; etc.)

- Individuals with access to or knowledge of data collection and analysis (lab engineers, computerized data analysts/ statistician, simulation experts, information research expert).The role of these individuals is to provide details on the way data is or can be collected and analyzed. In general, these persons are knowledgeable in wide areas of expertise and may provide useful insight on any issue. Their role will be even more pronounced in the later stage of model validation.

The team leader should consider adding more experts on a case-by-case basis to achieve the most complete set of models. If there are several process steps or independent functional systems that could be involved, knowledgeable individuals (tool owners) are required from each system. You may drop some of these participants right after the model building stage and include others that could better assist in data collection and model validation stages. Record the name of the individuals who suggested the models. There could be another iteration of in-depth, more detailed modeling suggestions based on investigation progression (down the problem definition tunnel). In this case, you would like the person whose line of thinking was found to be correct to participate in the next model generation phase.

Chapter summary

In this chapter, you learned that a problematic outcome could be related to a sequence of dependent events or to the coincidence of independent events. In a sequential event, you may progress in the investigation by repeatedly asking why and following (in reverse order) the sequence of actions or conditions that led to the observed problem. However, in processing lines it is not rare to face a coincidental event or an event caused by a problem in an early stage of a process that remained latent until end-of-line.

It was said that a complete model is achieved when knowing the conditions or actions that were in place, the properties generated or altered by these conditions, and the reflectance of these conditions and properties on observable behavior. It was also explained that in cause analysis, one of the aforementioned three elements (conditions, properties, and behavior) may be concluded by learning another.

Conditions and properties trees are tools that map and arrange the potential conditions and properties hierarchically. The team is free to judge in each case with which modeling tree it is more appropriate to start.

The intention is to look for ways (data) to confirm or deny the involvement of branches in problem appearance. Segmentation and categorization are used in this hierarchical arrangement to isolate the most relevant branches in problem creation. Performing this in the highest level of the hierarchy may speed up the investigation.

Wise selection of team members with complementary expertise is essential to progress in the analysis. The team should have the knowledge and skills required to build modeling trees, to suggest and collect the required data to cut or point branches.

CHAPTER
5

Model Validation

You and your team raised one or several models that provide a potential explanation for the appearance of the unexpected event. You already started to build a conditions tree, properties tree or both. However, how can you choose the correct model out of the several suggested models (scenarios) or branches that appear in the tree? Even if you have only one model that explains the event, how can you be sure that this is the right model?

A good model is one that can explain all existing data, but it can also predict something new or something that was not yet found. Checking that the data complies with a suggested model, and/or verifying that a prediction about a model is true is called model validation. You may think that model validation is a one-time action for final confirmation of a well-established model, but this is not so. Validation is the way of using the data items for practicing segmentation and categorization techniques on conditions and properties trees, as discussed in the previous chapter. It is a way of placing any data item against every possible alternative (model or branch) and testing its validity. You need to look at the existing data and also look for non-existing data, and use it to confirm or deny one or few of your branches/models. Do so repeatedly until you end up with only one well-confirmed model.

This chapter describes how to deal with existing data, but it also discusses several aspects related to generation of new data.

The following topics will be covered in this chapter:

- What the data can tell
- The data / model matrix
- Defining missing data
- Experiments

What data can tell

In many cases, during characterization and in the initial model-building stage, a lot of data is collected. Not every data item is collected with the aim of differentiating between specific branches of any tree. Still, there could be a whole lot of useful information in this data. It is important to incorporate this data into the validation process, and it may save unnecessary data collection by telling something about the models.

What can a data item tell when placing it against each model/branch or category?

There are five indications that a data item may provide on a tested model or branch.

Pointing data
This data item strongly supports the assumption that this model is the probable cause of the problem.
(**If** this data item shows this, **then** it is most probably this model / branch)

Supporting data
This data item does not oppose the assumption that this model is a possible cause of the problem.
(**If** this data item shows this, **then** it could be this model / branch)

Eliminating data
This data item indicates that this or these models / branches are not the cause of the problem.
(**If** this data item shows this, **then** it cannot be this model / branch)

Objecting data
This data item indicates that this or these models / branches are less probably the cause of the problem.
(**If** this data item shows this, **then** it is less probably this model / branch)

Not indicative
This data item cannot be used to draw any conclusion regarding the suggested model. Note that a data item that could be used as

indicator (eliminator or pointer) for some models could provide no indication of the validity of other models.

(**If** this data item shows this, **then** it can neither contradict nor support the tested model).

How can we test a data item and learn its indication on a checked model? We will first look into the rationale behind how to do this, and then reach the understanding that this is a relatively easy task, which in most cases can be performed intuitively.

The sequence of testing a data item against a model

Each data item can be tested against a model by asking the same question in four ways. Can this data item say that this model **is not** / **is most** - **unlikely** / **likely** to be the correct model? We can place this question in a small matrix (Figure 5-1) and see the meaning of a positive answer for each possible question.

Figure 5-1. Testing data against model matrix

		Unlikely to be the correct model	**Likely** to be the correct model.
Can this data item say that this model	**is not**	A possible model (supporting data)	A less probable model (objecting data)
	is a most	Improbable model (eliminating data)	probable model (pointing data)

If the sequence of questioning is arranged in a flow chart (Figure 5-2) it will be easy to see that all four questions will never be needed to cover all five possibilities (four that appear in the matrix as well as the not indicative conclusion).

Figure 5.2 Testing data against model - questioning flow chart

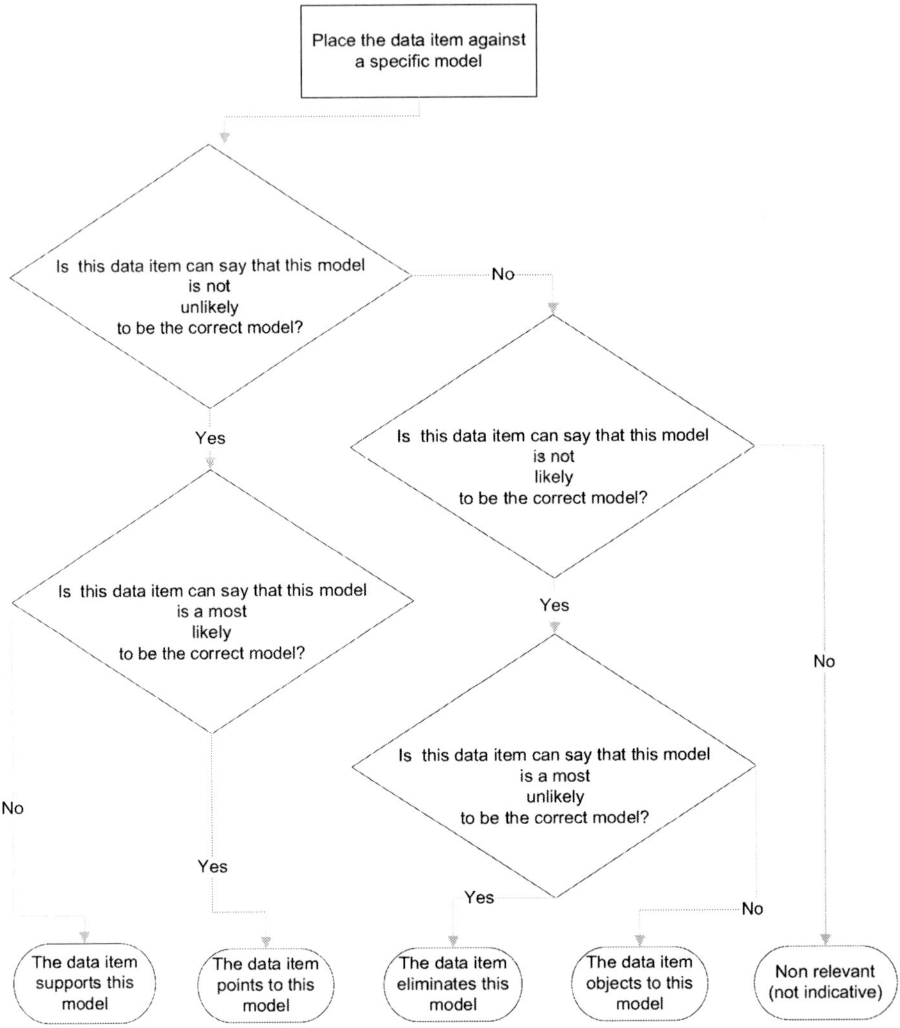

Based on this flow chart, we can see that no more than three questions are required to make a decision about the meaning of the data item in respect to a model. Now let's return to the matrix described earlier (in figure 5-1).When following the possible sequences on the flow chart, "1" indicates a positive answer and "0" indicates a negative answer in the matrix (see figures 5-3A to 5-3E).

Figure 5-3A. Supporting data
This data item says that this model **is not** **unlikely** to be the correct model.

	Unlikely	Likely
Is not	1	0
Is most	0	0

Figure 5-3B. Pointing data
This data item says that this model **is not** **unlikely** to be the correct model, and it also says that this **is most** **likely** to be the correct model.

	Unlikely	Likely
Is not	1	0
Is most	0	1

Figure 5-3C. Objecting data
This data item says that this model **is not** **likely** to be the correct model.

	Unlikely	Likely
Is not	0	1
Is most	0	0

Figure 5-3D. Eliminating data
This data item says that this model **is not** **likely** to be the correct model, and it also says that it **is most** **unlikely** to be the correct model.

	Unlikely	Likely
Is not	0	1
Is most	1	0

Figure 5-3E. Not indicative data
This data item **cannot** say that this model **is not** **unlikely** to be the correct model, and **cannot** say that this **is not** **likel**y to be the correct model (neither supports nor objects).

	Unlikely	Likely
Is not	0	0
Is most	0	0

All five possible situations that were discussed earlier appear on the matrices. You probably observed that a pointing data item is also a supporting data item, but not vice versa. An eliminating data item is also an objecting data item, but not vice versa.

At first glance, it appears as if this is going to be a very exhausting process. However, most of us do it intuitively without investing too much thought. You know intuitively whether certain data contradict the tested model and eliminate the chance that this is the cause of the problem. This is called eliminating the model. However, from time to time you may feel that certain data does not totally eliminate the model, but it does not "fit nicely" to the model. You may call this objecting data.

You can tell if some data fit a tested model and say that this data can support the model. However, you also know when data lead to a strong preference for one model, and this is considered as pointing to the model.

You may ask what the purpose is of the above distinction. How can it help us to progress in root cause analysis and how can we relate it to the conditions and properties tree with which we are working?

Data model matrix

The data model matrix is a tool for connecting observations made by the data items and the models that are, or appear on, or drawn by the modeling trees (condition and property trees).

The idea is to list all observations (facts found in data) in a row and arrange all models in columns. Then check each observation with respect to any suggested model and mark the proper indication. The example in figure 5.4 is a schematic matrix showing the suggested concept followed by the possible scenario.

Figure 5-4. Schematic data model matrix

	Category A			Category B	
	Model 1	Model 2	Model 3	Model 4	Model 5
Data item 1	V	V	V	V	V
Data item 2	V	V	V+	V+	=
Data item 3	=	V	V	=	=
Data item 4	V	=	=	V	V
Lab data 1	V	V	V	E	E
Exp # 1	O	V	V	=	=
Exp # 2	E	E	V	=	=

V	Supporting data
V+	Pointer
O	Objecting data
E	Eliminators
=	Non-indicative data

The team working on the problem had some initial data that was collected in the problem characterization stage. Based on the information they built, a few possible models may be supported by this data (data item 1). As more data continued to be accumulated (data items 2-4), it was found that either model 3 or model 4 is probably the cause of the problem, but all other models are still a possible explanation as well. At this stage, the models were categorized based on phenomenon and lab analysis was performed to confirm the existence of this phenomenon. The lab results eliminated Category B (models 4 and 5) as a possible cause for the problem. Model 3 turned out to be the most probable one; however models 1 and 2 were still possible. Two experiments were performed with the intention of differentiating between the suspect models. The observation in Experiment 1 just said that model 1 is less likely to be the model. Experiment 2 proved that models 1 and 2 are not valid models, and Model 3 remained the only model consistent with all data collected.

Looking at this simple matrix, it is easy to see that all suggested models, except for Model # 3, were eliminated by the collected data. However, in complex problems, there could be many rows and it will be harder to see the full picture in one quick glance. Therefore, it will be useful to be able to filter out all rows, except for those with the information that made the real progress in cause analysis.

It is recommended to filter out all rows except for those with eliminators and pointers as first level indicators for progress. If there are no sufficient eliminators, it is possible to add all rows indicating objecting data as well.

The data model matrix is the main tool for following the validation process throughout the cause analysis process, since it lists all data items collected so far. Start to build it as soon as you start the investigation. Keeping it alive will be easier than building it from scratch at a later stage of your investigation.

More hints on data model matrix

Column headers: Ideally, the headers of each column in the data model matrix should reflect every single box in the modeling tree. However, I find that this approach is very tedious and hard to follow. You will need to dedicate a number of rows just for the column headers to reflect the number of levels in your tree. Any change in the tree will require a change in the matrix. This is a rather exhausting and time-consuming task. Instead, it is suggested to look at your modeling tree and place, on your data model matrix, all possible scenarios (models) built by the modeling trees. If there are too many possible scenarios or you have only a rough estimation of what could go wrong, use model categories instead. Keep in mind that the connection between the modeling tree and the matrix should be kept. The column headers should reflect the situation on the tree that you are using. Whenever a model is added to your tree, check whether this should be done to the matrix as well. If you find a way to categorize models, check its impact on your matrix. When adding models and categories, make sure you don't shift the entire marking under this column from its header, as this will mess up your matrix.

Rows: The description of each observation should be written clearly so that the team members will understand the meaning of this data item. Do not place just ID numbers or vague descriptions in these rows. It is also recommended to link the rows to the actual data. Arrange the rows according to the order of receiving the data. This will enable you to follow the logic behind the conclusions that were made, and the rationale behind the next data items you decide to explore.

Dedicate one row to one observation. From time to time, you may receive experiment results with several different observations. In this case, break the experiment into several rows, treat each observation as a separate data item and indicate the experiment that this observation comes from.

During investigation, place future data collection tasks in a proper row and see whether the anticipated conclusion will help to differentiate between models (columns). If it does, count this task as key data, and prioritize it accordingly.

Problematic data in data model matrix

The sequence of data collection and placement against the models is not totally free of confusion and complications. Below you'll find two of the most frequent situations that you may face.

Data is inconclusive

A data item that should provide an indication on a certain model failed to do so. This data item should have been either a pointer or eliminator by proving a certain fact, however you've reached a situation where there is no conclusive observation to make a clear cut decision about the model. The simple solution is to mark this data item as Not Indicative and ignore it. However, it is not always wise to do this. The data collected or experiment conducted aimed to provide an indication about a model. You should invest some thought and try to figure out why it failed to provide the anticipated results. In many cases you'll find that by repeating this experiment more thoroughly, using a different analytical technique, or expanding the sampling of the same data, you will reach a firm conclusion. If you do not have resources to repeat this at the current stage, mark it a little bit differently than Not Indicative. You may want to return to this direction at a later stage.

Contradicting or conflicting data

This situation is even more confusing than inconclusive data.

- Two different data items point to different models as the cause of a problem. Each data item points to another model and eliminates the other.

- Two data items that draw different conclusions on the same model.

  A subset of this kind of contradiction is the situation where a certain data item that indicated something about the model is repeated, and is now telling something else.

The basic question in this situation is: Which data should I believe in?

The first thing to do is to double check the data source. How was the data picked and analyzed? You may find that the contradiction is related to the way that the data was picked and analyzed, or the way the experiment was run, and so on.

Next, when there is conflicting data on the same model, think again. Is it probable to anticipate that data may show inconsistent results, based on previous behavior or problem understanding (such as cases where performance fluctuates)? If you have reason to believe that this data could provide a noisy or inconsistent signal, then the conflict is expected.

If both are checked and the data is confirmed as true and meaningful, then you need to settle the conflict by an explanation that should come from the model.

Two strong pointers directing you into two separate branches of your tree may indicate that an integrative effect is involved. Think about a reasonable model that connects the relevant branches.

A more problematic situation is when two observations point to different branches as a correct model, and at the same time each eliminates the model that was pointed at by the other. If you are pretty convinced about the data, you either drew a wrong conclusion by interpreting the data as an eliminator, or a different model that may satisfy the conflict should be developed.

Summary table

The data model matrix can be very detailed and long, as it lists all the data items and observations collected during the investigation, and all the models you have worked on. It is often found to be more convenient to use the tree itself for relating data items to branches by adding a note or link on the relevant branch indicating the data items that support or eliminate it. There are numerous software applications that make this work pretty easy. Either way, it is not easy to follow how conclusions were made and what the future course of action is, especially for those who are not deeply involved

in the investigation. So, you may need to present the information more concisely.

This may be performed by a simpler table (Figure 5-5), which in a way is a subset of the main data model matrix.

Figure 5-5. Summary table of models

	Supporting data	Objecting data	Validation direction
Model A			
Model B			
Model C			

For each model, place all pointing and supporting data items appearing in the relevant column of the data model matrix and place it under supporting data in the respective cell in the summary table. If the list of supporting data is too long, delete unnecessary items, and leave only the key observations required to clarify the reasoning for the respective model.

For each model, place all eliminating and objecting data items from the relevant column of the data model matrix and place it under objecting data in the respective cell of the summary table. Place data collection activities that you anticipate to provide an indication of the respective model in the validation direction cell. This is the key information that will make progress in the root cause analysis investigation. Keep the table concise and clear. Do not overload it with unnecessary information and do not use it to track team tasks.

Defining missing data to progress in RCA

So model validation is just a name for another data collection cycle, isn't it? Well yes, but at this point you need to redirect the data collection to a new way of thinking. The basic way of thinking required for data validation is: If ... Then ...Else. **If** this data shows **X**, **Then** the valid model / segment / category is "A", **Else** it cannot be "A". The **X** represents any evidence you can think of that may differentiate between parallel branches of your tree.

Thinking about proper X
When trying to think about ways to progress in RCA and differentiate between branches in your trees, you need to think again about what was said about the three elements that were discussed in the Model Building chapter.

"...Learning every one of the three elements may promote understanding of the others.
- Identification of the problematic resource may provide understanding of the product's failure mechanism (learn the inputs).
- Localization and understanding the flaw within the product may point to the problematic resource or process step that caused it (learn what is going within).
- Thorough learning of the product behavior or its measurable properties may help to understand the flaw within it and/or the conditions that created it (learn the outputs).
..."

In a validation process, you need to use every one of the model elements to confirm or deny possible models.

Learn the outputs:
We have already said that the item under investigation externalized behavior. This behavior could be in measurable values (such as resistance, weight or dimensions), or it could be in visible form (such as shape, color and position). In a validation process, there is an attempt to check any aspect and phenomenon that is observed, measured or sensed and draw conclusions for the condition or properties that are responsible for generating this effect.

Learn what is going on within:
The IUI itself may have components or structures that are related to the failure. In a validation process, by learning the properties (of an object) or the unexpected change in properties (of a defective structure or system), it is possible to draw conclusions for the required conditions responsible for generating the observed phenomenon.

Learn the inputs:

There is a given set of process parameters and conditions that are required to generate the product (physical outcome or IUI). This set of conditions is also responsible for the behavior detected on the product (or IUI). In a validation process, there is an attempt to understand the connection between the provided conditions and the resulting properties and behavior. This is either by drawing conclusions about the connection based on known facts of conditions, or by active manipulation of the suspect conditions.

There are three basic validation categories or ways of thinking that are required for a validation process: 1. Syllogistic validation. 2. Active validation 3. Predictive validation

Syllogistic validation

Look into existing effects or phenomena that characterize the problem, infer what possible condition or property could cause it, and draw conclusions for the possible models. "If this effect/phenomenon exists, then this is the possible model, or else this effect/phenomenon would be different".

Active validation

Examine the existing effect or phenomenon (like pattern) that characterizes the problem, try to alter this effect by manipulation, and draw conclusions for the model based on the result. Note that an attempt to repeat the problematic conditions that existed during the event and learn the results is part of this validation category). "If this effect/ phenomenon is altered or regenerated by this manipulation, then it validates that this is a correct model or else it denies it".

Predictive validation

The third way is to predict an effect or phenomenon that was not yet observed or known, and try to confirm it by a certain analysis or by manipulating condition, and then draw conclusions for the model.
"If this data / experiment / analysis demonstrates this effect / phenomenon, then it confirms that this model is correct or else it denies it".

Some people are more creative than others in raising ideas to practice the above basic techniques. Team knowledge and creativity is the key to progress in the validation process. A team may reach a dead-end situation in the investigation just because they couldn't find a good way to validate possible models. It is important that once an idea of how to verify a model is raised, the team will

think about a way to translate the idea into an actual workable task (recheck data, take a sample to a lab for analysis, run an experiment, and so on).

To further stimulate your mind in thinking about model validation, here are some more ways of thinking that you may use during investigation. These are subsets of the three main validation categories mentioned earlier.

Learning a similar system or structure
Look for another structure/system that shares similar properties to the failing one. The rationale: similar properties should be affected by the same conditions. **"If the failing structure or system shows a specific effect (X) and another structure or system with several similar properties also shows it, then it is related to a property or condition that is common to both** (concentrate your effort on the simpler structure and the common properties), **or else it is related to the differences"** (concentrate on understanding the differences).

Learning companion effect or phenomena
Look for things that are unusual in the affected material. The rationale: If a problem is accompanied repeatedly by a certain "stamp" or unusual phenomenon, then this effect is related to the same condition that causes the problem.
If the phenomenon (X) appears with the problem (and not on healthy material) in this specific way, then it may be related to the specific condition/property that caused the problem, or else it would not appear in that form. Concentrate on learning the possible conditions and properties that are able to create this "stamp". Look for possible ways to change material **order or orientation** and verify whether the "stamp" was changed.

Learning by altering potential causing factors
Look for the effect on problem appearance while changing or skipping **process-steps, conditions, or timing**. The rationale: Try to segment the possible modulating factors by changing or skipping them.

If factor (X) is manipulated and an effect on relevant properties or behavior is sensed, then this factor is related to problem creation, or else this factor is not related to problem creation.

This is the most familiar way of thinking that motivates teams to conduct line experiments with the intention of recreating the problem. Be careful not to blind yourself with rough manipulation that will lead to catastrophic failure with meaningless or misleading results. Keep in mind that there are cases where manipulation of different factors may lead to the same behavior. Either each factor (condition) could cause the same effect independently or each is a contributing factor in a combined effect.

Learning by reaching a different trait

Look for other ways to detect the problem. The rationale: Another way to detect the same problem means that there is another behavioral aspect to the same conditions or properties. **If this different effect (X) can also detect the same problem, then these are the potential properties or conditions causing the problem, otherwise it cannot be these properties or conditions.** Finding another way to detect the problem could describe the property or conditions that are required to produce this new behavior. It may also provide a better signal to noise ratio for problem detection, or a shorter response time to detect the problem.

The above ways of thinking should stimulate your mind on possible ways to look for or generate evidence that could assist in differentiation between models (branches in the condition or property trees). It does not matter whether this evidence is computerized data, physical analysis, experiment or simulation. Check whether this will help you to progress in cutting or confirming relevant braches in your tree.

When there are a number of possible models, it is typical for you to collect many pointers and establish a pretty good model, but still not have confidence in it. It is best to look for a data item that will be a pointer (to a certain model) and eliminator (to other models) at the same time. In most cases, this kind of data is not easy to find. So, whenever possible, use eliminators to isolate a model and gain more confidence in your conclusions. Note that an eliminator is a stronger indication than a pointer, since it will assure you where not to go, while a pointer indicates that you are probably going in the right direction. When you have an intuition (probably based on experience) about the problem you are working on, and the data item appears to support your intuition, follow this intuition positively. This means that when saying that a certain branch is more likely, you can continue and explore this direction more

intensively. However, when saying that a branch or model is less likely, you cannot ignore that possibility, so do not discard this branch or model.

Experiments

Running an experiment is active generation of data while altering conditions or properties in a controlled manner. The DOE (designing of experiments) is a well covered issue that is beyond the scope of this book, and has rich literature for further learning. Experiments will be covered here briefly, and further learning is recommended for those who are going to use it. The golden rule for experiments in root cause analysis is (how surprising): know the expected. So, when planning any experiment, never forget to include the control group (reference). When saying that we are running an experiment, it means that we are going to make a deliberate change in a certain controllable parameter and compare the results to the situation without a change. In the simple case, the experiment has only two sides: the changed side and the one that is used as a reference. To make the results more meaningful, it is quite usual to take several samples per experiment side, thus gaining more confidence in the results. So in this case the reference will also be called the control group.

Manipulating two parameters

When running an experiment, we may try and alter several parameters and learn the impact of each one of them separately, and testing the interaction effect between parameters as well. Let's first check a situation in which two process parameters are to be evaluated. Each parameter will be tested in increased and decreased values with respect to the control group. The increased value is denoted as high and the decreased value is denoted as low. The matrix below (Figure 5-6) demonstrates a plan of a simple experiment.

Figure 5-6. Matrix of experiment for two process parameters

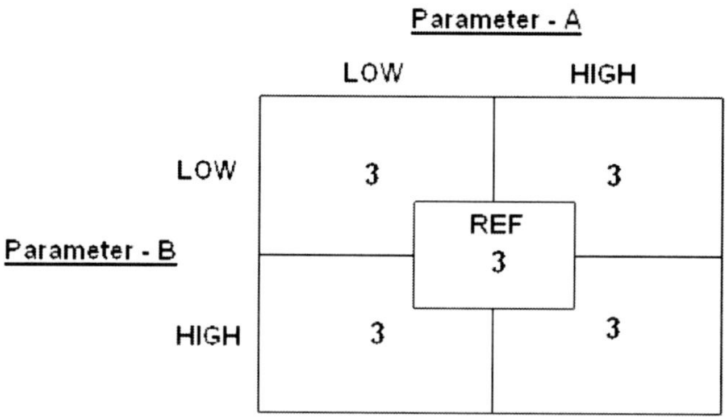

In this experiment there are five groups (or split-sides), and each group has three samples (as in each cell in the above matrix). So, the total number of required samples for this experiment is 5 x 3 = 15.

It can be seen that the net effect of both parameters, as well as the interaction effect between these parameters, can be tested. This can easily be understood by looking at the matrix. The net effect of Parameter A is learned by comparing Column Low to Column High in the matrix. The net effect of Parameter B is learned by comparing Row Low to Row High in the matrix. So, net effects are learned by comparing the matrix cells vertically or horizontally. Interactions are learned by comparing the cells of the matrix diagonally. (Both parameters in Hi vs. both parameters in Lo; and A-High B-Low vs. A-Low B-High). Figure 5-7 shows a more conventional way to present the same experiment plan.

Figure 5-7. Experiment plan (two process parameters)

Total # of samples	# of samples for Parameter A	Parameter A Condition	# of samples for Parameter B	Parameter B Condition
15	6	High	3	High
			3	Low
	3	Normal	3	Normal
	6	Low	3	High
			3	Low

<u>More than two parameters</u>
The same methodology may be employed for learning a larger number of parameters. Let's look at figure 5-8, which shows a plan of three process parameters (A, B and C).

Figure 5-8. Experiment plan for three process parameters.

Total #	# of samples for A	A condition	# of samples for B	B Condition	# of samples for C	C condition
18	8	Hi	4	Hi	2	Hi
					2	Lo
			4	Lo	2	Hi
					2	Lo
	2	Normal	2	Normal	2	Normal
	8	Lo	4	Hi	2	Hi
					2	Lo
			4	Lo	2	Hi
					2	Lo

Experiments designed in this way usually aim to optimize and explore the working window of a certain process module. However, in our case we are more interested in the ability to generate data to achieve progress in root cause analysis. So, we should test the potential outcome of the experiment and its contribution to the progress of our investigation in some way.

<u>What-if scenario</u>

Two techniques are suggested for self-evaluating the potential outcome before running an RCA experiment, and both are borrowed from the IT world. These are the Truth Table and the Flow Chart.

Truth Table

When testing the contribution of a certain parameter to problem creation (by experiment), one would expect the experiment to provide a yes or no answer to the question: "Does this parameter contribute to problem generation?" So, when planning an experiment for failure analysis, one needs to check the meaning of a possible response from each parameter to model building and validation. A response from a tested parameter is represented by 1 (yes), and no response is represented by 0 (no).

Example: The resistance of a deposited metal layer in a certain process step indicated a step change. A laboratory analysis verified that the layer thickness was not changed. When checking the metal deposition tool, it was found that three conditions had been changed in the suspected time frame: a metal target from a recently arrived batch was installed, an MFC (mass flow controller) was replaced in the machine, and a new TC (Thermo Couple) that controls the target temperature was replaced. It was decided to check the impact of each of the above parameters on metal resistance results. The engineer suggested reinstalling a target from the old batch in the tool as the first parameter to check, test the impact of high and low gas flow as the second parameter to check, and test the impact of higher and lower temperature as the third parameter to check.

Figure 5-9. Initial partial truth table for three suspect parameters

Target	Gas flow	Temperature	Conclusion
1	0	0	Target is most probable cause
0	1	0	MFC is most probable cause
0	0	1	TC is most probable cause

The above truth table (Figure 5-9) aimed to justify the suggested experiment. However, there are some flaws in the way of thinking. First, not all possible scenarios are presented in the truth table. The engineer wanted this scenario, but more confusing situations are still possible. Second, there is a built-in assumption that if a certain parameter has the ability to control resistance, its respective component is the one that causes the problem. However, this is not necessarily correct, since there is a chance that several independent parameters have the same effect (including some that are not checked by the experiment). So, an interpretation based on the above built-in assumption may provide misleading conclusions. Some missing parts were added to the truth table (Figure 5-10) to show the missing possibilities.

Figure 5-10. Missing possibilities that may appear in the experiment.

Target	Gas flow	Temperature	Conclusions
0	0	0	None of these components caused the problem
1	0	1	Target and TC probably caused the problem
1	1	0	Target and MFC probably caused the problem
0	1	1	Either MFC or TC caused the problem
1	1	1	All three components are still suspect

This indeed addresses the first concern, but it does not help much in the second concern. Bearing in mind the second concern that was mentioned earlier, we may encounter confusing situations described in some of the rows of the full truth table.
For example:
- A response from two parameters could be interpreted as: both components are bad; one of the two components is bad; neither of these two components is bad.
- A response from one parameter could be interpreted as: this component is bad; this component is not bad (still, ruling out the other two parameters is a significant finding).

If the component related to the parameter showing a response was replaced by a new one, and the problem was fixed, this confirms that this is indeed the cause of the problem. In this case, even if it seems slower and labor consuming, replacing components and check results, or finding an alternative way to verify proper functionality of the suspected components, could provide a more conclusive indication than indirect learning of parameter impact on process results.

From this we can learn that the experiment plan that fits process characterization is not always ideal for root cause analysis. Experiment results for root cause analysis should be interpreted carefully. Invest thought when placing the conclusion in each row of your truth table. Try to make the response as digital as possible. Make it either yes or no rather than maybe.

The truth table discussed earlier is a nice way of evaluating experiments. It tells you the potential understanding that you may gain from a planned experiment. However, sometimes you may need to evaluate and show the possible outcome from a sequence of activities that each depends on the results of a previous action. In this case, it is better to present the what-if scenario in a flowchart.

Flow chart

Figure 5-11 shows an example of a flow chart showing a set of actions intended to isolate a problematic component within a system.

Figure 5-11. Flow chart of analysis sequence

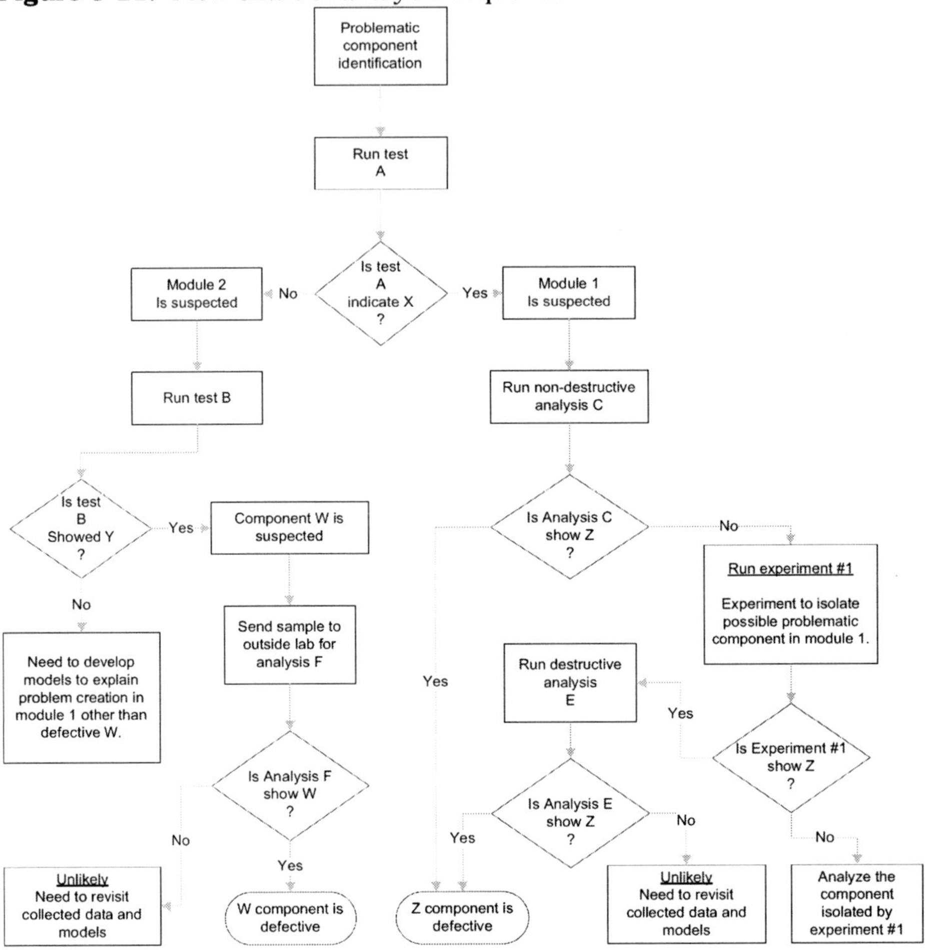

Let's discuss the above flow chart.

The system of interest has two main modules, and a simple test (Test A) can differentiate between them.

The first scenario is that Test A proves that Module 1 is the problematic one. The favorite model for a problem in this module is a defective Component Z, but other module components could also be the cause. This component is pretty expensive, so it was decided to check it by non-destructive analysis that is fast but is not 100%

reliable. If this test indicates that this component is defective, then it is really so, but if it indicates that it is not defective, then it is not necessarily correct. In that case, a more time-consuming experiment will be performed. If Experiment #1 indicates that Z is the problem, then a destructive test will be performed for final validation that component Z is defective. If Experiment # 1 isolates another component within this module, then a different set of analyses will be required. It is unlikely that the destructive test will provide an indication that component Z is good. This situation means that it will be necessary to review all the collected data and the conclusions that were drawn, to find the reason for the discrepancy that led to this outcome, or to find a new model to satisfy all findings.

The second scenario is that Test A suggests that Module 2 is the reason for the problem. There is another test (Test B) that can tell whether the problem is in Component W or in other components within this module. If this test provides a clear indication that Component W is the most suspect, then this component will be sent for an Analysis F, which cannot be performed locally, and this will be used to understand the type of failure in Component W. If this analysis reaches the conclusion that component W does not have any flaw, then an unlikely situation is reached and the procedure mentioned earlier should be followed. If Test B indicates that the problem is in another component in Module #2, then the investigation should be directed to this set of possibilities.

The above example demonstrates the use of the flow chart for root cause analysis. During this what-if scenario, it is frequently observed that some tests are redundant (and can be skipped), or an action that should be performed in sequence can actually be performed in parallel.

As in the example, the end result should not always be covered in details. It could end with a brief indication of the necessary direction to follow, or it could even lead to a dead end. A dead-end means that a certain sequence of actions is directed into an end box saying that this situation is either unlikely or does not make sense. In most cases, you'll see that it is only a hypothetical situation, and in real life the data will always be reliable and all your conclusions will always be correct. But... just in case you reach a dead end, the flow chart is an excellent tool to reverse your line of thinking.

Chapter Summary

This chapter explained that model validation is a process that employs data (existing or needing to be acquired) for identifying the correct model for problem creation.

A data item could be in agreement with a model (supporter), indicate the correctness of a model (pointer), indicate that a model is less likely to be the one (objector), eliminate a model as a possible one (eliminator), or provide no indication about a model (non-indicative data).

Proper placement of data items against possible models will clarify what was achieved by the data collected so far and what is needed to progress in the event investigation. A data model matrix or summary table indicating the supporting data and objecting data may help to clarify the next necessary validation steps (validation path).

The way of thinking in validation by data collection is "if... then...else". The intention is to find a way to confirm or deny branches that are high in modeling-tree hierarchy. In other words, try to find data items that can differentiate between main branches rather than small leaves.

Experimentation is a well known data-collection method in root cause analysis. What-if learning is recommended before running experiments or a set of analyses. This may be done either by a truth table, flow chart, or any other means. The intention is to ensure that the experiments/analyses are conducted in a reasonable order, efficiently, and have the best chance of providing a conclusive result.

A compelling reason for saying that a model is a correct one, is that when all data items are in agreement with it, there is no objecting data to this model, there is some data that point to it (preferably a pre-predicted data), and all other possible models were denied. If there are several valid models, the validation process should be continued by looking for a data item that could tell which is the correct one.

CHAPTER 6

Data Collection

Progress in RCA is made by fitting pieces of information together to obtain a full picture of event generation. Generally speaking, every piece of information is a data item. A data item, in its wide definition, may come in any form or shape. It may assist cause analysis in several ways and in every phase of the event investigation (problem characterization, model building, and model validation).

As mentioned in previous chapters, a very important part of cause analysis in process industries is extraction and manipulation of process control parameters (in-line and end-of-line measurements) by computerized tools. The techniques for drawing conclusions on events based on this data have been discussed in detail in the Problem Characterization chapter. However, as thorough as this may be, it is not always sufficient to provide all the information required to define the root cause or apply a solution to a process problem.

Other data sources should be employed to enhance RCA, either by telling what went wrong or by thinking what could go wrong.
This chapter will introduce and discuss other data sources, some of which are described in detail, and others which are presented briefly.

The following topics will be covered in this chapter:

- Ad-hoc data collection: Getting new data
- Walk-through
- Literature research
- Lab analysis
- Interviews and verbal updates
- Simulation

Ad-hoc data collection: Getting new data

It has already been mentioned that extraction and manipulation of process control parameters (in-line and end-of-line measurements) that were collected and stored in a database play a significant role in event investigation. One may think that anything needed to identify the cause of any event can be found somewhere in the factory's database. However, this is not necessarily correct. We cannot rely on the database to have all the information needed to explain every event. The fact is that some process parameters are sampled and controlled adequately while others have either poor sampling or no record at all. When facing the cause analysis challenge of a certain problem, you may learn that the data recorded is insufficient to support the investigation. Either more frequent and even different sampling is required for an existing parameter, or the collected data is not the information required for the investigation and a new type of data should be collected.

Why is new data collection needed?

Support problem containment

Some of the material run on the line is suspected to be bad. Still, most of the material emerging from the line is healthy, so why bother with an extra check that may apply significant strain on the line? The reason is to contain the problem and prevent further damage.

Prevent bad material from reaching the customers. If there is a wave of problematic material, you need to consider whether the product tests are good enough to catch every defective product. If this is not so, a denser mesh is needed to filter out any bad products.

Prevent bad material from causing further damage to later process steps in the production line (such as contamination or mechanical breakage). Problematic material is a potential threat to the line. Depending on the kind of problem, you need to consider the potential consequences of running suspect material through the line. If you think that it is too risky for the line, you may need to identify a good way to detect any defective material in the earliest possible stage and intercept this material before it causes further damage. If the material has already progressed and you suspect that it may cause an unwanted effect, you may apply a special measure to test this effect.

Prevent the waste of good material that may enter a problematic tool, and reroute the production through a healthy channel. In some cases, there is a problem in a later process step that only affects material with special characteristics in an earlier process step. In this situation, you may consider a meticulous test right after the early process step, and direct the material to the best tool or treatment for optimal results.

In the above situations, a decision to apply a more demanding check and sampling applies strain on the manufacturing line and slows down the operation. Since it is clear that this is needed to contain the problem, it is usually well accepted. In many ways, the special data collection that is applied to contain the problem also serves the needs of RCA. However, sometimes special collection tasks are driven solely by root cause needs, and when trying to apply this kind of constraint for cause analysis purposes, it is frequently accepted as an unnecessary burden. So it is important to emphasize the contribution of this action to problem elimination and minimize constraints by defining the required sampling and duration of this data collection.

Support problem characterization

It was already discussed that during problem characterization, differentiation between good and bad material is required. As the distinction between bad and good is more accurate, there is a better chance that the data analysis tools will be able to identify the source of the problem. This distinction may be blurred by incomplete sampling. If the routine is to skip a few products and test only occasional samples, then the bad material could be skipped. The existing sampling can also be performed without skipping, but the measured points are not in the optimal location to catch the problem. So the intention is to redefine data collection so there is the best chance of catching problematic material by the correct test, in the most sensitive location, with proper sampling.

When running problem characterization, it is particularly important to look for patterns in problem appearance. Random sampling and partial test coverage do not usually provide enough data to do this. It may be necessary to avoid any skipping and look for a repeat or other significant pattern in material order through the line. A pattern in lot sequence may provide a hint about the source of the problem. In addition to a pattern in the material running sequence, it is rather important to learn the problematic phenomenon by checking the appearance (pattern) over the problematic material. This may require full mapping of products or lots with an appropriate test or measurement.

So learning the problematic material may require changing the frequency and the way material is checked. Yet there is another reason for special checking during RCA.

Support model building and validation

When model building was discussed, it was explained that segmentation is an attempt to isolate a problematic process step, tool, system or component. If a problem is detected in a late process-step, attempt to identify the earliest process step to demonstrate that problem should be a part of the segmentation effort. Even if there is no routine checking or testing of material after each one of the earlier steps, it should be added as part of the investigation. Identification of the problem in earlier steps reduces the number of suspect process steps or tools, and in certain cases it may point to the exact source of the problem.

In the validation stage, the team tries to either confirm or deny suggested models to a problem. For this purpose, there may be an attempt to gather more information about potential correlation that may exist between input parameters and output results. Naturally, collecting more information will require adding tests or measurements needed for this purpose. In addition, experiments that aim to prove or disprove a certain theory may require special data collection to check the results.

Considerations in getting new data

From all the above, it is clear that there are good reasons to incorporate special data collection in the case of a problem. The situation is relatively simple when the required information is a test or a measurement that already exists in line. The required tool to run the test is available, the technique is known, the knowledge exists, and it is just the matter of employing it for a larger sample size or to alter an existing testing or measurement program.

It is more complicated when the required information is something that is not collected routinely in line. When the aim is to gather information in a new way, there are numerous questions and considerations.

As an example, let's take the case of a phenomenon that repeatedly occurs in a certain tool and this should be visible. However it occurs randomly, and when it happens, it is in a twinkling of an eye. The problem is that a person cannot just sit there and stare at the system 24 hours a day, hoping to see it happen. Even if someone is there at the time of the event, it is too fast to be captured by the human eye. A simple idea is to place a TV camera that will constantly record the action of the tool. Still, this requires some thought. First, it is necessary to decide about the technical aspects of the camera and recording media (how many frames per second is needed to properly capture the event? What is the required resolution? What is the required lighting?). Second, the best location for the camera is required. It should be placed so the tool will be viewed constantly without being blocked by persons or items that may disturb the field of view. On the other hand, it should not disturb the actual work on the inspected tool. It is also wise for the recording instrument and the inspected system to have some time synchronization, so it will be possible to look at the recorded information at the exact time, and save the need to go over the entire recorded information.

So, when considering collecting new data the team should ask:

What needs to be detected? What tool should be used? What is the base line for this test? How often is it needed? What is the implication of adding it to the line or to the system under investigation?

The team should think first about the property, phenomenon, or action that needs to be measured, sensed or viewed and look for the best tools or methods to reflect it. You may ask yourself what characterizes the best tool or method. Well, the way to judge it is by sensitivity of detection, ease of implementation, and speed of results.

Sensitivity of detection: Check whether the method that you are considering using can easily detect the phenomenon or property in which you are interested, and has the potential to clearly differentiate between a normal and abnormal situation (ease of data interpretation).

Ease of implementation: An existing or already-known system may save time required for installation and extra training. If a new instrument or procedure is to be implemented, look for the one that will be easy to learn and install, and that will cause minimal interference to the normal working mode.

Speed of results: Achieving results as close as possible to the time of occurrence may greatly contribute to the ability to identify the source of the problem. A shorter delay time may require minimal sampling to achieve results, and the response time will be fast and immediate.

Once the proper tool or method is identified, the risk involved in applying it to the system under investigation should be carefully assessed. It is extremely important for this data collecting tool to be inert to the process under investigation. This is for two reasons: one is not to jeopardize the line or the system under investigation, and the other is not to question the validity of the collected data.

Ad-hoc data collection frequently applies an extra work load on the process line. Invest some thought on the frequency and/or the sample size that should be employed to minimize this burden. Make sure to remove any implemented ad-hoc data collection if found to be ineffective or upon completion of this task.

To summarize ad-hoc information gathering, here are some hints for consideration.

- Prefer automatic data logging, chart recording, or other recording methods over manual measurements.
- Potential items to be monitored are: set-points vs. actual, input quality and stability, dynamic behavior conditions, components and human behavior and output-results.
- Apply best monitor (existing or new)
  - Sensitivity: best chance to detect the problem
  - Sample size: minimum interruption maximum chance of detection
  - Response time: fast and immediate

Walk-through

Walk-through is field data collection. A team could convene in a conference room and discuss a problem for hours and days without reaching results, just because the answer to the problem is in the field. Needless to say, walking around in the field of the event is extremely important.

The effected material moves from one machine to another and travels through the process line as any other production material. However, this material experienced something different from the usual process that provides healthy material. You may ask yourself what this could be. There is a significantly higher chance of realizing what could happen to a product, tool, or system by walking through the sequence of working. It could be that the same event will not recur in this exact walk-through, however it is more probable that you'll be able to raise more intelligent scenarios about things that could go wrong along the way.

You may suspect that a walk-through is needed when someone is asked to describe a sequence of operations or activities, and this description raises too many questions. An attempt to fully understand how that material is handled and processed, or how a machine works or is maintained by a theoretical explanation in a meeting room is not always successful (this is an understatement). It is unlikely that a team will capture a problem in a certain operation by this kind of learning. Why? The problem is in the **gap of knowledge**. We can map our knowledge by saying that there are things that **we know that we know**, there are things that **we know that we don't know**, and there are things that **we don't know that we don't know**.

The first part is simply having knowledge and being able to answer a question. The second part is recognizing a gap in knowledge and being able to ask a question with the intention of closing the gap (this is also a level of knowing). The third part is a gap in knowledge of which a person is unaware and therefore unable to ask any questions.

The problem in the meeting room is that we acquire knowledge from what we were told and the image we create in our mind. We can ask questions based on what we were told and understood, but what about things of which we were unaware? The aim of the walk-through is to minimize this last part and maximize the first two parts. In other words, the person or team that conducts the walk-through will acquire enough knowledge to either get answers or to be able to ask relevant questions.

What is the best way to conduct a walk-through? What needs to be observed? How should the trip be recorded?

Before you start
1. Define the activity, procedure or system that you are going to cover.
2. Find a knowledgeable person to walk you through this procedure.
3. Learn a bit about the theory of the issue that you are going to cover.
4. Define the way to capture your impression.

What is going to be covered?

You or your team should ask what you intend to gain from this walk-through. It is different if the intent is to conduct an audit of a certain activity, or if it is just an educational visit to gain a first-hand impression and be introduced to a tool, system, or procedure in its natural surroundings.

A walk-through in audit format means that a previous assumption was made that something may be different or is done in a different way than it should. Therefore, every step of this walk-through should be compared to an existing situation or a known demand. The intention of this thorough checking is to capture a specific fault.

The intention in an educational walk-through is to be there, look around and acquire enough information and knowledge to ask questions that may lay the basis for building a modeling tree.

System auditing

Auditing a system for RCA is very demanding. It requires covering all details related to the system under investigation. There should be meticulous checking of all system components and verification of proper performance of all required activities. To do this properly, it is advised that the person running the audit is familiar with a similar system and is still detached from this specific site and its personnel. Otherwise, the person assigned to conduct the audit should spend some time in learning the system and familiarizing himself or herself with the related procedures.

When running the audit, the person conducting it should follow a pre-prepared checklist. This checklist should be marked while walking through the sequence that was defined for checking. All system and human aspects should be scrutinized.

System or tool aspects:
As mentioned earlier in this book, try to check all S.Co.T.T sides.

Supplies: everything that enters the system. Think about: supplier, shipment procedures and conditions, handling procedures, storage conditions, replacement procedures, and so on.

Components: all hardware. Think about: source and originality of component, versions, dimensions, consumables, maintenance procedures, alignment procedures, calibrations, and so on.

Treatments: all conditions and actions that have a potential impact on supplies or components. Think about: process recipes (set points and actual), environmental issues, working procedures (handling, loading and unloading, measurement and information recording), and so on.

Timing: all time-related issues. Think about: times in recipes, typical and unusual delays, idling periods, duration of activities, and so on.

Human aspects:
Adherence of performed activities to procedures: Follow the performance of activities. If a certain activity appears strange, ask for clarification. Wait until the task is completed, so as not to interfere with work that needs concentration or extra care. Verify what is based on the written procedure and what part is on-the-job training.

How is a new employee qualified to do the job? What kind of training is required?

Integrity of records: How are records taken, automatically or manually? Where are records kept? What are mandatory records and what depends on good will? Does the person involved care about keeping things in order? What is the chance of having wrong or misleading information in records?

If a discrepancy is observed, the auditor may ask for and receive a convincing explanation. However, any discrepancy, whether or not it is well justified, should be recorded either by writing a comment, scribbling a drawing or taking a picture of the problematic issue.

All discrepancies should be discussed by the cause analysis team to evaluate their potential contribution to problem generation. Those that are highly suspect or could fit a suggested model of failure will require further checking.

If a certain discrepancy is found later on as the cause of failure, it is important to understand what led to this situation. Something that was not compatible with the requirements led to a failure, but what caused this discrepancy to be there?

Educational walk-through

In the educational walk-through, the intention is to familiarize the person or team members with the system, tool, or procedure discussed during the meetings. There is no intention to make anyone expert in the one or more visits dedicated to the educational walk-through, and there is a very low chance of identifying the cause of an event during the walk-through. However it is rather important to capture as much as possible during the visit, with the intention of being able to ask relevant questions. So the benefit of this kind of walk-through is in the new learning it provides and the list of relevant questions to ask, rather than a list of discrepancies as in an audit.

When performing an educational walk-through, look thoroughly, listen carefully, be curious and ask questions. First ask yourself, and if you can't figure things out by yourself, ask the person walking you through the system.

Look how it's built, and how it's done.
Look at, and look into it.

Look around.
Look up, and look down.

Think and wonder:
Is it possible that it looked different at the time of the event? Consider the possibility that conditions were different, that the surrounding environment was changed, or that there was interference by neighboring systems.

If you try to imagine how things are done in reality, or how conditions can be different at different times, you may reach simple, yet interesting observations. A nearby pump that was idling during the visit could have caused vibrations at the time of the event. A door that is closed during the visit could be open at the time of the event, and thus the air flow, temperature or humidity could be different. A fine alignment that appears easy to perform with bare hands, is much harder to perform with coarse gloves.

When looking into a structure of a tool or system, ask:
- What is the role of each component? What is it made of? Why?
- Is a situation subject to a constant change over time? How does it look at the beginning and at the end?
- What are the potential problems with this component under given conditions? What if...?
- How is proper functionality and performance ensured? What is the procedure for this?

When looking into a performed procedure, ask:
- What is the trigger for the activity? What is the frequency of performance?
- Who is to perform it? How will they know how to do it? What and where are the requirements they need to follow?
- What is replaced and what is placed back?
- What are the challenges or difficulties that a person may face while doing it?
- Why is it done this way? Is there another way?
- How it is recorded? How it is verified to be OK?

There are way too many possible questions for me to mention, and too many possible things to investigate for me to list. The amount of learning that can be acquired is up to the person or persons performing the walk-through, and the time available for this. You may not get complete answers to all of the questions, but at least you are able to ask questions, and as we said earlier, being able to ask questions is a level of knowledge.

Literature research

Searching for literature to support the RCA effort could be a very frustrating task, for two main reasons. The first is that sometimes it is simply hard to find relevant material related to the specific issue you are dealing with. The second is that after investing effort and finding most appropriate literature, there is a tendency not to consider the literature content seriously.

The first is a more technical difficulty, while the latter is more of an attitude issue. Let's start with the latter.

Attitude towards literature research

When directing professional personnel to look for assistance by searching for information in literature, it may be perceived as challenging their professionalism. If this request is accompanied by a sarcastic statement like "Do not re-invent the wheel," even an intelligent and enthusiastic person could take it as a statement that underestimates his or her ability. A long silent response is an expression of reluctance to adopt any suggested idea coming from an outside source. This overprotective attitude on professional territory is known as NIH syndrome (not invented here).

We all have to admit that we cannot know everything about everything. If someone paved a way for us by documenting experience and knowledge, it would be wise to learn from it. Therefore, when facing an event that needs to be solved, searching for existing information on topics that are related to the relevant issue may help a lot. It is unlikely to produce the direct answer to any specific problem, but it will most probably lead to information that will open our minds to different analytical techniques, to more complete model understanding, and maybe even to possible solutions.

The literature research should be considered as a virtual member of the problem-solving team that is especially effective in brainstorming or in providing background information.

What is going to be covered?

Obviously, when talking about literature research these days, we are no longer thinking about going to dusty libraries and archives to get data. It is either the Internet, if we are looking for public domain information, or the Intranet if we are seeking information within our organization. This section deals with literature research on the Internet.

This discussion will not provide details on Internet structure, search engine syntax, or list any specific resources. Instead, it will briefly review the data arrangement and placement on the Internet and its relevancy to the literature research. This will be followed by a short discussion on the approach to literature research. Then, some hints (that work fine for me) on searching arrangements will be provided, and finally, a few words on the way to evaluate material quality.

Where does the relevant material reside?

Information accessible by the Internet is spread over a huge number of servers and computers and there is no need to register or get approval for placing any page on the web. So, no one is responsible for listing the contents of the pages in any methodical way. Still, we are able to look for and find material within this amorphously arranged information.

When talking about searching for information on the Internet, the immediate connotation is a search engine like Google. However it is important to understand that this is not always the best default to start with when running a serious and professional literature research. To understand why, some elaboration is required on Internet searching possibilities.

We can distinguish three main directions to look for information.
1. Subject directories
Volunteers or people who are paid to review Internet pages and catalog them according to categories and subcategories: These people decide what is relevant to the subject directory they are working for and under which directory and subdirectory it should be placed.

Some subject directories are generic (and more commercially oriented) and cover a wide range of categories (such as Yahoo). Other subject directories specialize in a more narrow range of scholarly or professional issues and are reviewed by professionals from academic institutes or organizations (such as Librarians' Index or INFOMINE). Since some judgment is involved in selecting the pages, better quality material is expected. However, the material is usually more generic in nature, and one cannot expect to find a specific paper on the relevant issue.

In some subject directories, you need to browse and go down the hierarchy of the selected category to find the necessary material. Most of the subject directories are equipped with a search within capability that provides quick identification of the most relevant URLs.

2. Search engines
Search engines index Internet content by running programs called spiders or crawlers. These programs cover the web by going from one link to another, and every page is indexed in the search engine database. The search engines differ in the way the engine "decides" the relevancy of the page in response to the terms you enter and it ranks the page accordingly. Boolean operators are usually employed for more precise searching. Since there are small variations in the syntax used by different search engines, invest a few minutes in learning the proper syntax once you get into a new search engine. In some engines you have the option to select between "all", "any", or "phrase", but employing the syntax provides more flexibility and power when running a search.

Since no judgment or selection is made by the automatic processing of the search engine, you may receive a mixture of very good material and poor quality stuff. The only way to learn the material quality is by entering the site and reviewing it.

3. The invisible web
This may be surprising, but there are more web pages that will not appear in a typical search done by a search engine than pages that will. Funnily enough, the pages that are not shown are often more useful for professionals who are looking for high quality material. Why is this so?

The search engine crawler is a robot that depends on the continuous ability to travel freely from one link to another. If, for some reason, it encounters a barrier, it will not be able to continue and learn the pages behind it. If, for example, the crawler reaches an entry page of a professional database that requires entering information or a password, the crawler will not be able to do so. All pages within this database will not be explored by the crawler and will stay invisible to you when using the search engine.

Papers scanned to image format instead of printed text are not readable by the crawler, and will not be visible to you even if the exact phrase exists in the paper. Sometimes, search engine companies choose to exclude certain file formats that are not popular or rarely used. Why do we care about the invisible web?

A significant number of professional searchable databases and reference index sites require completion of an entry form to enter, or even a membership fee with a password. These sites focus on technical, engineering and academic topics and contain high-quality papers, such as publications, proceedings or articles that are potentially the most valuable for the serious literature researcher.

What is the approach?

The way you run the search depends on what you intend to gain by this search. It may be a generic search that you need for basic fundamental understanding of an issue, or it may be a very detailed research about a specific aspect directly related to the problem you are working on.

If you intend to learn a new topic that you are not familiar with, then look for more generic and introductory material. In this case, subject directories are the natural direction to start with. This usually leads to better quality material and may save time wasted in filtering out lean or poor quality sites found by search engines.

For example, let's assume that you are involved in a team investigating a problem in refractive index of a silicon dioxide layer deposited by a chemical vapor deposition system, and you are not familiar with such systems. You may want to learn the basics of chemical vapor deposition systems. So you will start by searching introductory material about chemical vapor deposition, and probably also generic material about silicon dioxide properties. The way to reach the most relevant material is by selecting key words providing a broad definition of the topic, and narrowing down the search within this definition if needed.

If you are using a search engine (such as Google) for this task, the same key words will most probably produce an overwhelming amount of material, most of which does not meet the expectations for well-arranged introductory material on the topic of interest.

On the other side is the situation where you need to learn about a very narrow aspect of a specific professional problem. This kind of material typically appears as a research summary or study presented at professional conferences, or published in a professional magazine. This kind of material will not be found in subject directories, and it is most likely that a search engine will not provide satisfactory results either.

To look for this kind of material, go to searchable databases or index directories that are related to your profession. Since you are searching material that is very specific to your problem, use more distinct terminology that fits the particular case. If the specific wording does not produce the expected results, broaden your definition slightly and search again.

If you are working in a well-established organization, you may have free access to some professional databases related to your job. If you are not aware of this capability in your organization, make enquiries with the librarian or colleagues. For example, a few sites that I find useful for my day-to-day work are: IEEE Explore (technical literature on electrical engineering, computer science, and electronics); IngentaConnect (comprehensive collection of academic and professional publications); INSPEC (comprehensive index to scholarly, scientific journals and conference proceedings); Sciencedirect (science, technology, and medicine).

The advantage and the disadvantage of the search engines are in their coverage and ranking. They cover a huge variety of topics and diverse levels of material quality, and the most relevant link may have a low ranking for the most irrelevant reasons. However, search-engine usage is suitable when you are looking for an issue that is loosely defined or when looking for specific information. The results improve when thought is invested in keyword selection and the search is given a few trials. It may provide excellent findings if you have time to invest in refining the search or/and filtering the results.

To summarize: Go to the subject directory for introductory material or background learning of a certain topic. Search professional databases for papers or publications relevant to a specific issue. Use the search engine for reaching many results on any issue (specific or generic) and don't forget that relevant material may be invisible or appear low in ranking.

A few more hints on running a literature search

* Pick the three or four best or strongest topical databases, subject directories, and search engines that fit your regular interest, and place their links on your desktop. Get URLs from your own experience or from your colleagues.

* Invest time in learning the syntax and advanced search capabilities of these search engines, directories and databases.

* Before running a search on a topic, prepare a folder for placing all documents that you find appropriate during the search, with **their respective links**.

* Open a new blank Word document and use copy and paste to save contents of html pages as document. This way, page elements such as graphs and images will be included with the text in one document.

* Use proper Boolean operators wisely on your pre-defined keywords. Adopt appropriate keyword synonyms when you find good ones during the search or when reading relevant articles.

* When looking for basic learning of a new issue in a search engine, include keywords such as basic/s, fundamental/s, elementary, principals and tutorial.

* Consider excluding .com sites from your search (Limit it to .edu; .gov, .org, as appropriate).

* When studying search results in a search engine, favor URLs ending with .pdf , .doc , .ppt (documents formats) over others (such as .html, .asp). Proceedings and articles usually appear in these formats.

* Do not read the full article during your search. Briefly review the abstract and summary. This should be sufficient to decide whether it's worth saving for later in-depth reading.

* When saving a document or an article on your computer, change its name, link, and the reference information, to a meaningful full title (such as the full name of the article) instead of the meaningless default file name that usually appears. For convenience, use Copy and Paste (or Text Select in pdf) from the paper title while it's still open, and paste it into the Save As dialog box.

Evaluate material quality

It is important to realize that Internet data was not collected and edited by experts and professionals in any subject. The information is placed on the Internet voluntarily by anyone who is interest in doing so. Therefore the data could be reliable and accurate, but it could be superficial or even false. It is important to treat the information with caution.

The quality of the information you get may be judged by the source behind it, the credibility of the author and the reason for the paper to be there.

- Reviewing the site and who is behind it

  Look at the URL and check the domain name. If it ends with .org .edu .gov it is already a good sign. Truncate the URL and check the main page. Look for links or buttons that say "Who we are", "About us", or similar and learn about the site and the motivation for placing the material there. Does this appear to be a trusty institution? If the above self introduction is missing, try to get more information about this URL by placing it on Alexa.com and learn the details provided in traffic ranking.

- Learning the paper and the author

  If the paper resides in a well-known professional or academic database, this is already a good sign. See whether the paper carries an author name or whether the page has an email address enabling contact with the author. Run a search and check whether there are other papers published by the same author or organization. If there are references in the paper, the ability to trace these is a good indication of the paper quality and may provide more information on the same topic.

- Learning why the paper is there
  The motivation for placing a paper on a commercial site is not the same as the reason that paper is in an academic or professional database. If the paper intends to promote sales or ideas, suspect that the contents are biased. Try to trace back papers like this and check whether their original content was not altered nor has missing parts. Do not disqualify material just because it is in a commercial site. There is a whole lot of useful information in these sites as well. Equipment manufacturers provide background information required to understand their tools. This is sometimes excellent introductory material to a topic of interest.

Last but not least, if you are a professional in the searched matter, you need to have a gut feeling about the page content.

Physical lab analyses

What does it look like, what is it made of and how much of it is there? This kind of question can be answered by lab analysis. Lab analyses are extremely effective in supporting RCA and should be used as early as possible in the event investigation. The lab information may lead to source identification, but more than this, it may provide crucial information required for model building. Frequently enough, the whole model building process and validation depends on lab analyses, and without lab work it simply becomes a guessing game.

However, just by saying "I'm going to submit material to lab analysis" and dropping some material off at the lab for analysis does not guarantee useful results. There are several important things that should be carefully considered in order to achieve meaningful lab results, otherwise you may receive useless or even misleading information that will divert your team in the wrong direction in event investigation. So, make the lab analyst part of your team.

When considering lab analysis think about:

- Expected and unexpected!!!
- Picking the correct sample for lab analysis
- Choosing the correct analytical technique
- Using proper sample handling and preparation
- Correctly interpreting the lab results

Expected and unexpected!!!

One of the most common mistakes in lab analyses, causing a delay in event investigation, is not having a reference. As we mentioned earlier in other event investigation issues, the key for achieving significant results from lab analysis is by knowing what is expected. Without this knowledge, interpretation of the lab analysis will be rather speculative.

When choosing the lab technique, you must either have a known baseline for this analysis or provide a reference sample for comparison. If you fail to do so you, your team and the analyst will sit in front of the results and wonder, "Is the result really abnormal?", "Is this within or beyond the normal variation?" without having a definite answer. In some cases, this result will be inconclusive and the analysis will be repeated with proper reference, but in other cases it may lead to wrong conclusions.

Picking the correct sample for lab analysis

When confronted with an event, you probably want to select the sample that will have the best chance of catching the problem. Your choice is either to take a representative sample lying somewhere within the affected population (typically affected material) or to take the extreme case (most severely affected material) in the belief that there is a better chance of catching the problem on it.

The question is, when to pick what?

If the failing population is distinctively apart from the normal population, it will be good to take representative material that failed and use it for the analysis. It is important to pay special attention to selecting a sample that represents the affected material and has all characteristics of the problem of interest.

In some cases, the affected material is not so far apart, or even overlaps the normal population. In this case, to avoid ambiguous results, it would be wise to select the material with an extreme effect. However, keep in mind that this material is not typical affected material. So, make sure that this failure is part of the problem and not an outlier with a different problem.

As said earlier, it is also important to have a reference sample. Again, to avoid confusion there should be some thought behind the reference. It is important to compare apples with apples. A reference sample of good material should have minimal differences (that are not relevant to the problem) compared to the affected material, while considering tool, location, treatment, timing and so on. Otherwise the unrelated source of variation between the analyzed samples may provide misleading results.

Choosing the correct analytical technique

Persons or teams often face the question of what analytical method should be used for best results. Those who are not well experienced in lab work look for the ultimate technique that will provide all the required information in one instance.

In the semiconductor industry, a request for TEM analysis is typical, since this tool provides the highest magnification. Selection of the analytical tool is not always straightforward. First, it is important to emphasize that there is no ultimate analytical tool, and complementary data from several techniques may be used to gain a clearer picture of the cause of a problem.

When considering lab work on a sample, one should weigh the advantage of each technique vs. its limitations, and decide on the appropriate technique according to the given problem and the analytical tools that are available. An analytical technique may have a fast or slow throughput time. It may have a high or low chance of succeeding, and it could be destructive or non-destructive.

When a one-of-a-kind sample is available for analysis and urgency is less of an issue, then non-destructive analytical techniques should be used first. A destructive method with the best chance of succeeding will be used only after exhausting these techniques. If the level of urgency of the required analysis is high and back-up samples are available, it is possible to run a fast test with a lower chance of success, parallel to a slower technique with a high chance of success. Preserving the sample is not an issue in this case.

Every analytical tool has its own limitation regarding resolution, concentration, accuracy, and so on. Available lab capabilities and analytical techniques are not common knowledge. A lab expert with broad knowledge of analytical techniques could be an asset to any team. If this person was not part of the team in the first place, then the team should consult with one when deciding to use analytical lab services. Before making an effective recommendation, this person should have proper background information about the problem as a whole, as well as specific expectations from the lab analysis.

Using proper sample handling and preparation

Once a decision is made to perform lab analysis, there is usually an attempt to grab the material as fast as possible and let the lab persons work on it. In this case, haste makes waste. Don't rush. Consult the expert of this specific technique about the procedures to follow to achieve the best results.

The lab analyst should have a clear understanding of what you expect to learn from this sample and should have detailed information about the material to be analyzed.

Proper material selection
It is rather important to know that the material and structure selected for analysis perfectly fits the selected technique. Every analytical technique has its own limitations and these should be considered when selecting the material or structure to be analyzed. Things like physical structure, dimensions, materials, phase (liquid, solid, gas), concentration and process stage are important details that could determine whether analysis will be possible or even whether it has a good chance of success.

Proper test location
The affected location should be clearly defined for the analyst and should be indicated on the analysis results. Save frustration and confusion by clearly defining the location to be analyzed.

Proper sample treatment
Any treatment or handling applied to the sample prior to analysis should be inert to the sample. Altering or contaminating the sample by improper treatment will cause errors in analysis. Contamination could come from the environment or from the handling procedures that are in use. Keep this effect in mind while dealing with delicate samples subjected to contamination.

In some cases, it will be necessary to run certain procedures deliberately to enable or improve the performance of the analysis. It is important that the reference sample receives exactly the same treatment to produce valid reference results.

Example: If the structure size is too large to fit into an analytical tool, one would like to cut it or saw it into smaller pieces. During sawing the material heats up. Will it have an impact on material characteristics? If cooling liquid is used, will it contaminate the sample?

Correct interpretation of lab results

When interpreting results, the key is again to understand what is expected and what came out unexpected. Even with this in mind, interpretation is not always so easy, and understanding how meaningful the results are to understanding the problem can be tricky.

When realizing that the affected material differs from the reference sample, you may ask yourself whether this difference is **real** and **meaningful.**

Meaningful: the results are not exactly the same for both reference and affected material. The immediate question is whether this change is the natural variation between samples or this is a significant finding that relates to the event you are dealing with.

Understanding the significance of the findings is part of the know-how acquired with experience. Part of it is related to understanding the analytical tool and part of it is related to the technology under investigation.

Real: There are sometimes findings that appear to be significant, however they are not. These artifacts may be caused by improper handling and preparation of the sample, by effects related to the analytical technique, or even by trivial things such as order of analysis and difference in exposure time of samples to the environment. An inexperienced analyst may interpret these artifacts as a real problem, while an expert will avoid falling into this trap.

If you have a strong feeling that physical evidence should appear in the lab analysis, thoroughly review the process of sample selection, point of analysis selection, and sample preparation sequence. **Note that 90% of your chances of achieving a meaningful result in lab analysis depends on preparation for running the technique**. If you doubt whether the selected analysis method is not good or sensitive enough to provide the explanation, look for an alternative way to analyze the problem.

When no problem is detected in the analysis and results are similar to reference or background, you may feel a bit frustrated, because you expect to see something. **Remember that negating something is also a meaningful finding.** So, if you are in model building and validation, you have a new data item to work with.

Interview and verbal updates

A team of experts may spend days on endless discussions without a definite understanding of what went wrong. The team may even possibly guess the real reason for the event but this could not be confirmed by any solid evidence. This is especially correct in cases where human behavior contributes to event initiation.

Even where there is a well established system, procedures, and controls, there are always workarounds and shortcuts that are being made for some reason. Things that were performed informally and were not recorded, and the reason for doing so, are exactly the kind of information you would like to learn.

One hint from a person who was at the scene of an event, or who spent time near the tool or system, could provide the key to understanding the problem.

What is the best way to get spoken information about an event? Naturally, the best way is by having this key person as part of the team in the first place. However, even if this kind of person is on your team, his willingness to provide the data depends on how he perceives the investigation process.

If the individual perceives the environment as a threatening situation that could have a negative implication on him and on his colleagues or friends, he will not provide data openly. He will only suggest things that are neutral or expected to be heard. This is even more correct when dealing with interviews that are not part of the team meetings, with persons that are not part of the team.

So, here are several things and ideas that may help you when interviewing individuals about an event.

- Pick the right persons.
  This is correct for both the interviewer and the interviewee. When an unfamiliar face appears at the scene following an event and asks questions, it is perceived as an interrogation. Since the motivation of this person as well as the consequences of the investigation are not known, the people involved will be reluctant to provide too much information, especially if they were directly

involved in the event. So, it will be better if someone familiar with the area and trusted by relevant personnel conducts the interview or accompanies the person that is to conduct the interview. It is better to start by interviewing a person that is very familiar with the actual day-to-day work in the area of interest, but is not directly involved in the specific event. It is important to interview a person that knows how things are actually done (operator or tech) rather than how things should be done (such as supervisor, manager or engineers).

- Set the right environment.
  A neutral location is the best location for conducting an event-related interview. I find that a public location such as a cafeteria or dining room is better than a meeting room. A special room appears to be too formal and it is harder to break the ice and achieve an open discussion. The impact of creating a casual environment in the cafeteria is far more beneficial than the small risk of distraction or inconvenience from background noise. If there is a need to interview at the scene of the event, it is better to start the interview somewhere else, and then visit the site as part of the interview, when the conversation is more fluid and mutual trust has been established. It is best for it to be a continuation of an explanation that is more natural near the tool or system of discussion. The presence of someone higher up in the hierarchy is very often a limiting factor. The interviewee may be reluctant to mention things that could imply that the situation under this manager is not perfect. The interviewee will be busy thinking how things will be heard or perceived by the manager, and this will limit the flow of information.

- Get the information without making the person defensive or protective. I find that the best way to get information is by drawing the interviewee over to your side. Tell the interviewee the story of the event as it is known up till now, explaining that the intention is to use his qualifications and familiarity with the area to identify ways to prevent reoccurrence of an event in the area. Ask him to suggest events like this, to point to similar potential failures and ways to prevent them. This will usually produce surprising results. When a person that is not directly involved in the event, but knows details about it, is asked to provide examples of failures that recently occurred in the area, this recent event will almost always come up as an example (with no names). It is simply because this is still fresh in his mind and can serve as reinforcement of his knowledge about what is going on in his area.

- Listen to what is said, how it is said and why it is said.Try to get into the interviewee's head. Consider how much he knows about the damage, risk, and implication of the discussed event. Is he scared or excited? When there is a lot of damage, and the plant is noisy and agitated by the event, the interviewee's usual reaction is to focus on his relation (or absence of relation) to the event, such as: I was not there at the time; It was not on my shift; I was busy doing something else. If there is a code of loyalty in a certain group, the interviewer may face selective memory syndrome. People may provide many irrelevant details but once the discussion approaches the sensitive issue, their memory slows down.

Body language: Many books dealing with interviews attribute great importance to this. Even if you consider using it to learn something about your interviewee, be careful as not to misinterpret his verbal information because of that. Body posture, hand waving and expression is sometimes different between cultures and personalities, so be careful and sensitive when interpreting body language. This is also relevant for language and manner of speech. If the interview is not conducted in the interviewee's native language or dialect, it may alter the original intention. Even if it sounds as if the interviewee is fluent in the acquired language, be aware that he is still missing some nuances that may be interpreted by a native speaker as rude or insincere.

- Try to understand whether there is something that should be said but was not said. This is especially correct when there are several interviewees that should share the same knowledge or have the same information. When comparing what they have to relate, you may observe that one or more of them avoided mentioning meaningful information, and it is hard to believe that the interviewee has forgotten it or regards it as unimportant.

- Get opinion and facts but remember that they are not the same. Even if the interviewer prepares questions ahead of time, the interview should not be conducted as if filling in a questionnaire. The conversation may sometimes digress with useful information and other times it may just build the proper environment for the interview. The interviewer should pay attention and know when the interviewee is telling real facts and when he understands, interprets, estimates or guesses.

It was said earlier that the interviewer should listen to what is said and what is not said by the interviewee. When doing so, the interviewer interprets things that were not said or intended to be understood in that manner. This is OK as long as the interviewer realizes that this was done to keep the interview running and get more facts.

Things that someone with firsthand experience has to say should not be underestimated, even if this person does not have formal background on the issue under question. Frequently, this person may provide a fact or description of a situation that is important but is wrongly interpreted. Listen carefully to the facts and observations. Do not overlook it just because the interpretation is wrong.

- Don't jump to conclusions and don't share suspicions. When there are several sources of information on hand, you may sometimes have more knowledge about an event than someone who was actually there during the event and saw only a part of it. Avoid using this advantage to undermine the interviewee's credibility.

- Apply pressure as a last resource to get information and avoid doing so in cases that are not related to sabotage or criminal negligence. Consider that applying pressure on an innocent person will lead to loss of trust and bitterness and may also prevent future cooperation by others. Implying that failing to provide information will lead to termination or removal from position, or will affect promotion, is applying pressure.

- Appreciate contribution. Make the interviewee feel that the information is important and significant, and that the contribution is appreciated, not at this moment but in general. Remember, openness and frankness should work for, and not against, the interviewee. Someone who voluntarily shares critical information should not suffer because of it, unless that person was involved in sabotage or criminal negligence.

Simulation

Reconstructing a situation is a way to repeat or mimic the sequence of events that leads to the unexpected result. Repeat means a real attempt to re-create the actual situation that occurred at the time of the event. Process line experiments are this kind of reconstruction effort. Mimic, on the other hand, is an attempt to simulate the situation that occurred during an event. Simulation means creating a mathematical or statistical model based on known or estimated behavior of the involved process parameters, and using this model to predict results in an unknown situation.

Simulation concludes a real life situation based on a theoretical model. How reliable are the results of the simulation? When should simulation be used? What are the advantages of using simulations, and what are the pitfalls? These issues will be discussed in the next few pages.

Advantages of simulation

The validation process of an assumed hypothesis of a certain event involves data collection that aims at confirming or denying the suggested hypothesis. In most cases, validation is performed by collecting actual data. This data may be results of experiments or an outcome of a corrective action in an attempt to fix a problem (such as replacing a component that is assumed to be defective, or tweaking a suspect process parameter). This kind of learning can be expensive, time consuming and even risky. The material cost and the time required to run actual experiments for a comprehensive checking of many possible situations may be intolerable.

In simulation, it is possible to test different possibilities, in a fast turnaround time, with no risks. Using simulation, a high number of experiments can be run in a very short time, enhancing effects that cannot be easily controlled in real life. It is possible to run the time faster in simulation and manipulate parameters beyond the usual tolerance used in actual situations.

We do not always have the technical tools or ability to look directly into a system or sequence and to gain a direct impression of what's going on in there. Sometimes it's too small, too large, or too hostile to get in. However by correctly understanding and simulating it, we can have a pretty good view of what's going on.

Let's take an example of an ion beam that is accelerated towards solid material. We would like to see what's going on with the ions that are getting into the solid. What will be the situation if the energy of ions is altered? What if different ion species are used? No tool can get into the solid and look around and see what's going on in real time. However a Monte Carlo simulation can do this, and computer animation allows us to see it. (The name was coined by Von Neumann when he worked on the development of the atomic bomb at Los Alamos, and used random number generation to create his model).

So simulation may save time, money, material and effort. It can reduce risks in making decisions about certain changes or when designing a new system or process. Simulation may suggest an explanation to problem appearance or it could predict scenarios in case of changes to a given.

It seems to be a perfect tool to assist in RCA, and it is indeed. However, it is typically seen that simulation is dismissed as a low added-value tool for RCA. Unrealistic expectations from a simulation and improper understanding of its limitations may lead to frustration and loss of its potential benefits. Obviously, study of proper operation of simulation is required to achieve realistic expectations.

Simulation, simulators, and graphics

To build a simulation program, information should be collected about all system components to be analyzed, the different supplies and conditions fed into the system, and the potential changes and interactions between all these. A mathematical or statistical model then should be built, describing all interactions occurring in the system as a function of changing conditions and/or time. Naturally it requires in-depth knowledge of the system, the ability to represent the involved interactions in a mathematical or statistical model, and the ability to translate it into a computer simulation program by simulation language.

Since it is not always so simple to concentrate all resources for every given problem, a more generic computer program that enables easier running of simulations is frequently generated. This program is called Simulator, and it enables the user to insert or alter values of predetermined variables and check results. Simulators are intended to help those that are not involved with simulation programming to run simulations in a user-friendly environment. Since simulators are intended to cover a wider selection of systems or situations that may differ in construction or conditions, they are usually less accurate than a dedicated and specially written simulation program.

Computer graphics are often used for easier viewing of the simulation process and results. The use of graphics or computer animation creates a clear user-friendly interface and interpretation of the results is easy and nice. Animation makes the simulation look more like a real-life situation.

Building a simulation

Before developing a simulation, you first need to know the objective and scope of the project. What do you expect to achieve from the simulation? Yes/no answer, general direction or impression, rough estimation, or exact quantitative analysis? Naturally, quantitative analysis with high accuracy will demand more detailed and time-consuming effort in building the simulation.

Next you need to learn all the details required to create the mathematical or statistical model to describe the relevant process. This includes:
- All system components and sub-components with their respective functionality
- Every occurrence or action that leads to a change in the system, and its timing
- Every interaction between components or supplies that ends with generation of a byproduct

After collecting the above details, it should all be correctly modeled mathematically. The sequence, timing, interdependencies and interaction results should all be modeled correctly to achieve proper results. Following mathematical modeling, the simulation program is written. Computer graphics may be added for visual running of the simulation and to make it easier to interpret.

From the above, it is clear that simulation development is a team effort. No simulation analyst can possibly know everything about every tool or process. Tool experts, process experts (physicists or chemists), mathematicians or statisticians, programmers, and graphic experts should cooperate, led by a simulation analyst, to build the most accurate model for the required system.

Simple simulation programs that require limited resources can be generated for RCA tasks. However, it is hard to justify large-scale simulation development for RCA in cases of process events, unless the problem is big enough to justify any required project. Existing simulation programs or ready-made simulators are often employed for RCA. One should consider how useful this simulation is in predicting problematic system behavior.

Issues in employing simulation for cause analysis

Simulation is usually used for predicting and checking scenarios during project planning, designing or development stages. The intention is to avoid costly mistakes during construction or before introducing a real product into the manufacturing line. If simulation can be used to predict or test a problematic situation, it can also be used to identify the cause of a problem. However, as we have seen, building a simulation is not an easy task. It needs a variety of talents and knowledgeable resources to be identified and orchestrated to achieve proper results.

In RCA, the symptoms that are investigated are unexpected, based on team knowledge and experience. To achieve successful results from simulation, our knowledge and experience is required. This appears to be somewhat contradictory. If we can produce the knowledge required to build a simulation model that can predict the problem, why can we not figure out the problem using the same knowledge?

Indeed the wisdom of simulation lies in the knowledge and information that was invested in it. The simulation is just stronger in running calculations and figuring out different scenarios; it is still based on facts and assumptions.

Assumption is based on known behavior and estimates that the known behavior will be kept beyond the known region. But, as the model moves away from the region of knowledge, the validity of the assumptions may be wrong. We may consider dependency as linear for a region with which we are familiar, and calculate accordingly, while in fact it is non-linear. We may think that a certain dependency is continuous, while in fact it ends with an abrupt change (a cliff). It could be that a contributing factor was counted as insignificant or totally neglected, and in fact it is rather critical to the proper operation of the system.

How can we trust the simulation?

When receiving simulation results, first look for the facts and assumptions that were made for building the model. As less factual information enters the system and more assumptions are made about the system, there is a higher chance of the simulation failing. As the model calculations are more dependent on assumed facts than on known ones, the output could be less accurate. If you see a significant factor is missing, you may suspect that the results are wrong.

As well as checking the inputs to the system and the formulas and calculations that were made for running the model, you may check the validity of the simulation program. Large-scale simulation programs that are built for development or design usually go through some kind of validation process. If the simulation program is something that was developed previously for other purposes, you may ask about the validity checking on the program, or how successful previous simulations were in predicting actual results. If the program is written for the specific problem you are facing, consider running a limited number of experiments to validate the simulation results and gain more confidence in simulation validity.

If the simulation is something that is build for this specific RCA task, check the attitude of the analyst that developed the program. If the analyst had the end result (failure) in mind and tried to build the program to reach this end result, you may suspect the program is biased and you may challenge the validity of the contributing factors leading to the result. However, if the simulation program does reflect the expected behavior (based on previous knowledge) and still led to the correct prediction, you may have more trust in the simulation result.

As the graphics show more resemblance to the actual system or to the image that person has in mind about the system or process, there is a higher tendency to believe in the simulation result. Nice animation may be misleading. It is the model behind the graphics you are interested in and not the animation itself.

Use simulation for what-if learning

We mentioned the analyst's ability to tailor the simulation to achieve the end results (failure) as a pitfall and a way to test whether simulation is reliable. However, this very attitude may be used as a benefit when using simulation for RCA. Approach the simulation analyst and ask exactly that. What are the parameters in the system that I need to manipulate to achieve the actual problematic results that were detected? After achieving the results, do a sanity check with the analyst on the manipulated factors. Is it the law of physics that were manipulated? Is it something that will probably happen? Be careful with the outcome. Regard this information as a direction to check and not as factual data.

So, is simulation good or bad?

Do not hesitate to use simulation whenever possible for RCA. If a simulation program is already available, use it. If simulation is not available, weigh the required resources to build one vs. the problem in hand and decide accordingly.

Simulation may be a very strong tool that may help in RCA, either as a tool for raising what if scenarios, or to reconstruct situations that may require a long time to perform or have a risk in running in real life. It may deepen the understanding about interactions and processes that are inaccessible, invisible, or simply hard to grasp intuitively.

The outcome, however, should be treated carefully and further verification of the simulation outcome is advised, either by other supporting evidence or by running experiments to confirm the validity of the simulation model.

Chapter Summary

It is impossible to identify root cause without collecting information (data). This information could serve every stage of the investigation and have different kinds of data.

The chapter devoted to Process Characterization indicated that if proper analytical techniques/ tools are used with well-characterized statistical material, it is very possible that the source of the problem will be identified. In the Data Collection chapter, other sources of information were discussed with the intention of progressing towards cause identification. These data sources were not presented in order of importance, because all mentioned sources are equally important and should be used as needed.

Things to keep in mind:
- The data already stored in the database is not the only source available for the investigation. It is possible to generate more accurate and relevant data by changing the sampling plan or by establishing a different way to check material or systems.

- Close the knowledge gap. Get to the field, look, and learn what you didn't know that you don't know. Then, ask the right questions.

- It is possible that someone has already invented the wheel. Search written resources. Even if the exact information is not to be found, you may gain new insight about your problem.

- To gain the full benefit from an analytical lab, all you need is the correct sample and reference, proper handling and preparation, the right analytical technique, and someone to provide accurate and relevant interpretation.

- Get people to tell about the event, by being a true and empathic listener. There is something to learn from everyone.

- Simulation can achieve the impossible. It can get into places that nothing can get into. It can run time faster, it can even predict the unknown. However, it all depends on the accuracy of the model on which it is based.

CHAPTER 7

Team Tools and Techniques

Up till now this book has discussed the tools and techniques required for progress in RCA. No part of the book addresses team building and team management, and this is indeed beyond the scope of this book. There are numerous good books focusing on these subjects, and you can find details of some in the Recommended Reading chapter.

However, as part of team work, it is very often necessary to look for new directions or to raise new ideas. This could occur while looking for hard-to-get data, or when new models and scenarios should be raised. The ability to converge a variety of ideas coming from many individual minds into an unambiguous working direction is important for team progress. This chapter deals with two aspects related to generation and convergence of team ideas. The first part very briefly covers several techniques related to group thinking, and the second part discusses and presents several team decision-making techniques.

- Group thinking
  - Brain-storming
  - Fishbone diagram (Cause and Effect diagram, Ishikawa diagram)
  - Buzan's mind-mapping

- Decision-making tools
  - Simple voting: Tally Sheet
  - Nominal group technique
  - Weighted decision matrix
  - Paired decision matrix
  - Combined methods

Group Thinking

Brainstorming

In problem solving, brainstorming is widely used as a way to achieve a breakthrough in situations that appear to be somewhat stuck. It is used to raise ideas about potential causes to a problem (model), find ways to get required data, or suggest creative solutions.

There are numerous brainstorming methods, but the basic idea is common to all. The idea is to create an environment free of filtering or criticism and provide an equal opportunity for everyone to suggest any idea, thereby generating many ideas in a very short time. If this type of environment is achieved, individuals with different ways of looking into issues will not hesitate to raise ideas, others will feel free to piggyback on them by association, and many ideas will keep flowing in.

The basic steps for holding a brainstorming session are pretty simple and straightforward.

- The team is assembled in a room.
- The leader explains the subject to the team, and the basic requirement to be achieved by the brainstorming is clearly displayed for everyone.
- The rules of the brainstorming are explained to the team:
    - Every idea is welcome, with no concern about its practicality.
    - Any idea that is built upon or is a subset of a previous idea is welcome.
    - No discussion or criticism of any idea is allowed.
    - Everyone in turn may suggest an idea.
- Each idea is immediately captured. The capturing aid should be visible to the team.
- The session will continue as long as ideas keep flowing in.

The way to capture and visualize brainstorming output has a significant role in streamlining brainstorming. Since the whole concept is based on raising ideas wildly by association and without a structured order, ideas will come in random order and will usually be a mix of generic statements and small details. Putting it all on one "laundry list" will make it hard for the participants to easily follow what has already been said, and will create many repetitions of similar ideas.

There are several capturing techniques available in brainstorming. The one that is most frequently associated with RCA is the Cause and Effect diagram, also known as the Fishbone or Ishikawa diagram. Another technique is the Mindmapping® technique developed by Tony Buzan.

Cause and Effect diagram (aka Ishikawa or Fishbone diagram)

This tool was developed by Professor Kaoru Ishikawa from Japan. The intention is to identify and arrange every potential cause in a certain hierarchy. The problem statement will appear on one side as the head of fish, with a long backbone connected to it. Several branches will emerge from this backbone, and each branch will be dedicated to one category of potential causes. Any potential main cause related to one of the categories will appear as a stem coming out of the related branch. Finer details will appear as smaller stems under main stems.

The initial set of categories should be defined correctly, so that any potential cause will be included in one of the categories. It is quite common to see readymade fishbone templates with predefined main categories. However, it is not necessary to follow these, and the team may tailor the main branches (categories) according to their specific need. The end result should look like a fish skeleton with many items arranged in a hierarchy according to defined categories.

Mindmapping®

Mindmapping® was developed by Tony Buzan, based on the idea that the mind does not necessarily think sequentially and hierarchically, and could work associatively. Therefore, tables and lists are not the best methods to record thoughts.

The basic idea is to place the issue of interest in the center as a focal point and to start to branch outwards. Any idea should be defined and written by one or two keywords so as not to get into a long discussion about it, but to allow stimulation of the mind to the next idea. Ideas that are associated with or related to a branch will be connected to the relevant branch. Symbols, strange characters, and small drawings instead of or in addition to words are welcome, and may be used as a reminder or to emphasize a certain idea. Do not hesitate to write down any idea so as to free the mind for the next association. An idea that is not captured is usually stuck in a person's mind and will not free the mind to think about other possibilities. Use of colors, symbols and drawings are all good and are encouraged for mind stimulation.

There are several software packages in the market that provide an easy way to produce computerized mind maps. As well as easy map creation, they enable attaching files or symbols to any branch or stem of the map.

A few words of caution

There is no guarantee that brainstorming will extract you from a dead end, but sometimes brainstorming does provide surprising results. However, brainstorming output should be used with caution. The exact same things that make brainstorming efficient and attractive may cause it to be an obstacle that delays progress rather than being helpful.

Since brainstorming is not a structured way of thinking but is built on free association, a certain direction may be totally overlooked. The lack of criticism may also lead to directions that are speculative or "look promising" and the team may be swept away to trial and error kind of work instead of the required step-by- step process.

So, remember that when practicing brainstorming, the raw output should never be used to assign actions, or to define a direction to go in the investigation. The output of brainstorming should serve a more coherent and comprehensive way of thinking as described throughout this book.

Reaching decisions

Data (facts) that have certain implications on a group or individuals within a team are often not well accepted. In this case they may look for ways to dismiss this data. Should a team vote or make decisions against these facts? Facts will continue to exist even if the team votes against them. Would you consider a model that was decided by voting as the correct reason for failure? A decision that root cause has been identified should be based on solid model establishment. A model is based on factual data. If the team has confidence in the collected data, then the model should be the natural outcome. So, employing decision-making techniques as a "best guess" tool for deciding about problem cause, or as a way to accept or reject factual data, is not a wise idea. It may take the root cause process completely off track or even put the process line at risk.

Teams make decisions when they are able to consider risks or implications from one side, and see the potential and benefits from the other side. It could be a yes/no decision or it could be a selection between several options. In problem solving, it could be a decision about the course of action to take to prevent further damage, the best way to get data, and most frequently, the best solution to adopt.

Since individuals evaluate and weigh certain risks and benefits differently, a decision made by an individual may not be well balanced or unbiased. The team's power lies in the ability to cover more aspects of any given issue and to reduce the chance that a decision will be made according to a narrow aspect that an individual considered as important. A number of techniques for team decision-making are presented in the next few pages.

Simple voting table

This technique is the most simple to implement. As a result of a previous discussion or brainstorming, several alternatives were suggested. The pros and cons of each alternative were discussed, and it is time to make a decision. The leader prepares a table similar to the one in figure 7-1. The alternatives are written in a column and each team member in turn states their preferred option. The leader marks a sign (tally) next to it. At the end of the process, the number of marks per alternative is summed up and the alternative with the highest number of marks is the one decided on by the team.

Figure 7-1. Simple voting table (tally sheet)

Alternatives	Team's vote	Score
Option A	////	4
Option B	~~////~~ /	6
Option C	/	1
Option E	///	3

Nominal group technique

The decision made by selecting one option per person may appear to be somewhat problematic. The decision in the above vote was made by six team members, while the opinion of the other eight team members was totally ignored. This is especially correct where there are two or more options that are very close in quality.

To have a better chance for the opinion of every member to be reflected in the final score, each member will need to rank the options in descending order. Since there are four options in the table, four points represents the highest score and one point is the lowest. The number of scores for each option will be equal to the number of team members (Figure 7-2).

Figure 7-2. Nominal group technique voting table

Alternatives	Team's vote	Score
Option A	3,4,4,2,3,3,3,4,3,2,4,1,3,3	42
Option B	4,2,1,4,2,4,2,2,4,1,3,4,4,2	39
Option C	1,1,2,1,1,1,1,1,1,3,1,2,1,4	21
Option E	2,3,3,3,4,2,4,3,2,4,2,3,2,1	38

The team decided that Option A is the best. If you look carefully, you will observe that the results are actually the same as before. Six team members gave the highest score to Option B and only four gave the highest results to Option A. So, how come Option A got a better score? Because almost all the team members considered

Option A as good, while there were strong disagreements about Option B. If there are many options, it could be good enough for each member to rank the top three options and the calculation will be made the same way.

Is there a better way for the team to make decisions?

Weighted decision matrix

It was said earlier that the pros and cons of each option were presented to team members. During voting, it was left for the team members to weigh every option and decide upon the most appropriate one to address the requirements for an optimal decision. The question is: Do all team members see the requirements the same way? Naturally, in most cases, they do not. How can a team incorporate the level of importance of required considerations into the decision-making process? It is most likely in decision-making that there are considerations that are critical or very important, while others are less important or only nice to have.

Before getting into decision making, the team should prepare a list of requirements for the optimal alternative. Each requirement should be judged and a level of importance is assigned to it. The requirement could be crucial, important, and nice to have (3, 2, 1 respectively). It is important to emphasize that a higher score means the most desired situation, whether it appears as a positive or a negative characteristic.

Let's look at the example in figure 7-3. The team decided to implement a new monitor in a process line, with the intention of gathering data that is needed for RCA. Four optional monitors were suggested. To make the optimal decision, two requirements were defined as crucial, three requirements as important, and two requirements as nice to have.

The team needed to provide marks on a scale of 1 to 5 for each option and for every requirement. These marks were multiplied by the weighting factor assigned for the relevant requirement and marked on the table. The total scoring for each option was summed up and the decision was made based on the highest score achieved.

Figure 7-3. Simple weighted matrix

Requirement	**Weight**	**Option A**	**Option B**	**Option C**	**Option D**
Efficient problem detection	x3	5x3=15	3x3=9	2x3=6	1x3=3
No risk to other operations	x3	4x3=12	5x3=15	1x3=3	2x3=6
Minimal impact on line performance	x2	3x2=6	4x2=8	3x2=6	1x2=2
Simple and fast to introduce	x2	4x2=8	2x2=4	1x2=2	4x2=8
No extra human resources	x2	5x2=10	4x2=8	1x2=2	3x2=6
Use of existing tools in line	x1	3x1=3	4x1=4	5x1=5	3x1=3
No special training	x1	4x1=4	5x1=5	4x1=4	4x1=4
Total score		58	53	28	32

Based on the results, Option A was selected by the team as the best option. However, one of the managers looked at the decision table made by team and said, "Under no condition will I allow introduction of a monitor into the line that poses even a remote risk to the line". The weighting of this requirement was changed to veto, meaning that any option that does not meet this requirement cannot be implemented, no matter how high the other criteria of this option are. Since only Option B was found to withstand the "no risk to other operations" requirement, this option was selected even though the ability of this option to detect the problem was not optimal.

By placing each option against the requirements, a team can be more confident in the decision that is made. However this technique is not free of problems. The results can be easily manipulated. Others may be convinced that a certain requirement should be given more weight than it really deserves. A longer list of low-level requirements with high scores may overcome a short list of important requirements. The scores that are given to each option are based on subjective judgment and this may cause an individual to give a higher score to their favorite option. Still, the need to judge every option against the requirements makes this method very popular and usually provides adequate results.

Paired decision matrix

When there is a need to decide between two options, things are simpler. The advantages of one option over the other stand out and a decision is easier to make. However, when the team is faced with several options that have significantly different characteristics, the decision may be less than optimal. Anyone could be biased by a certain advantage or disadvantage that he considered important, while ignoring other considerations that could also be important. A weighted decision matrix is one way to make a better decision, however it requires finding criteria that are common to all options, and judging the options based on these. This way unique advantages (or disadvantages) of a certain option may be lost. If a team wishes to scrutinize the possibilities, it must place every option against every other option and then discuss each pair separately, make a decision, and let the best win. How many discussions and voting sessions will be required to make a final decision? How should the voting table be arranged?

The answer to the first question is based on a well-known riddle. There are four guys that need to be introduced to each other. How many handshakes will be made in this introduction? The answer is shown in figure 7-4

Figure 7-4. Four options require six comparisons

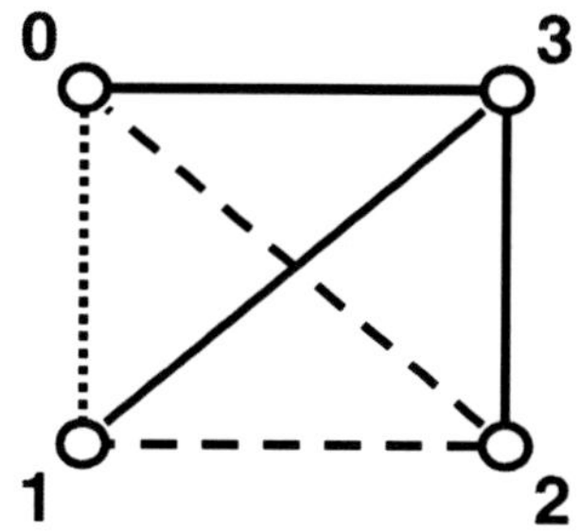

$$(n^2-n)/2$$

So, to reach a final decision about four options, six pairs need to be compared before making a decision. Figure 7.5 shows how the paired decision matrix is arranged. The results of voting for each pair should appear under the respective option. The sum of the two results that appear in each row should be equal to the number of voters. The scores for each column are summed up after completing the six voting sessions. The option with the highest score is the one the team finds to be the most appropriate.

Figure 7-5. Paired decision-making matrix for ranking four options

	Option A	**Option B**	**Option C**	**Option D**
A vs. B	7	7		
A vs. C	11		3	
A vs. D	10			4
B vs. C		11	3	
B vs. D		8		6
C vs. D			2	12
Total Score	28	26	8	22

Note that in figure 7-5, the team could decide between Option A and Option B. However, when placing these two options against Option D, it looks as if Option A has some advantages that B was missing, and this made Option A the better one.

Combined methods

In the weighted decision matrix, everyone is able to see how each option addresses every required consideration. As well as being a decision-making tool, the weighted decision matrix may be used as a memory system that captures the rationale behind making a certain decisions. However, it was already mentioned that preparing the list of considerations in decision making, assigning a weighting factor to each consideration, and then giving marks to each option for every consideration, is a lengthy process that may be manipulated in favor of one option over the others. In addition, unique advantages of a certain option, or unique flaws in another, are sometimes neglected.

The nominal group technique provides good representation of the team impression from the suggested solutions. The paired comparison technique eases the comparison between the options by placing one option at a time against another. But both do not provide a tool that captures the rationale behind making the decision.

There is a way to get both: capture the rationale behind a decision that is made, and make the decision by comparing one option at a time against another. The first step is intended to learn the requirements for reaching a resolution and deciding the criteria that will be used to judge any available option. Unlike in the weighting factor, there is no weighting process. Only mandatory and important criteria should be included. Requirements with lesser importance or nice to have ones are excluded. This process is shown in the simple list in figure 7-6.

Figure 7.6 Decision criteria table

Mandatory criteria (Veto)	1. Imply no risk to line
Important requirements	2. Good problem detectability 3. Low impact on line performance 4. Low cost 5. And more

Next, prepare the first pair of options for comparison as in figure 7-7. Place the two options against the pre-defined criteria. List important advantages, disadvantages or special risks that are unique to an option under the respective column.

Figure 7-7. Pair comparison

		Option A	Option B
Mandatory criteria (Veto)	Imply no risk to line	Go	Go
Important requirements	Good problem detectability	0	1
	Low impact on line performance	1	1
	Low cost	1	0
	And more	0	1
Score		2	3
Unique important advantages		Tool exists in line. Immediate implementation is possible.	Inexpensive new tool
Unique important disadvantages or risks			10 days to install and train
Decision		0	1

Now the team needs to decide which of the two is the better option. An option that does not withstand a mandatory criterion is immediately marked as no-go. The team should decide the better option for each important requirement by a simple vote. Mark the better option for each criterion as 1 and the other as 0. Mark 1 for both if two the options are found equal for this requirement. Calculate the total score per option by summing up the 1s. Now the team should look again, and when considering the score and unique properties of each option, decide which of the two is the better option by voting.

Count on your team members to judge correctly between the two options. They have all the necessary parameters in front of them. Note that by looking at this comparison, the team may consider a combined option, such as immediate implementation of Option A as a temporary solution (for 10 days) and order the better tool of Option B to replace it.

If the result of the voting is even, add another unbiased person to the team and explain the decision that should be made. Then let one person that is in favor of one option to present his or her arguments, and let a person that is in favor of the other option to present his or her arguments, giving each argument five to ten minutes. Then repeat the voting.

This paired comparison should be performed one after another. The winning option will be placed against the next option for comparison, as in the King of the Hill game demonstrated by figure 7-8.

Figure 7-8. King of the Hill decision-making table

	Option A	**Option B**	**Option C**	**Option D**
1st pair	0	1		
2nd pair		0	1	
3rd pair			1	0

The better option decided by the comparison of first pair (B in figure 7-8) will be compared to the next option (Option C in figure 7-8) in the same way as for the first pair. The better option of the second pair will be placed against the next option, and so on.

The rationale behind this is that if Option B is better than Option A, and Option C is better than Option B, then Option C is better than Option A. The option that was left with 1 in the last row (after completing the comparison) is the best option. Note that if the team wishes to rank all options, instead of defining the best one, a full pairing process should be conducted.

Decision-making summary

When a team reaches a situation where a decision should be made, it is necessary to look for the best way to make the decision. The risks and benefits of each alternative should be clearly defined (pros and cons), and the importance of each requirement should be clarified. In simple cases, there is no need to get into a deep discussion and the most basic voting will be adequate. In other cases, deep discussions may be needed and more time-consuming techniques will be required to achieve appropriate results. It is important to bear in mind that when a team is asked to make a decision, it is because there are doubts. The team needs to pick the best option under known circumstances. Saying later on that a decision was wrong is usually post factum wisdom. So, do make decisions, but evaluate the alternatives in the most appropriate way possible.

CHAPTER
8

EVENT DOCUMENTATION

Relations between Root Cause Analysis and Knowledge Management

Knowledge management is broadly defined as a way to capture, store, and retrieve accumulated information in the most appropriate way. The people dealing with this issue struggle to manage the acquired information in a way that it will be most helpful when needed. We can imagine it as a small "knowing all, experienced in all" person sitting inside the computer who jumps out and shouts, "I know, I know" when needed, providing everything that is needed to solve a problem in the most efficient way. Or even better, this small person will do some of the work for us.

We can consider the Internet and search engines as some kind of knowing all person, but is it also an experienced in all person? An experienced person is someone that has toured unknown territory and therefore has a map to lead others through it. It is not only about having the information. It is also about knowing how to get to information sources. It is about understanding the relevancy of the information and it is about knowing how to use that information. Hence, it is not surprising that the term know-how has become a common way to name the elusive capability that comes with experience. So, transferring experience also involves learning the way of thinking as well as pure information exchange. Therefore, the internet does not meet the "experienced in all" expectation.

In RCA, the basic idea is learning from experience, meaning that we are running through the investigation sequence to apply a proper solution and prevent reoccurrence of a problem. Persons or teams that passed through RCA of a specific problem already chose tools, collected and evaluated data, suggested hypotheses, confirmed or denied them, made experiments, suggested solutions, etc. They are experienced because they have both the information and the thinking process that leads to cause identification.

How can we capture and transfer this kind of experience and information to another person or team that will face a similar problem, and make the way easier for them? Why does this not work in most of the current knowledge management systems?

Document repository, virtual library or any other such names are the typical attempt of organizations to keep information for future use. In general, most of these information storing systems are differentiated by the way the data is arranged or classified and/or by the way to retrieve it. The person that was in charge of a task is responsible for summarizing it and placing it in the proper location. This kind of summary, if well arranged, will contain all relevant information about the problem, such as the symptoms, cause, relevant data that led to cause identification, and the selected solution. Typically it will not include all other hypotheses, data items, tools and techniques that were in use but were found to be irrelevant to this specific problem. However, all this may be extremely valuable and may save time and effort for another person or team that will face a similar issue. It may save time in suggesting hypotheses; it may contain useful experiment results, important data or techniques and so on. However, all this is no longer accessible, or at least not arranged in a way that it can be retrieved in an easy to read manner.

There are some other systems and ways that attempt to preserve the acquired experience. For example, we can mention the meeting management systems. The usual way of running a team is by calling meetings. In these meetings, the problem is presented to all, hypotheses or models are suggested, data is presented, and required actions are stated. So it looks as if being able to store all these meeting minutes, data, updates, and summaries, and add a retrieving system to it, will be a good knowledge management system. Well, it is not exactly the case. Going over the rolling history of event investigation by reading meeting minutes can be rather exhausting and boring. Usually the information is not structured in an easy to follow arrangement and it is relatively hard to relate a document containing a certain experiment or analysis to the relevant stage in the investigation process.

How can we create a system that on the one hand, will serve the team leader while an investigation is running, and on the other, will be easy to understand by someone who is looking for relevant material at some point in the future?

In this book, two major techniques were thoroughly discussed: the modeling tree and the data model matrix. The modeling tree helps to keep the team's line of thinking and provides the rationale behind the required task, while the data-model matrix lists the observations made by the collected data items (analyses and experiments) in order of information arrival. So it serves the team while progressing through the RCA process. However, if at some point in the future, someone wishes to learn this event investigation thoroughly, this person may use the exact same tools to follow the team's line of thinking. This person will go over the modeling tree, and if interested in learning a specific analysis for which a certain observation was made, it will be easy if each observation appearing in the data model matrix is linked to the respective analysis document. So ideally, all material related to a certain event, such as lab reports, data analyses and experiment results, will be accessible from the basic documents that were used for running the task (as long as the links are not broken).

We may call this arrangement an associative database, since all documents associated with a certain event are linked to one basic document with all required information. However, there is one big flaw in this idea. A person that is busy with a current problem would like to gain a quick impression about the relevancy of a past event. Nobody wants to dive blindly into a past event and spend valuable time learning it deeply when it may be totally irrelevant.

So, we should bear in mind someone who is looking for past experience and interested first in an easy-to-read document. Once this person realizes that this past event is relevant to his current needs, he may be interested in further learning of the line of thinking and the data items that were used in this event.

So, the easy-to-read event summary should be written, and once this document is spotted, it should be possible to access all associated information using the exact same document.

An Event Summary on One Page

As said earlier, by following the modeling tree and data model matrix, one may learn the line of thinking and the data that was required to complete an investigation. However, this may be rather confusing. The short scripts that may appear on a modeling tree could be sufficient for those who are involved in the investigation, but may not be clear enough for a person who intends to learn from it at a later stage. A long list of data items appearing in a data model matrix may add to the confusion of this future learner, since a few data items made a significant contribution to investigation progress while many others did not.

It is important to make it easy for anyone not deeply involved in the event to learn about the event. There is often much investment in preparing detailed progress reports for updating management during the investigation. However, summarizing the event in an easy-to-read manner after the problem was resolved depends on the organizational culture. In many organizations, an event is not summarized routinely, and unless it is presented as a paper in a conference or publication, no proper documentation is prepared for the potential reader.

There is no intention here to explain how to assimilate a documentation culture in the organization. However, I find it appropriate to suggest a simple template that will be easy for both the person involved in an event that needs summarizing, and for the person who is going to read it sometime in the future. I call this simple template AESOP. Aesop was a slave who lived in Ancient Greece in the 6th century BC, and at some point was freed from slavery. Aesop was famous as a talented teller of fables. His short, simple fables were easy to understand by all and provided a moral lesson. His fables survived for centuries and inspired many creators in generations to come, and are still read by many today.

Apart from the name being inspired by this unusual person, AESOP stands for An Event Summary on One Page. The intention is to present the event story concisely. Don't take the "one page" literally. The intention is to make it short but also to make it useful. So, it should include relevant and helpful information, and only this. Lengthy discussion and extra information is considered an unnecessary burden that should be avoided. It is quite natural for an individual or team that is enthusiastic about the results of their hard work to insert it into the event summary, so that others will realize the work invested or will appreciate the achievement. Something like: "I can imagine the praise of those who will read what we've done". However, the person responsible for documenting the event should keep the potential reader in mind. So, only information that will directly contribute to reader understanding should be included. Other information, no matter how much hard work was invested in it and how much brilliance shines from it, should be left out. Use of abbreviations or uncommon terminology should be avoided or explained clearly in the first use. The proper test for learning the quality of this type of document is by having a person who was not involved in this event read and understand it in 10 minutes.

Aesop: **A**n **E**vent **S**ummary on **O**ne **P**age

Event name:

Define the naming convention to be used, such as: SITE, PROCESS, WWYY, Problem-Nickname. The intention of the WWYY is to avoid duplication of names. Use the work week in which symptoms were first detected, or the week that the team was established.

Problem detection:

Describe the symptoms that characterize the problem in an easy to understand way.
Attach a graph, drawing, image, or any other means to clearly show the detected phenomenon. Use minimum to explain maximum.

Cause identification (sequence):

List and briefly describe only the key data items that led to cause identification. Arrange the list in the same order that the data arrived during the event, and make the progress of investigation easy to follow. Attach supporting info that clarifies these key data items, such as a graph from data analysis, image from lab analysis and a table of experiment results. Use minimum to explain maximum.
Do not include information collected during investigation that did not directly contribute to identification of the root cause.

Solution / fix:

Briefly describe the solution that was selected, and the indication that it was successful.
Attach a supporting graph or other means to demonstrate this indication.
If applicable: list other solutions that were suggested. Mention whether these were checked or not.

Other relevant documentation:

Att-1, att-2 / Link-1, Link-2.
Attach documents with concise information, such as modeling trees, data model matrix, and summary tables. Avoid attaching large files that will make the Aesop document heavy to upload.

Contact persons:

Name1, Name 2.

Recommended Reading

- **Root Cause Analysis and Problem Solving**
  - Dennis Daniel P. "How to Organize and Run a Failure Investigation" ASM International, 2005.
  - Wilson Paul F., Larry D. Dell, and Gaylord F. Anderson. "Root Cause Analysis: A Tool for Total Quality Management" ASQ Quality Press, 1993.
  - Nelms Robert C. "What You Can Learn From Things That Go Wrong: A Guidebook to the Root Causes of Failure" Failsafe Network, Inc. 1994.
  - Gano Dean L. "Apollo Root Cause Analysis – A New Way of Thinking" Apollonian Publications, 1999, 2003.
  - Latino Robert J. and Kenneth C. Latino. "Root Cause Analysis : Improving Performance for Bottom-Line Results" CRC Press, 2002.
  - Ammerman Max. "The Root Cause Analysis Handbook : A Simplified Approach to identifying, Correcting, and Reporting Workplace Errors" Productivity Press, 1998.
  - Andersen Bjorn, Tom Fagerhaug. "Root Cause Analysis : Simplified Tools and Techniques" ASQ Quality Press, 2000.
  - Robitaille Denise E. "" Root Cause Analysis : Basic Tools and Techniques" Paton Press LLC, 2004.
  - Kepner Charles H., and Benjamin B. Tregoe "The New Rational Manager" Princeton research Press, 1981, 1997.
  - Jones Morgan D. "The Thinker's Toolkit: Fourteen Powerful Techniques for Problem Solving" Three Rivers Press, 1995,1998.
  - Higgins James M. "101 Creative Problem Solving Techniques: The Handbook of New Ideas for Business" The New Management Publishing Company Inc. 1994.

- **Statistics, SPC, DOE**
  - Harrington James H., Glen D. Hoffherr, and Robert P. Reid Jr. "Statistical Analysis Simplified: The Easy-to-Understand Guide to SPC and Data Analysis" McGraw-Hill, 1998.
  - Amsden Robert T., Howard E. Butler, and Davida M. Amsden. "SPC Simplified : Practical Steps to Quality" Productivity Inc. 1998.

- Anderson Mark J., and Patrick J. Whitcomb "DOE Simplified : Practical Tools for Effective Experimentation" Productivity Press, 2000.
- Drain David. "Statistical Methods for Industrial Process Control" Chapman & Hall, 1997.
- Ronald E. Walpole, Raymond H. Myers. "Probability and Statistics for Engineers and Scientists" Prentice-Hall International, Inc. 1993
- Porkess Roger. "The HarperCollins Dictionary of Statistics" HarperPerennial, 1991.

- **Team management and human interaction**
  - Daniels William R. "Group Power I: AManager's Guide to Using Task-Force Meetings" University Associates, 1986.
  - Daniels William R. "Breakthrough Performance: Managing for Speed and Flexibility" ACT Publishing, 1995.
  - Lundy James L. "TEAMS – Together Each Achieves More Success: How to Develop Peak Performance Teams for World-Class Results" The Dartnell Corporation, 1994.
  - Seagal Sandra, David Horne. "Human Dynamics: A New Framework for Understanding people and Realizing the Potential in OUR Organizations" Pegasus Communications Inc. 1997.
  - Fisher Roger, William Ury, and Bruce Patton "Getting To Yes: Negotiating Agreement Without Giving In" Penguin Books, 1981,1991.

- **Analytical Lab tools and methods**
  - Mix Paul E. "Introduction to Nondestructing testing: A training Guide" John Wiley & Sons Inc., 2005.
  - Vickerman J.C. "Surface Analysis: The Principle Techniques" John Wiley & Sons, Inc. 1997.
  - John C. Riviere, Sverre Myhra. "Handbook of surface and Interface Analysis: Methods for Problem Solving" Marcel Dekker, Inc. 1998.
  - Wulpi Donal J. "Understanding How Components Fail" ASM International, 2000.

- **Computer simulation**
  - McHaney Roger. "Computer Simulation: A Practical Perspective" Academic Press Inc. 1991.
  - Jerry Banks "Handbook of Simulation: Principles, Methodology, Advances, Applications and Practice" John Wiley & Sons, Inc. 1998.

INDEX

Lightning Source UK Ltd.
Milton Keynes UK
UKOW052153040713

213276UK00001B/76/P

9 781425 139773